G. Allen Fleece Library
Columbia International University
Columbia, SC 29203

International Students and Academic Libraries

A Survey of Issues and Annotated Bibliography

Diane E. Peters

The Scarecrow Press, Inc.
Lanham • Toronto • Plymouth, UK
2010

Published by Scarecrow Press, Inc.
A wholly owned subsidiary of The Rowman & Littlefield Publishing Group, Inc.
4501 Forbes Boulevard, Suite 200, Lanham, Maryland 20706
http://www.scarecrowpress.com

Estover Road, Plymouth PL6 7PY, United Kingdom

Copyright © 2010 by Diane E. Peters

All rights reserved. No part of this book may be reproduced in any form or by any electronic or mechanical means, including information storage and retrieval systems, without written permission from the publisher, except by a reviewer who may quote passages in a review.

British Library Cataloguing in Publication Information Available

Library of Congress Cataloging-in-Publication Data
Peters, Diane E.
  International students and academic libraries : a survey of issues and annotated bibliography / Diane E. Peters.
     p. cm.
  Includes bibliographical references and index.
  ISBN 978-0-8108-7429-9 (pbk. : alk. paper) — ISBN 978-0-8108-7430-5 (ebook)
  1. Library science—Bibliography. 2. Library schools—United States—Bibliography.
3. Library schools—Canada—Bibliography. 4. Students, Foreign—United
States—Bibliography. 5. Students, Foreign—Canada—Bibliography. 6. Library
science—United States—Bibliography. 7. Library science—Canada—Bibliography.
8. International librarianship—Bibliography. 9. Foreign study—United States—
Bibliography. 10. Foreign study—Canada—Bibliography. I. Title.
  Z666.P475 2010
  016.02—dc22

2009048167

∞ ™ The paper used in this publication meets the minimum requirements of American National Standard for Information Sciences—Permanence of Paper for Printed Library Materials, ANSI/NISO Z39.48-1992.

Printed in the United States of America

Contents

A Survey of Issues

In the 1990 article "Trends in International Education: New Imperatives in Academic Librarianship" (no. 319), Martha L. Brogan described new directions in international education during the previous decade. Five major areas of development were highlighted: foreign language instruction, study abroad, internationalizing the curriculum, foreign students and scholars, and technical assistance and international development. Brogan noted that in academic institutions the argument for increasing the international competence of students was twofold, stemming from educational and economic imperatives; developing the skills required to succeed in a multicultural, interdependent world in which North America is only a partner in a global marketplace is "both educationally responsible and the only means of survival—economic and otherwise—in the twenty-first century" (p. 196).

In the almost two decades since Brogan's article appeared, the international dimension of higher education has become increasingly important and more complex. Jane Knight outlined a number of current developments and initiatives in the October–November 2008 issue of *Academic Matters*, the journal of the Ontario Confederation of University Faculty Associations ("The Internationalization of Higher Education: Are We on the Right Track?" pp. 5–6):

- the creation of new international networks and consortia;
- the growing numbers of students, professors, and researchers participating in academic mobility schemes;

All numbers in the text in this format refer to the numbered entries in the bibliography, as do the numbers in both the author index and the subject index.

1

- the increase in the number of courses, programs, and qualifications that focus on comparative and international themes;
- more emphasis on developing international/intercultural and global competencies;
- stronger interest in international themes and collaborative research;
- a steep rise in the crossborder delivery of academic programs;
- more interest and concern with international and regional rankings of universities;
- an increase in campus-based extracurricular activities with an international or multicultural component;
- investment in recruiting foreign students and dependence on their income;
- the rise in the number of joint or double degrees;
- growth in the numbers and types of for-profit crossborder education providers;
- the expansion in partnerships, franchises, and branch campuses;
- the establishment of new national, regional, and international organizations focused on international education.

Knight went on to discuss a number of the challenges and consequences that arise as a result of the internationalization process. She concluded that "it is imperative that the international, intercultural, and global dimensions of higher education continue to be proactive, responsive, and innovative, while keeping a close watch on unanticipated spin-offs and implications" (p. 9).

As part of the growing emphasis on globalization, North American universities are increasingly devoting resources to recruiting students from around the world. International students bring cultural and intellectual diversity, and in times of decreased public funding and increased costs, they contribute essential income. Success in attracting large numbers of international students, in particular at the graduate and post-graduate levels, may also be seen as a source of prestige for universities, indicating their world-class reputation. It has also been pointed out that "the reputation associated with gaining a postsecondary or graduate education from an American institution is still an enticing motivator for students who wish to solidify success in their careers when they return to their homelands" (Kaetraena Davis, *Global Evolution: A Chronological Annotated Bibliography of International Students in U.S. Academic Libraries*, no. 142, p. 5).

The Open Doors Online website maintained by the Institute of International Education (http://opendoors.iienetwork.org) reported in November 2008 that the number of international students at colleges and universities in the United States had increased to a record high of 623,805 in 2007–2008, an increase of 7 percent over enrollment in the previous academic year. This 2007–2008 growth built on a 3 percent increase reported for 2006–2007 and exceeded by 6 percent the previous all-time high of 586,323 reported in 2002–2003. Open Doors data showed an even stronger increase in the number of "new" international students, those enrolled for the first time at a U.S. college or university in the fall of 2007, with new enrollments increasing by 10 percent, following increases of 10 percent and 8 percent for the previous two years. The majority of international students—61 percent of the total number—came to the United States from Asia.

According to a February 7, 2008, report issued by Statistics Canada in *The Daily* (http://www.statcan.gc.ca/daily-quotidien/080207/dq080207a-eng.htm), 80,200 students from other countries were enrolled in programs at Canadian universities in 2005–2006, a total which was up 6 percent from the previous year. International students represented 7.7 percent of the total registrations, nearly double the proportion of a decade earlier. Half of these students were from Asia, with China accounting for 46 percent of Asian students.

The following discussion is based on a review of the literature outlined in the following bibliography. It highlights issues faced by both international students and by librarians in academic institutions who work with them, and offers suggestions on how to make the relationship between students and librarians more positive and productive.

INTERNATIONAL STUDENTS AND LIBRARIES

A survey of educational literature from the mid-1960s to early 1980s indicates that very little was written on international students in post-secondary institutions. Mention of libraries, if it occurred at all, was peripheral. Library literature on the topic is even more sparse, with only isolated examples, such as Mary Genevieve Lewis's 1969 article "Library Orientation for Asian College Students" (no. 93), to be found.

Both scholarly and anecdotal writings dealing with international students began to appear with increasing regularity in library literature from the mid-1980s onward. Much of the material focused on cultural differences affecting library use and library services to deal with them, especially services related to library orientation. Several important surveys appeared. Frank William Goudy and Eugene Moushey reported on their 1984 questionnaire completed by forty-four directors at large American academic libraries and designed to determine the proficiency of international students' library use, whether library instruction would be helpful to them, and how the instruction could be accomplished ("Library Instruction and Foreign Students: A Survey of Opinions and Practices among Selected Libraries," no. 63). Findings showed librarians perceived foreign students as having additional problems in using the library because of poor English skills, lack of adequate vocabulary, cultural differences, and a lack of library skills. The type of instruction offered international students and the degree of coordination that existed between the library and other areas of campus serving them differed considerably. It was concluded that library instruction should be more extensive than what was currently offered. Another 1984 study, this one of librarians at fifty-four American colleges and universities with large international student populations (Laura S. Kline and Catherine M. Rod, "Library Orientation Programs for Foreign Students: A Survey," no. 5), showed that while 98 percent of the campuses offered special orientations for new international students, only 56 percent of libraries followed suit. A 1988 counterpart to Goudy and Moushey's study conducted by Benhong Tsai (*Special Bibliographic Instruction for International Students: A Survey of Academic Libraries in Medium Sized State Universities*, no. 134) presented results from a survey of library directors at sixty medium-sized state universities. Results at that time indicated 58 percent of libraries offered some form of bibliographic instruction exclusively for international students, with most instruction programs consisting of brief introductory sessions and individual assistance at the reference desk. Few programs were mandatory and student participation rates tended to be 50 percent or lower. Lack of funding and staff were cited most often as reasons for not providing specialized instruction.

Such studies are notable in that the focus was on librarians' perceptions of student needs. However, some attempts were made to solicit information from students themselves. Dania Bilal's 1988 Florida State University dissertation, *Library Knowledge of International Students from Developing Countries: A Comparison of Their Perceptions with Those of Reference Libraries* (no. 214), examined the relationship between international students' understanding of the importance of library knowledge and their success in using the library, particularly with respect to certain variables (length of stay at an American university, participation in library instruction programs, sex, region of origin, English language proficiency, previous library experience). Reference librarians' perceptions of students' success in using the library and the importance of library knowledge to them were also examined, as well as differences between student and librarian perceptions. The study sample included 53 librarians and 104 students at 42 large Association of Research Libraries (ARL) member institutions. Results indicated that reference librarians underestimated student needs.

Since the 1990s themes in the library literature have expanded to include discussion of technological skills, bibliographic instruction, information literacy, library programming, and information-seeking behaviors of international students. It is clear that as a result of such factors as the expansion of technology, the popularity of worldwide online social networks, and the growing strength of information infrastructures in previously underdeveloped countries, international students are perceiving and using North American academic libraries differently than in the past. The educational, linguistic, and cultural barriers that have been long recognized in the literature on international students and libraries remain important considerations, but current literature also raises new questions regarding what international students expect from North American libraries, the library skills they bring with them from home countries, and ways in which librarians should respond.

In addition, as internationalization initiatives in universities expand, theoretical research on the impact of globalization on libraries is becoming more common. Much of this theoretical literature emanates from Australia, which has one of the largest international student populations of any country in the world. More of this type of research is likely in the future.

STUDENT-RELATED ISSUES

As noted above, there are a number of themes that have remained constant over the past three decades in library literature regarding international students. Sally Wayman's seminal articles "The International Student in the Academic Library" (no. 307) and "The International Student in Your Library: Coping with Cultural and Language Barriers" (no. 308) were published in 1984 but continue to be cited in almost all subsequent articles dealing with the barriers faced by international students using North American libraries. These barriers include:

General Culture Shock

While international students are deeply involved in their academic work, they simultaneously struggle to adapt to a new environment. Australian librarian Hilary Hughes, who has conducted extensive research on international students, has noted that

> overseas students are likely to experience a range of emotions prior to and during their course. . . . The excitement of new experience is tempered with anxiety, due to: leaving relatives, friends, and familiar environment; coping with daily routines, finances, and relationships, alone in an alien culture; homesickness. Often intense pressure to succeed academically and/or fear of failure is compounded by reluctance to seek advice from peers and counselors, through concern to maintain face. The rate and degree of adjustment varies with each individual, and "highs and lows" occur throughout their stay. ("The International-Friendly Library: Customising Library Services for Students from Overseas," no. 236, p. 2)

Donna Gilton, a professor at the University of Rhode Island Graduate School of Library and Information Science, elaborated further:

> There are several phases of culture shock—euphoria, anxiety, adjustment, and readjustment. Short-term visitors and people who are very new to a culture see the new culture as exotic and exciting. Many people who go to international, multicultural, or ethnic fairs or who eat at an ethnic restaurant of a group not their own also experience the first pleasant stage of culture shock.

The second stage is not so pleasant and usually strikes people who have been in the new culture for awhile, and who are planning to stay longer, but it can also affect those just encountering a new culture. The written and unwritten rules that work so well at home no longer work, and in some cases the new culture makes little or no sense. At worst, people in this second stage see the new culture as a disaster and their home cultures as ideal and they may experience much anxiety and even paranoia during this time.

People who stay in a new culture and who learn enough of the culture's rules and logic usually adjust. This is the third stage of culture shock. By this time, the sojourner can see the merits and demerits of both the new culture and the home culture. Last, sojourners may experience culture shock again, as they return to their home countries. ("Culture Shock in the Library: Implications for Information Literacy Instruction, no. 60, p. 425)

Gilton's article then goes on to provide an overview of the literature dealing with international students in libraries, including discussion of some of the issues addressed below.

Communication/Language Issues

The title of Karen Bordanaro's 2006 article "We All Have an Accent" (no. 360) highlights an important issue. Most of us recognize accents in the speech of others, but we usually do not consider ourselves as having one. However, there is no "standard" form of English and students studying in North America are likely to be confronted by a myriad of ethnic speech patterns, idioms, and local expressions. Many students for whom English is a second language will have learned a form of standard "British" English that may bear little resemblance to the form of English spoken in the country in which they study, although the worldwide popularity of North American television and the advent of global social networking systems have likely had some impact on familiarity with North American speech patterns. Even students from English-speaking countries who study in another English-speaking country may have difficulties understanding words, phrases, and accents that are unfamiliar. I certainly found this to be true when I attended Oxford University in England as a Canadian graduate student.

While most international students from non-English-speaking countries have studied English and presumably passed a language test such as the TOEFL—the Test of English as a Foreign Language—their written skills are often better than their spoken language and comprehension skills. Most international students are familiar with a technically correct form of English, but everyday North American speech may be more imprecise in word choice and usage, especially with respect to grammatical constructions. It has been noted that the average international student has one-half the reading comprehension speed of American students and less oral comprehension (Greenfield, "Training Library Staff to Reach and Teach International Students," no. 391, p. 46).

In a 2007 study investigating international students' perceptions of issues they faced using English as a second language while attending American universities (Li, Fox, and Almarza, "Strangers in Stranger Lands: Language, Learning, Culture," no. 351), Hong Li, a doctoral student from China, described the sense of frustration experienced:

> My limitations in speaking and listening created a great deal of stress for me. When conversing with native speakers, I often felt helpless because I could not speak freely what was exactly in my mind. I often became easily lost in conversations, just due to missing a word or a sentence. The worst situation occurred when I sometimes heard only the sound of peoples' voices in English but knew nothing of what they were saying. Whenever this happened, the feeling of being an illiterate, struggling in a modern society, tortured me.
>
> On the other hand, I was shocked to realize how little I actually knew about the English language, its tons of vocabulary, let alone the colloquial expressions of Western culture. These unexpected but bursting feelings of failure and embarrassment were so overwhelming, that I even doubted my original goal of improving my English proficiency in this country. At such times, this goal seemed like an impossible dream.

The author comes to an interesting and rather startling conclusion:

> Based on my personal experience and the stories told by many other international students from Latin America with whom I shared experiences, the training we received in English in our home countries was a waste of time. In order to be able to operate in a society with a different language, the second language learner has to learn the culture in which that language is embedded. Unfortunately, the English teachers in our countries believe the second language learners of English are better off if they learn "standard" English that could be used everywhere, that is, a language without any cultural context.

Nonverbal communication issues are also a concern since both librarians and students send silent signals that can be misinterpreted. If a librarian sees a student nodding his or her head, the movement may be seen as a sign that the student understands. However, in certain cultures, head nodding is a negative rather than an affirmative signal. A firm handshake may be considered disrespectful by some students. Even friendliness toward strangers may be interpreted as rudeness.

In a 1994 article entitled "Did I See You Do What I Think You Did? The Pitfalls of Nonverbal Communication across Cultures" (no. 352), Dr. Annette Lopez noted that only approximately 37 percent of face-to-face communication is verbal while 63 percent is transmitted nonverbally. She went on to discuss a variety of nonverbal features that can have an impact on intercultural interactions. With respect to pitch, tone, and intonation, she pointed out that loud, excited discussion may be a standard way of speaking and does not necessarily signal an argument. Gestures are not universal; puckered lips do not always signify a desire to kiss, but rather are just another way to point for many Caribbean Spanish speakers (as the author, a Puerto Rican, found out to her chagrin when studying in the United States). The OK gesture of rounded index and thumb may be considered obscene by students from some parts of the world. The establishment of eye contact has contradictory meanings across cultures; while North Americans tend to encourage it as an indication of attentiveness and respect for authority, in some cultures it may be perceived as defiance or overfamiliarity. Some cultures, such as Latino and some Middle Eastern societies, are touch oriented, while others, such as mainstream North American culture, are not. Lopez suggested that the best way to determine if a particular culture is touch or nontouch oriented is to observe their patterns in greetings and taking leave of one another. The distance maintained during face-to-face communication is also culturally coded. The Japanese, for example, consider a distance of approximately four feet appropriate in greeting and taking leave, for this behavior requires bowing, while for many from the Middle East, to feel another's breath on one's face is comfortable. North American mainstream and Latino cultures prefer a distance somewhere between these extremes.

Other Cultural Differences

There are many other culture-based differences that affect the relationship between librarians and international students. North American informality is often confusing to those from other cultures. This issue has an impact on various aspects of intercultural interaction, for example, the form of name by which people are addressed, the use of job titles, or attitudes toward age. A librarian's gender can be either inhibiting or advantageous when dealing with students having different gender role orientations; for example, female librarians may not be granted as much respect or considered as knowledgeable as male librarians by those from male-dominated cultures, while the opposite may be true for those from female-dominated cultures. There may also be differing attitudes toward time and punctuality; what is considered lateness in one culture may be perfectly normal and acceptable in another.

Students from stratified societies may be reluctant to come to library service desks out of fear of acting inappropriately and placing themselves in a position where they may experience ridicule. Yoshi Hendricks points out that many Japanese students are reluctant to speak a foreign language because making mistakes is strongly discouraged in their homeland ("The Japanese as Library Patrons: An Intercultural Perspective on Information Literacy," no. 70). Librarians need to be sensitive to the need for students from some cultures to "save face" and should be prepared to offer positive reinforcement and support.

Recent literature on international students suggests that the transition to independent research is often one of the major challenges faced, and the development of critical thinking skills is identified as one of the most important facets of information literacy instruction programs. However, library self-sufficiency may be an especially difficult concept to grasp for those from countries with a societal structure in which lower classes do the bidding of the wealthier upper classes. Librarians may be regarded as simply clerks expected to fulfill the students' requests.

While knowledge of other cultural norms may be helpful when interacting cross-culturally, it is still extremely important to keep in mind that cultural stereotyping is an obstacle to communication on the part of both librarians and students. Stereotypes often contain elements of truth, but they prevent real understanding of individual needs.

Learning Styles

There is a considerable body of literature dealing with differences in learning styles between North American students and those from other cultures.

North Americans tend to be verbal, and from early childhood onward they are encouraged to learn through question-and-answer sessions. It is common to question teachers, even if doing so counters the teachers' authority. Independent research and creative original work are promoted. In many other societies, in particular Asian and some Middle Eastern cultures, students are taught to defer to the authority of the teacher, to respond only to direct questions, and to learn by observation and imitation. Memorization is expected, and independent research not a priority. As a result, plagiarism is not viewed as negatively as it is in Western cultures (see, for example, Deckert, "Perspectives on Plagiarism from ESL Students in Hong Kong," no. 49).

In many cultures children grow up in an environment that encourages them to be strongly identified with an extended family. Group achievement is considered more important than individual identity and accomplishment. This orientation leads to a perspective on such issues as individual testing and evaluation that is much different from that in the West.

Information-seeking behavior is also often culturally based. Mengxiong Liu points out ("Ethnicity and Information Seeking," no. 258; "Library Services for Ethnolinguistic Students," no. 259) that in many ethnic communities, including Chinese, Japanese, Korean, and Latino groups, gatekeepers play an important role in this process, providing links between their communities and the appropriate information resources. For this reason, international students may consider it more appropriate to seek assistance from intermediaries within their ethnic group— friends or relatives—than to ask for assistance from outsiders such as librarians.

Differences between Libraries in Host and Home Countries

Initially, even locating the library building may prove confusing for those from cultures accustomed to *borrowing* books from the "bibliotheca" or "bibliothèque" and *buying* books at a "libreria" or "librairie." Once inside, procedures in American libraries may be very different than those in other parts of the world, especially for those from developing nations. In cultures where lectures and textbooks are considered the major means of disseminating information, the library may not be seen as having much significance. The breadth of materials available to Western students can be overwhelming to students from countries where information is restricted or unavailable due to cost or bureaucracy. In addition, North American libraries do not generally engage in censorship, but this practice is common in many countries, in particular with respect to government materials.

Some libraries still have closed stacks and students do not have free access to library holdings. This situation, previously the norm in most European and Asian countries, is now changing but is still the case in many older libraries. Many books are noncirculating, and there may be limits on the number of items that can be taken out at one time.

In many parts of the world libraries are considered to be primarily quiet places for study. They are run by students or clerks whose principal responsibility is to retrieve books.

Library reserve collections may be totally unfamiliar or confusing for those for whom these collections exist primarily as repositories for multiple copies of course textbooks. Such concepts as bibliographic instruction and inter-library loans may also be unknown, as are professional librarians and the practice of seeking reference assistance in finding information.

Library classification schemes in North America are often different from those to which students are accustomed, and the use of different classification schemes within the same library—for example, one form of coding for books and a separate form for government materials—may be particularly confusing. The Library of Congress system, which is the standard system used in North American academic libraries, may be inadequate to international students' needs, since it is Western-focused and does not always provide detailed access to subjects such as Asian literature, Middle Eastern history, or non-Christian religions.

Certain aspects of the North American approach to book arrangement on library shelves are confusing even to domestic students, for example, "call numbers" which begin with letters. Many students have trouble alphabetizing if they are from countries that do not use a Roman alphabet, and this can cause problems when trying to locate books on open shelves. Even the North American practice of shelving books from left to right is not standard in some parts of the world.

Students from some countries may not be accustomed to libraries where all material is indexed in a single library catalog. For example, at Phillips University in Marburg, Germany, which I visited in 2003, online cataloging began in 1987 and at that time the catalog included all materials from 1974 onward, except that entries from 1974 to 1986 were incomplete (S–Z entries were not yet available). Retrospective cataloging was continuing on these titles. There was also an online catalog of works dating from 1930 to 1973, accessible through a larger union catalog maintained in Frankfurt. However, this consisted of scanned catalog cards, so was accessible only through main entry, with no keyword searching. For subject access to the scanned material, it was necessary to use the old book catalogs. Finally there was a printed catalog of pre-1929 works, which also consisted of scanned catalog cards, and a separate catalog for dissertations from various German universities. Marburg has a decentralized library system, and most of the branch libraries used their own classification schemes and maintained their own catalogs of holdings. In contrast, most North American academic libraries have a single integrated online library catalog. However, access to information usually still involves learning to use a bewildering variety of search engines and interfaces. While the implementation of meta-search engines designed to allow a "one-stop shopping" approach to information retrieval is becoming increasingly common, these systems present their own problems, in particular, information overload.

Recent literature suggests international students are increasingly computer literate. In a 2000 article ("Trends in Computer Use among International Students," no. 190) Carol Taylor, Joan Jamieson, and Daniel Eignor reported on computer familiarity among English-as-a-second-language students learning English for higher education programs in North America. The 191,493 participants in their study were Test of English as a Foreign Language (TOEFL) examinees, who were tested twice. Frequency of computer use, frequency of using English word-processing software, and Internet use were among factors used in developing profiles and determining if the profile was changing. Results indicated increased use of computers, English word processing, and, most notably, the Internet over the test period (one and a half years), with dramatic differences evident from what had been reported in a similar study done in 1989. A 2003 survey conducted at San Jose State University in California and designed to assess incoming international students' library and computer experience before coming to the United States (Jackson, "Incoming International Students and the Library: A Survey," no. 240) showed that 94 percent of incoming international students used a library in their home country, and of those, 84 percent had used a computer inside a library, 96 percent regularly used the Internet, and 93 percent had used e-mail. Around 80 percent had conducted some form of computerized library research before coming to the United States, although over half had never used a chat room or instant messaging. A 2005 survey undertaken at Virginia Tech University in Blacksburg, Virginia (Liao, Finn, and Lu, "Information-Seeking Behavior of International Graduate Students vs. American Graduate Students: A User Study at Virginia Tech 2005," no. 256) suggested that online information resources and searching tools are becoming the favorite choice of graduate students. During the general information-seeking process, searching the Internet and exploring library electronic resources were the top starting methods used by all respondents (224 American students and 91 international students). However, information in library books and the library catalog played a more important role in international students' information-seeking behavior.

While it is obvious that the technological skills of international students coming to North America are changing, library automation may still be a new experience for students from some developing countries. It also needs to be recognized that prior computer use does not necessarily imply familiarity with library systems. Philip Howze and Dorothy Moore reported on a 2003 survey of international students' knowledge of terms in the American College and Research Libraries Instruction Section's Committee on Instruction for Diverse Populations multilingual glossary ("Measuring International Students' Understanding of Concepts Related to the Use of Library-Based Technology," no. 178). The 153 respondents were enrolled in the Intensive English laboratory course at Wichita State University in Wichita, Kansas. Results indicated a significant disparity between self-reported or perceived understanding and actual understanding of the terms in the glossary.

The advent of online systems that allow keyword searching has meant that gaining an understanding of controlled vocabulary and standardized subject headings may be somewhat less relevant than it was in the past. However, it must be kept in mind that keyword access may be difficult for those whose vocabulary, in particular their knowledge of synonyms, is limited. In addition, keeping up with the ever-changing technology in libraries can be difficult for all students (as it often is for the librarians as well) and that the most effective use of the library requires a sophisticated knowledge of search strategies despite efforts to create systems that are "user-friendly."

Library Anxiety

Linguistic, cultural, and technological issues such as those outlined above often lead to library anxiety on the part of international students. The issue of library anxiety has been the focus of a number of studies conducted by Anthony Onwuegbuzie and Qun Jiao. One of their later articles, published in 2001 (Sources of Library Anxiety among International Students," no. 242), concluded that mechanical barriers (e.g., computer indexes, online facilities, printers, photocopiers, and change machines) caused the greatest degree of library anxiety, followed by affective barriers (e.g., feelings of inadequacy about using the library, barriers related to staff, comfort with the library, and knowledge of the library).

There have also been several noteworthy recent dissertations dealing with library anxiety. Abdulaziz Ben Omran's 2001 Ph.D. research (*Library Anxiety and Internet Anxiety among Graduate Students of a Major Research University*, no. 171) considered the correlations between selected variables (year of study, major, grade point average, number of library instruction sessions attended, gender, age) and whether these variables could predict anxiety. Results indicated that library anxiety and Internet anxiety existed among the subjects of this study, who were graduate students at the University of Pittsburgh in Pennsylvania, but age was the only variable that predicted library anxiety. The frequency of Internet use and subject major were significant in predicting Internet anxiety. Joel Battle's 2004 study, conducted at Richland College in Dallas, Texas (*The Effect of Information Literacy Instruction on Library Anxiety among International Students*, no. 21), concluded that library training reduced both general anxiety and library anxiety for international students.

LIBRARY-RELATED ISSUES

As international student populations in North America grew from the 1970s onward, debates arose in the literature about the degree to which librarians should accommodate this group. Some librarians thought they deserved no special treatment beyond that received by all new students, arguing that offering separate programs would delay integration into the academic mainstream. Others advocated the development of special programs to accelerate adjustment to North American libraries. At the present time, the focus is on recognizing and responding to the unique needs of international students.

Basic Library Orientation

Probably the most popular method of orienting international students are basic tours designed to point out the physical environment within the library building. Such tours are most frequently offered by reference staff. However, some libraries have had success with other approaches.

In the early 1980s, the State University of New York at Buffalo began a program in which orientation tours were presented in languages other than English by student volunteers recruited from international student associations and clubs (see Lopez, "Chinese Spoken Here: Foreign Language Library Orientation Tours," no. 7). This concept worked well, and it was noted that students appreciated the special effort made by the library to be proactive in reaching out to them. In the early 1990s Rutgers University Libraries also began offering non-English language tours (see Liestman and Wu, "Library Orientation for International Students in Their Native Language," no. 6). In this case Chinese language tours were offered by a librarian fluent in Mandarin, while Korean language sessions were conducted through a translator. Whereas the SUNY–Buffalo tours took place at the beginning of the term, those at Rutgers were presented during the third and fourth weeks of the semester, after students had had an opportunity to get settled in but before they became so involved in their studies that they did not have time to attend. The sessions covered such areas as: the services offered by reference librarians, how to search for books, how to locate books, using circulation, searching for periodical articles, locating periodicals, and getting materials from other libraries. Although initial attendance was low, those who participated found the sessions useful.

The design and implementation of orientation programs in the native languages of international students is a labor-intensive exercise for library staff and difficult to administer to a large and varied student population. It is still most common for libraries to offer international students brief library tours in English as part of their general orientation programs.

In addition to in-person library orientation tours, various types of audio-visual presentations have also been offered to international students. In the 1980s and 1990s these usually took the form of audio-taped walking tours (see, for example, Huls, Parsons, Peterson, and Vakili, *Planning, Producing, and Implementing a Multilingual Audiotape Walking Tour of The Iowa State University Parks Library*, no. 4). However, virtual tours are now more common. At Baruch College, City University of New York, a web-based tour was developed in the early 2000s and offered in the most commonly reported native languages of the college's students: English, Spanish, Chinese, Korean, Japanese, Russian, Polish, Greek, and Turkish (see Downing and Klein, "A Multilingual Virtual Tour for International Students," no. 3). The tour consisted of three sections: a welcoming text and audio-message, a twenty-eight-frame "slide show" presenting key features of the library, and a set of interactive floor plans. Reports emphasized that such approaches were meant to enhance rather than replace face-to-face interactions between library staff and international students, and that walking tours and other forms of basic orientation were still provided. However, a virtual presence was found to be useful in establishing an early rapport with international students and it supplied them with a format that was understandable and convenient.

The literature also emphasizes the importance of providing international students with written support materials. While these are most often in English, Oregon State University's Helping Hands Project provides an example of a multilingual venture (see Chau, "Helping Hands: Serving and Engaging International Students," no. 1). The aim of this project was to create a two-page handout in fourteen different languages. It was a collaborative project between the university's libraries and international office. Such efforts can be extremely helpful to international students, but projects of this scope, like audio-visual or web presentations, require a great deal of time and expertise and usually require grants or other special funding both to produce and to maintain.

Many libraries have also produced printed library guides in English aimed at international students (see, for example, *Georgia College Libraries Handbook for International Students*, no. 335, San Diego State University's *Library Research Guide for International Students*, nos. 337–338, or the Rutgers University *Library Guide for International Students*, no. 339). Libraries have also been encouraged to capitalize on other university publications. A review of current orientation guides from various universities indicates that few make mention of the library. Therefore, there is a need for librarians to be proactive in seeking to have library information included in general guides to campus life published by international student or graduate student offices and in packages sent to students before their arrival in the country or distributed during their orientation week.

Because of the difficulties in keeping printed library guides current, it is increasingly common for information to be made available on a web page specifically designed for international students. This page usually includes links to relevant library information (key contacts, borrowing information, how to locate materials, maps, glossaries of library terms) and could also include links to other helpful information such as other university services for international students, international news sources, worldwide weather information, online bilingual dictionaries or translation sites, contact information for local religious and ethnic groups, and local transportation information. While most web pages of this type are in English only, the University of Alabama Libraries developed an ambitious multilingual web page in 2005–2006 (see McClure and Krishnamurthy, "Translating the Libraries: A Multilingual Information Page for International Students," no. 366). However, once again it must be emphasized that complex projects of this type require time and expertise to produce, and usually require grants to cover initial and ongoing costs.

Bibliographic Instruction/Information Literacy

Much of what has been written on international students and academic libraries has focused on library instruction or information literacy. A number of questionnaire surveys have been conducted to determine the extent to which bibliographic instruction for international students has been offered and the nature of the programs implemented. Reference has already been made to the 1984 survey of forty-four directors at large American academic libraries conducted by Frank William Goudy and Eugene Moushey ("Library Instruction and Foreign Students: A Survey of Opinions and Practices among Selected Libraries," no. 63), the 1984 survey of librarians at fifty-four American colleges and universities with large international student populations by Laura S. Kline and Catherine M. Rod ("Library Orientation Programs for Foreign Students: A Survey," no. 5), and Benhong Tsai's 1988 survey of library directors at sixty medium-sized state universities (*Special Bibliographic Instruction for International Students: A Survey of Academic Libraries in Medium Sized State Universities*, no. 134). In addition, there have been several studies of Canadian programs, including Maureen Fanning Beristain's 1985 *Survey of Primary Bibliographic Instruction Methods and Aids Currently Used in Selected Canadian Academic Libraries* (no. 23) documenting efforts at twenty-nine academic libraries and designed to provide an update of a similar survey conducted in 1977, and Vivian Howard's 1994 master's dissertation, *Orientation Programs for International Students at Canadian Academic Libraries* (no. 75), which was based on data from thirty selected universities and degree-granting colleges.

Most articles dealing with bibliographic instruction begin with references to prior research. A particularly useful summary of earlier literature is found in Allen Natowitz's 1995 article "International Students in US Academic Libraries: Recent Concerns and Trends" (no. 275), which provides content analysis of eighteen journal articles written between 1985 and 1993 on international students and their use of American academic libraries and discusses implications for staff development and bibliographic instruction programs. This was updated by Sara Baron and Alexia Strout-Dapaz in the 2001 article "Communicating with and Empowering International Students with a Library Skills Set" (no. 20), which includes a chart listing pedagogical suggestions drawn from works published between 1993 and 2000. Also useful is Beth Ann Patton's 2002 master's thesis from Biola University (*International Students and the American University Library*, no. 279), which consists primarily of a literature review.

The literature dealing with bibliographic instruction and international students tends to be highly repetitive. However, individual writers focus on different aspects of the task. The following are common themes.

Responding to Language, Cultural, and Technological Barriers

Most articles discuss to some extent the linguistic, cultural, and technological barriers faced by international students, but a number concentrate specifically on those issues and responses to them.

Some of the entries included in the bibliography are drawn from general literature and do not deal with library instruction specifically. However, publications such as Shirley Peck's 1992 article "International Students and the Research Process" (no. 117), Susan Coleman's 1997 article "International Students in the Classroom: A Resource and an Opportunity" (no. 40), Janette Ryan's *Guide to Teaching International Students* published in 2000 (no. 124), Paul Kurucz's 2006 text *How to Teach International Students: A Practical Teaching Guide for Universities and Colleges* (no. 91), or Carolina Valiente's 2008 article "Are Students Using the 'Wrong' Side of Learning? A Multicultural Scrutiny for Helping Teachers to Appreciate Differences" (no. 135) all provide useful suggestions for librarians who teach. Much of the recent literature on teaching international students emanates from Australia, which has a high number of students from Asia in particular; see, for example: Arkoudis (*Teaching International Students: Strategies to Enhance Learning*, no. 12); Ballard (*Helping Students from Non-English Speaking Backgrounds to Learn More Effectively*, no. 15; "Overseas Students and Australian Academics: Learning and Teaching Styles," no. 16; "Sink or Swim: In Class or at Home," no. 17); Ballard and Clancy (*Teaching Students from Overseas: A Brief Guide for Lecturers and Teachers*, no. 18; *Teaching International Students: A Brief Guide for Lecturers and Supervisors*, no. 19); Biggs ("Teaching Across and Within Cultures: The Issue of International Students," no. 24). There is also a considerable body of literature dealing specifically with information literacy and overcoming barriers when teaching in the library setting, for example, DiMartino and Zoe ("International Students and the Library: New Tools, New Users, and New Instruction," no. 50), Jacobson ("Bibliographic Instruction and International Students," no. 83), Kflu and Loomba ("Academic Libraries and the Culturally Diverse Student Population," no. 87), Liestman ("Implementing Library Instruction for International Students," no. 94), O'Hara ("Bibliographic Instruction for Foreign Students," no. 107).

The 2001 article by Sara Baron and Alexia Strout-Dapaz cited earlier ("Communicating with and Empowering International Students with a Library Skills Set," no. 20), which was based on data collected by librarians and staff of international student offices at 123 colleges and universities in the southern United States, recommended a model for library skills training that integrated the ACRL Information Literacy Competency Standards. Australian librarian Hilary Hughes (*Information Literacy with an International Focus*, no. 76) also recommended the use of the information literacy standards produced by ACRL, along with those prepared by the Council of Australian University Librarians (CAUL), as practical frameworks for information literacy education designed to meet the needs of all students, including international students.

Miriam Conteh-Morgan's 2003 article entitled "Journey with New Maps: Adjusting Mental Models and Rethinking Instruction to Language Minority Students" (no. 43) is of particular interest. The author reviewed literature from the previous three decades, noting that two key points arise: the sameness in the issues discussed (language, culture, technology) and the semantic similarities between some of the terms used to describe international students' North American experiences—problems, obstacles of major proportions, deficiencies, difficulties, obstructions, barriers, challenges. She commented:

Taking these two observations together—that is, the recurring themes, and the terms used to describe these students' library experiences—what can be deduced is that (a) in the past three decades or so, there has been hardly any noticeable change in the profile of students who come to study in the United States, and (b) that their experiences continue to be marked by struggles. In short, the narrative constructed . . . presents international students as flat, non-evolving characters, continually laboring under the weight of their linguistic, cultural, and technological disadvantages, as they try to acquire an American education.

Conteh-Morgan acknowledged that these descriptions do reflect some aspect of reality, but argued that

the insistence on differences, the negative meanings attributed to them, and the persistence of these in the literature over the decades, have led librarians, whether consciously or unconsciously, to construct a one-dimensional image of international students. These students are depicted as constituting an accretion of deficits, and this image has stuck in the collective minds of librarians. And because the literature has, by adopting a problem-deficit stance, paid more attention to their less-than-positive characteristics, an essentialist image of international students has been constructed, which has led to fossilized mental models of them. The mental models in turn have affected instructional philosophies and the practices derived from them.

She went on to suggest that the standard assumptions regarding language and technology barriers may not accurately reflect the demographics of today's international students and that librarians need to adjust their perceptions and create more pedagogically and culturally responsive learning environments.

One method that has been proposed for dealing with linguistic and technological issues is to set up library databases to take advantage of interfaces and search functions in foreign languages. This function, which is available for products from such vendors as EBSCO, OCLC's FirstSearch, CSA, and JSTOR, can then be pointed out to international students during bibliographic instruction sessions. Fu Zhuo, Jenny Emanuel, and Shuqin Jiao reported on a 2005 survey conducted by librarians at Central Missouri State University and St. Louis University in Missouri involving 128 respondents (see "International Students and Language Preferences in Library Databases Use," no. 194). Data was collected on the use of multilingual features, bibliographic instruction given in the students' home nations, and questions about the literal translation of search keywords and terms. Results indicated most students were not familiar with the interface translation services provided by database vendors, but indicated that it would be useful to know about them. The survey report recommended that these features be activated. Librarians were then able to tailor their instruction to best meet students' database searching needs.

Responding to Specific Culture-Based Concerns

Some authors have examined specific culture-related issues that impact instruction for international students. A number have discussed learning styles. Some consider the issue from a general perspective—see Anderson and Adams, "Acknowledging the Learning Styles of Diverse Student Populations: Implications for Instructional Design," no. 11; Ladd and Ruby, "Learning Style and Adjustment Issues of International Students," no. 92; Niles, "Cultural Differences in Learning Motivation and Learning Strategies: A Comparison of Overseas and Australian Students at an Australian University," no. 104; Chattoo, "Reference Services: Meeting the Needs of International Adult Learners," no. 374. Others focus on the experiences of specific ethnic groups—see Chan ("The Chinese Learner: A Question of Style," no. 37); Nield ("Questioning the Myth of the Chinese Learner," no. 103); Griggs and Dunn ("Hispanic-American Students and Learning Style," no. 66, and "Learning Styles of Asian-American Adolescents," no. 67); Park ("Learning Style Preferences of Southeast Asian Students," no. 113); Rao ("Bridging the Gap between Teaching and Learning Styles in East

Asian Context," no. 120); Wong ("Are the Learning Styles of Asian International Students Culturally or Contextually Based?" no. 139). Mestre ("Accommodating Diverse Learning Styles in an Online Environment," no. 185) focuses on learning styles and the design of online tutorials.

Other authors have expanded upon the notion of differences of world view between international and Western students. Poping Lin ("Library Instruction for Culturally Diverse Populations: A Comparative Approach," no. 95) compares the more holistic and macroscopic world view of Chinese students and the specific mechanistic and microscopic world view of Western students and the implications for library instructors. Owens ("'Fitting In' in a 'Stand Out' Culture: An Examination of the Interplay of Collectivist and Individualist Cultural Frameworks in the Australian University Classroom," no. 112) examines the implications of differences between collectivist and individualist perspectives.

Classroom Communication

Most articles on bibliographic instruction place emphasis on principles of classroom communication. However, there is also information relevant to library instructors that can be gleaned from the general literature on teaching, for example, Brown, "Getting It Together: Tactics for Reducing Verbal Miscommunication between Native English-Speaking Instructors and Non-Native English-Speaking Students" (no. 32); Golemon, "Intercultural Classroom Communication" (no. 62); Jenkins, "Teaching the New Majority: Guidelines for Cross-Cultural Communication between Students and Faculty" (no. 84). Dawn Amsberry's 2008 article "Talking the Talk: Library Classroom Communication and International Students" (no. 9) provides a particularly useful review of the literature on classroom communication from both the second language acquisition and library fields.

Bibliographic Instruction/Information Literacy Programs

The library literature includes numerous descriptions of instructional programs specifically designed for international students. A few discuss credit programs. Both the University of Toledo in Ohio (Brock, "Library Skills for International Students: From Theory to Practice," no. 30; Brock and Archer, "Library Search Strategies for International Students: A Practical Experience," no. 31) and East Texas State University in Commerce, Texas (Correll, *Attitudes of International Students in Regard to Library Skills Development in the Academic Setting*, no. 45; Correll and Brooks, "The International Student and Use of the Library in Graduate Study," no. 46), successfully offered such programs in the 1980s. However, it does not appear that this practice is common.

Several exemplary bibliographic instruction programs are frequently mentioned in the literature. One is the LOIIS (Library Orientation and Instruction for International Students) project, developed and implemented at the University of

A Survey of Issues

California at Davis in the mid-1980s (Hoffman and Popa, "Library Orientation and Instruction for International Students: The University of California–Davis Experience," no. 73; Popa and Hoffman, "THE LOIIS Program: Final Report," no. 118). In this program efforts were made to actively involve all library staff members; they participated in special training programs, heard reports on research being conducted on international students, and were kept informed of the planning process. In addition, a network of twelve librarian volunteers was formed to provide support for students. International students were provided with promotional brochures, glossaries, printed tour guides, and evaluation questionnaires, then shown a slide presentation on the library and given detailed tours. Response to this project was extremely positive.

The bibliographic instruction program introduced for international students at Western Carolina State University in Cullowhee, North Carolina, in the mid-1990s is also of interest due to its focus on personalized library instruction tailored to individual needs (Watkins, "A Case in Point: Individual Library Instruction for International Students," no. 137). International students were identified through admission records and personally invited to participate in the program. They were taught in groups of one to four, and when there was more than one student, an attempt was made to group students from the same country. This approach allowed students to help each other understand concepts in their native language. The small group approach also meant that there was ample opportunity for hands-on experience. While this program was also deemed successful, it is noted that this approach would only be feasible in smaller institutions where numbers of international students were relatively low.

In 1995, Cynthia Mae Helms described the program undertaken at a small private university, Andrews University in Berrien Springs, Michigan ("Reaching Out to the International Students through Bibliographic Instruction," no. 69). Two kinds of library skills sessions for international students were offered: a basic workshop and an advanced workshop. Each session ran two hours or more, depending on student needs. The basic workshop provided an introduction to such topics as finding materials for a research topic, the Library of Congress classification system and subject headings, periodical indexes, and computerized bibliographic searching. It also included a library tour and brief social time. The advanced workshop built upon these skills, with a focus on computer searching. The library skills program was offered as a component of the overall international students orientation program. Helms outlined a number of factors that helped make the workshops successful. It was "given a professional look" by having students pre-register, then providing them with a portfolio containing handouts and name tags. Attendees were assured that this was a real workshop and that the time would be profitably spent. A friendly atmosphere was created by having participants introduce themselves and by including a brief social time with refreshments. Various teaching methods were used: lecture, discussion, demonstrations, and hands-on experience. Attempts were made to make the workshops as meaningful as possible by asking students to identify majors and topics of interest on the registration form so examples could be chosen appropriately. The workshops were widely publicized. Tours called attention to items of cultural interest. Students who registered were sent reminders to verify if they were coming, and when the workshops were over, feedback was solicited through formal evaluation forms. Those who did not return the form were personally contacted later for input. Although not all international students registered at the university chose to participate in the program, those who attended found it very helpful.

John Hickok has recently described "The Three I's" strategy developed and implemented at the California State University Fullerton Pollak Library in 2006–2007 ("Bringing Them into the Community: Innovative Library Instructional Strategies for International and ESL Students," no. 71). This approach combines elements of both outreach and instruction. *Inviting* involves proactively reaching out to international and English-as-a-second-language students and not just waiting for them to come to the library on their own. Librarians go to areas where students congregate, such as student cultural clubs and activities hosted by the international office, and make presentations on a familiar aspect of the students' culture, such as sports statistics or stock quotes. They then demonstrate how the library can assist in locating up-to-date information. The inviting process can also involve distribution of brochures outlining materials in the library relevant to students' home countries or cultures. The aim of inviting is not to teach library skills but to acknowledge the students' country/culture and to give them a reason to come to the library. After these initial visits, follow-up sessions can be scheduled by working with club presidents, student leaders, or ESL instructors. *Involving* calls for moving away from a direct instructional style and adopting a more experiential approach. Students who attend instruction sessions participate by going to open shelves and looking up books on their country or collaboratively assembling a correct citation. While students are being immersed in the library environment, instructors point out similarities and differences between libraries in their home countries and the United States. *Interfacing* involves two-way communication, for example, soliciting information about home libraries from international students, then sharing information, such as similarities and differences. This concept involves the idea of "scaffolding" advocated by Kamhi-Stein and Stein (see below), where new information is introduced gradually, building on already known information. Hickok notes that this approach to instruction has proven extremely successful but it is highly time intensive. He recommends a team approach to implementation, especially in the preparation of country- or culture-specific brochures.

Many library instruction programs have been designed in cooperation with other campus units working with international students. Most commonly, librarians allied themselves with teachers of English as a second language.

In the mid-1980s librarians at North Texas State University in Denton developed a program aimed at students enrolled in a non-credit English course prior to university admission (Cope and Black, "New Library Orientation for International Students," no. 44). Library orientation was modified to take into account the students' different cultural backgrounds and learning difficulties, and it emphasized both cognitive and attitudinal learning and development. ESL instructors, who were already known to students, actively participated in the library sessions as a liaison between librarians and students.

In 1989, Dick Feldman, an ESL teacher, and Joan Ormondroyd, a librarian, wrote of their experiences in working together over a number of years with international students enrolled in the Intensive English program at Cornell University in Ithaca, New York ("The International Student and Course-Integrated Instruction: The ESL Instructor's Perspective," no. 58; "The International Student and Course-Integrated Instruction: The Librarian's Perspective," no. 108). They discussed the development of a program involving course-integrated library instruction, where students completed research assignments under the supervision of the teacher and librarian. The need for ongoing evaluation and program improvement was emphasized.

More recently, in 1998, Lia Kamhi-Stein and Alan Stein, an ESL instructor and a librarian respectively, discussed their model for teaching information competency as a third language ("Teaching Information Competency as a Third Language: A New Model for Library Instruction," no. 86). The model was based on a number of principles that were grounded in second-language teaching theories, educational research, and library instructional practices: students should be provided with comprehensible input (i.e., a variety of approaches should be used to ensure that students understand); students should be provided with scaffolds (i.e., instruction should build upon what is already known and support for completing a task should be provided until it is no longer needed); library instruction should be an adjunct to course content; library instruction should be relevant to students' academic needs; library instruction should integrate information competence strategy training; library instruction should be hands-on. When these principles were applied at California State University, Los Angeles the model proved to have a positive impact on student learning outcomes.

Bibliographic instruction can also be fostered through the use of peer instructors or advisors. This approach is particularly useful for students from cultures in which gatekeepers play an important role in information-seeking, as discussed earlier. In 1989 Barbara MacAdam and Darlene Nichols described a peer information counseling program set up at the University of Michigan libraries in Ann Arbor ("Peer Information Counseling: An Academic Library Program for Minority Students," no. 96). Elaina Norlin described a similar program at the University of Tucson in Arizona in 2001 ("University Goes Back to Basics to Reach Minority Students," no. 106). These programs were found to be of value for both international and minority students. Helena Rodrigues's 1992 doctoral dissertation, *Bibliographic Instruction for International Students: A Comparison of Delivery Methods* (no. 123), completed at Simmons College in Boston, described various methods of instruction and recommended the implementation of peer-tutoring program for students at the Roger Williams College Library in Bristol, Rhode Island. Fu Zhuo, Jenny Emanuel, and Shuqin Jiao ("International Students and Language Preferences in Library Databases Use," no. 194) also recommended peer counseling as a way in which newer international students could learn from previous mistakes and gain insight into differences between North American libraries and those at home. They also suggested that libraries could employ international students to translate library materials such as handouts and tutorials into their native languages, and that libraries could then share these translations with the international students at their own institutions and with those at other institutions through knowledge banks and links on websites. While it does not deal with international students or library resources specifically, S. C. Ender and F. B. Newton's book *Students Helping Students: A Guide for Peer Educators on College Campuses* (no. 54) provides useful background reading for setting up a library peer training program.

A number of writers have discussed the value of doing a needs assessment before designing a library orientation program for international students. Information about student needs can be gathered through surveys (see Garcha and Yates, "Bibliographic Instruction for International Students in Academic Libraries," no. 59; Orr, Slee, and Evryniadis, "International Students and the Electronic Library Facilities at Central Queensland University," no. 109), through personal interviews (see Hughes and Bruce, "Cultural Diversity and Educational Inclusivity: International Students' Use of Online Information," no. 180), or through the use of focus groups (see Ishimura, *Information Literacy in Academic Libraries: Assessment of Japanese Students' Needs for Successful Assignment Completion in Two Halifax Universities*, no. 81).

Although most of what has been written on bibliographic instruction focuses on face-to-face methods of teaching, virtual learning environments are becoming increasingly important. Online tutorials allow students opportunities to learn important library concepts at their own pace and to review as needed. While the literature on e-learning and international students is still sparse, a notable example is the description of the online tutorial designed to support the development of international students' information literacy skills produced as a joint project of the libraries and Learning Technologies Centre at the University of Manitoba in Winnipeg in 2006 (Braaksma, Drewes, Siemens, and Tittenberger, "Building a Virtual Learning Commons: What Do YOU Want to Do?" no. 29). The tutorial addressed a broad range of topics in addition to information-seeking skills, including the enhancement of social and cultural skills. Web 2.0 functionality was incorporated in order to allow students to interact outside the classroom. The final product was placed in the university's Virtual Learning Commons.

Also of interest for those interested in general aspects of international students and e-learning are the 2002 paper by Elisabeth Kamentz and Thomas Mandl, "Culture and E-learning: Automatic Detection of a Users' Culture from Survey

Data" (no. 181), and the 2005 article by Joanne Bentley, Mari Vawn Tinney, and Bing Howe Chia, "Intercultural Internet-Based Learning: Know Your Audience and What It Values" (no. 172), both of which discuss the importance of knowledge about the culture of a user in the design of computer systems for use by multinational populations. Linda Main's 2002 text *Building Websites for a Multinational Audience* (no. 183) also provides useful insights.

As noted earlier, there is a great deal of repetition in the literature dealing with international students and bibliographic instruction in academic libraries. To summarize, the most common comments and recommendations include:

- recognize that instruction may take longer for international students than for domestic students;
- be selective about what is taught, since too much information can be overwhelming;
- speak clearly, but keep in mind that speaking too slowly or overenunciating may be confusing;
- do not speak more loudly than usual;
- avoid the use of intonation to convey meaning, and listen to words not intonation when engaged in discussion;
- keep sentence structure and vocabulary simple;
- avoid colloquial expressions, slang, and culture-specific references;
- avoid the use of library jargon, which can be especially problematic for international students. Words such as "stacks" and "serials" or acronyms are usually meaningless unless efforts are made to provide explanations. This advice applies to both oral presentations and written materials;
- repeat important concepts often, using synonyms where possible;
- summarize often;
- make use of appropriate graphic aids;
- include information on research and study skills support available, especially if the library is part of a broader information commons environment;
- be careful when using humor, as this is an area that can cause particular problems; sarcasm, satire, and jokes, which may be intended as "ice breakers," are often misunderstood or misinterpreted;
- if it is necessary to incorporate references to politics and religion in the discussion, avoid making value judgments;
- acknowledge different learning styles, for example, students whose learning style is characterized by a lack of independence will learn best by being shown rather than having something explained to them;
- provide opportunities for participation, ask frequent questions that require responses, and provide hands-on experience;

- distribute written handouts outlining important points so students are not distracted by keeping notes; written glossaries explaining important library terms can also be helpful;
- use visual clues to reinforce what is being said, for example, write unfamiliar terms on the blackboard or whiteboard, demonstrate processes such as logging in to the computer or locating books on shelves, use exhibit items such as spine labels on books, use PowerPoint slides or transparencies to reinforce information but be sure they are relevant, legible, and concise;
- hone listening skills and be alert to various accents; if you cannot understand a student, ask him or her to write down what is meant;
- be aware of differences in meaning in nonverbal communication patterns;
- be observant and adapt teaching approaches to the audience;
- design sessions to cater to varying levels of technological ability by building in self-paced elements and providing backup resources whenever possible;
- ensure that students have easy access to information about plagiarism and how to maintain academic integrity in the North American academic environment;
- develop patience and be sensitive to the emotional state of students, who may be under intense pressure and experiencing culture shock;
- become knowledgeable about other cultures;
- establish mechanisms for obtaining feedback from students in order to improve future instructional sessions.

A final publication of particular note with respect to bibliographic instruction is one written in 1985 by Eugene Engeldinger, then head reference librarian at the University of Wisconsin–Eau Claire. In an article entitled "Bibliographic Instruction for Study Abroad Programs" (no. 55), he pointed out a fact that was at that time, and still appears to be, generally overlooked in the literature, namely, that international study is not one-directional. Engeldinger discussed the role of academic librarians in preparing North American exchange students for research in foreign libraries and the bibliographic culture shock that may occur. He noted that librarians who are interested in addressing this problem can take a number of steps, including: identifying countries where their institution operates exchange programs and how many students and staff participate in each; learning something about how the cultures in these countries differ from that in North America; and finding out about such issues as foreign language skills expected of students, academic goals of the program (for example, some are culturally oriented while others focus on academic instruction), research and library project expectations of faculty in the foreign institutions, the extent of English-language holdings in the foreign libraries, types of reference materials available, ways in which materials are accessed (including types of catalogs and classification systems), library services offered, and library policies with respect to loan periods, interlibrary loan, stack access, and photocopying. In the present day, determining the use and types of technology available in the host country would also be relevant.

Reference Services

The nature of international students' interactions at the reference desk and the quality of reference service they experience is a topic that appears in the literature much less frequently than discussion of library orientation and bibliographic instruction with this population. However, reference librarians play a critical role in the international students' educational experience. Many of the issues faced are similar to those encountered in instruction sessions, and most articles on reference transactions cover similar ground with respect to linguistic, cultural, and technological barriers to service. However, public service transactions may require more in-depth interaction with students, and other factors often come into play.

A number of writers, including Christopher Brown ("Reference Services to the International Adult Learner: Understanding the Barriers," no. 373) and Li Zhang ("Communication in Academic Libraries: An East Asian Perspective," no. 355), discuss the impact of high-context versus low-context communication styles. In low-context cultures, such as the German, Scandinavian, Swiss, and American, most of the information is expressed explicitly in the language. Communication is conducted in clear and straightforward terms. In high-context cultures, much of the message is encoded in the physical context or assumed from existing cultural knowledge. Communication does not require clear verbal articulation and makes significant use of implied meanings. This communication style, which is common in most Asian countries, stems largely from Confucianism, which emphasizes consideration for others and prevention of embarrassment or conflict between communicators. Li Zhang points out that the Japanese, Koreans, and Chinese rarely use the word "no" when they disagree with others. As a result care needs to be taken to ensure that information given out during a reference transaction is really understood and it is not the case that the student is simply being polite. In addition, East Asian students tend to go from general backgrounds and finally to specific questions when at the reference desk or during research consultations. This pattern contradicts cultural thinking patterns of native English speakers, who tend to go from the more specific point to related subtopics. This can lead to confusion or misunderstanding. East Asian thought patterns also tend to be more circular than linear.

Li Zhang's article also notes that in addition to difficulties in the interpretation of meanings between languages, differences in language structures can cause confusion when a native speaker and a non-native speaker interact. For example, in Chinese, Japanese, and Korean there are no word equivalents to the English articles "a," "an," or "the." Thus in a reference situation, reference to "a book" may mean either "a book" or "the book." Furthermore, there is not normally a true form of expressing plurality in these East Asian languages, so the use of the word "book" may imply one or many books. It is also helpful for librarians to be aware that in Chinese verbs do not reflect time relations. The concept of time is expressed by adverbs, such as yesterday, always, and so forth, and contextual assumptions. In addition, since the pronunciations "he" and "she" or "his" and "her" in the Chinese language are the same, librarians may have to examine the context of the interaction when negotiating questions during the reference interview.

This discussion of differences between North American and East Asian grammatical structures brought to mind a conversation I had many years ago with a Chinese music student during which I tried to explain the difference between sitting "at" the piano, sitting "on" the piano, and sitting "in" the piano.

Trying to determine a library user's information needs can be problematic at times, and the issue is compounded in the case of international students. In a 1996 article ("Reference Work with International Students: Making the Most of the Neutral Question," no. 378), Yvonne de Souza discusses closed questions as barriers and the value of asking neutral questions. For example, a question such as "Do you want maps or statistics?" offers only two options, neither of which may be desired. A question such as "Do you need background material, maps, or something else?" leaves the field open, though the student still may not know exactly what he or she wants. De Souza recommends looking at the reference interview from the user's point of view and using a strategy that seeks to put the request into context. She suggests such questions as "Can you tell me what you have already found or what kind of things will help you?" or "Tell me more about what you are looking for and how this will help you." When reference librarians take this approach, they do not make predictions or assumptions or allow the student to wander aimlessly. However, neutral questions may still cause discomfort or confusion for international students, due to language difficulties, anxiety, embarrassment, or fear, and librarians should prepare students by explaining the intent of their questions and allowing them time to respond.

Evaluation or measurement of the quality of reference service is usually difficult. In the introduction to their report "Reference Service to International Students: A Field Stimulation Research Study" (no. 375), Dr. Ann Curry and Deborah Copeman discussed the guidelines for effective reference developed in 1996 by the Reference and User Services Association (RUSA), a division of the American Library Association. The RUSA guidelines emphasize that effective service is not measured entirely by an answer's degree of accuracy, but through the interaction between the librarian and the user. Curry and Copeman's 2005 study investigated reference service provided to non-native English-speaking international students at eleven college and university libraries in the lower mainland of British Columbia, Canada. Their research used a field simulation methodology in which an individual posed as a library user and initiated a reference encounter in heavily accented English with library staff at each institution. In each case the same question was asked and after the interaction observed behaviors were recorded. Each library was visited by the same individual twice. A number of themes emerged from the data as important factors determining reference interview quality. Many of the factors identified were similar to those suggested above when engaging in bibliographic instruction sessions. They included such things as offering advice and suggestions; being approachable; following up (offering an invitation to return, asking if the question was answered); asking questions; being attentive; showing an awareness of language barriers; explaining and instructing; avoiding library jargon; demonstrating sound listening skills; paying attention to nonverbal communication; showing patience; making referrals if necessary; repeating and rephrasing; showing resourcefulness; showing interest in the student's questions; and speaking clearly. Results indicated that in 75 percent of cases service was satisfactory or very satisfactory. However, reference librarians did not always take into account linguistic difficulties, frequently used library jargon without providing explanations, often failed to ask enough questions, and commonly rushed the interaction to closure prematurely. A relationship was found between some library staff behaviors and the user's level of satisfaction and likelihood to return to the staff member in the near future.

In 2006 Justina Osa, Sylvia Nyuana, and Clara Obgaa prepared a set of useful suggestions for communicating with international students during the reference process ("Effective Cross-Cultural Communication to Enhance Reference Transactions: Training Guidelines and Tips," no. 387). Their Model Communication Behaviors Checklist was based on feedback from a staff professional development workshop developed and conducted in the Penn State Libraries, University Park, Pennsylvania, and Texas State University Library in San Marcos, Texas. The checklist identified verbal and nonverbal behaviors a librarian or teacher should exhibit when helping students from other cultures. These included telling them what you are going to do, positioning the computer screen in such a way that there is co-browsing, audibly working through the search, stopping the reference transaction at various points and summarizing the session thus far, providing oral summaries using straightforward grammar and standard vocabulary, encouraging responses and questions during the interaction, using effective listening skills, giving specific feedback, and checking for user understanding. When speaking to students they suggested speaking slowly, repeating if necessary using different phrasing, avoiding use of local expressions and idioms, confirming that you have been understood and offering to clarify if necessary, focusing on what is being said and not on the accent, confirming that you have understood by paraphrasing, verbally encouraging students to fully express themselves, and asking follow-up questions. Again, many of these reference interview techniques are similar to those recommended in the literature on bibliographic instruction.

Virtual reference services, either via e-mail or through virtual reference software, allows users to connect easily to librarians online. Such services do not seem to be widely used by international students—McClure and Krishnamurthy

("Translating the Libraries: A Multilingual Information Page for International Students," no. 366) reported that an analysis of the first year of online chat transactions at the University of Alabama indicated only 10 percent of questions came from international students. However, this form of interaction does allow users who are uncomfortable approaching a librarian in person or uncertain of their oral skills to submit anonymous questions. In addition virtual reference may facilitate the provision of unbiased service to diverse user groups due to the lack of social cues. However, this is not necessarily the case. In their article "Are Virtual Reference Services Color Blind?" (no. 389) Pnina Shachaf and Sarah Horowitz reported on a 2006 experiment in which twenty-three Association of Research Libraries member libraries received one virtual request per week for six consecutive weeks. The targeted reference services received a version of the same request but with a different user name suggestive of a different ethnic group or religious affiliation. Findings indicated the quality of service librarians provided to African Americans and Arabs was lower than the quality of service provided to Caucasian, Hispanic, Asian, and Jewish students. This article highlights the necessity for librarians to make a conscious effort to avoid cultural bias in the reference process even when providing service in an online environment.

As in the case of bibliographic instruction, conducting formal needs assessments may enhance reference service. Such studies often report that results were not as anticipated; for example, Suzanne Li's article "Library Services to Students with Diverse Language and Cultural Backgrounds" (no. 255), based on a focus group study of thirty students at the City University of New York, reported that only one student mentioned timidity about approaching library staff for help and most students did not view their language and cultural backgrounds as major deterrents to satisfactory use of the library. It was also noted that most of the suggestions about facilities, collections, resources, and staff that came out of the study would be helpful to any library patron, regardless of language or cultural background. Paying attention to most of the points raised would not require the creation of new services devoted to a small segment of library users and would result in improvement of those already in place for all.

In summary, most of the points noted above under bibliographic instruction apply equally to the provision of reference service. Other key factors include:

- keep in mind that lack of language fluency does not signal a lack of intelligence;
- stay calm and if necessary politely ask the student to repeat what they have said or ask them to write down a misunderstood word or phrase; if not understood initially, rephrase information or directions using different words;

- encourage dialogue and discussion in order to both clarify questions and to make sure information is clear;
- take care to avoid misleading body language and offensive gestures; as a general rule, limit eye contact and touching;
- avoid stereotyping. Diversity within as well as between ethnic groups needs to be recognized. International students are not a homogenous group, and even students from the same country do not necessarily have the same cultural background;
- strive to appear approachable and interested in helping. Students may be reluctant to approach a library service provider because they misunderstand the purpose of the library; they may not wish to bother library staff or to ask questions about things they feel they should already know, so they should be openly encouraged to seek help.

Marketing/Outreach

It was previously noted that reference service is among the concepts that are often unfamiliar to international students. Marketing is therefore of primary importance to inform students of the wealth of both information and assistance that is available to them in the North American academic library.

Librarians have demonstrated a variety of ways to reach out to international students. The 1984 survey by Kline and Rod cited earlier ("Library Orientation Programs for Foreign Students: A Survey," no. 5) showed that most of the fifty-four libraries that participated offered some kind of library orientation. This usually included tours, with explanations of basic sources such as periodicals, reference tools, and indexes and abstracts. Other methods identified were credit courses, subject seminars, freshman English and technical writing seminars, self-guided tours, term paper clinics, and course-related instruction.

Other types of specialized outreach to international students were offered as early as 1973. Montez Bryson's article "Libraries Lend Friendship" (no. 361) described the Foreign Student Outreach Program at the University of Denver in Colorado, which was designed to help international students develop library skills. Librarians participated in relationship-building activities such as offering in-library luncheons and tours, holding regular afternoon coffee hours at the Center for Foreign Students, visiting English-as-a-second-language classes and answering library-related questions, and donating materials to the foreign student lounge. Communication barriers were lessened as a result of this program.

Various subsequent writers have offered additional suggestions for library outreach. Nancy Seale Osborne and Cecilia Poon advised creating displays of culturally diverse library materials, allowing students to create displays for the library, encouraging students to recommend materials for purchase, hosting brown bag discussions with students, and developing culturally sensitive library staff ("Serving Diverse Library Populations through the Specialized Instructional Services

Concept," no. 111). Karen Bordonaro recommended highlighting recreational material available to international students in their own languages, arranging library displays on topics that support speakers or lectures on campus dealing with international topics, greeting international students by creating a sign at the entrance of the library that welcomes them in various languages, and educating domestic students by displaying a large map of the world that highlights the home countries of their fellow students ("We All Have an Accent: Welcoming International Students to the Library," no. 360). Cuiying Mu suggested using an e-mail list to send out a welcome message and introduction to library services at the beginning of terms and issuing regular e-mails throughout the term highlighting new library resources and tips on finding information; creating displays of different language study tools such as bilingual dictionaries, English thesauri, and dictionaries; displaying photos of librarians to help students identify contacts for their subjects; making efforts to meet students in a variety of settings, for example, by attending academic lectures; and getting to know the staff from the international students' center and encouraging them to refer students needing assistance ("Marketing Academic Library Resources and Information Services to International Students from Asia," no. 367). Moira Bent, Marie Scopes, and Karen Senior suggested having wall clocks displaying the time around the world in the library entrance/reception area; having a "watching wall" of televisions showing international news programs with headphones and comfortable seating; providing a selection of print newspapers from India, China, and the Middle East in the newspaper area; posting compass signs around the library to allow students to determine a direction of prayer; recognizing international holidays and festivals on library signs or web pages; providing information on local English language courses and activities of interest outside the university both at service points and on the library web pages; staging a multicultural library event; identifying multilingual library staff and their contact information on the library web pages; making use of international symbols and images instead of words on library posters and signage, where appropriate; and using pictures of people of different nationalities in library publications and posters (*Library Services for International Students*, no. 298). Terry Buckner and Tiana French proposed offering library space for art displays by members of local cultural groups; they also reported that the practice of inviting visiting faculty and librarians from international partner institutions to visit the library to observe and discuss library operations allowed all involved to learn from each other and to gain insights into ways in which both library outreach and library services could be improved ("International Students and the Academic Library: How One Library Is Working to Make Its International Students Feel at Home," no. 218).

The increasing use of specialized library web pages for international students as a form of information dissemination has already been noted. Web pages permit libraries to reach out and promote the library to large numbers of students in a systematic way. Wei Wei, science librarian at the University of California, Santa

Cruz, noted that the web had become the tool of choice for reaching engineering students at the university and the creation of a website was a top priority when the Science Library International Outreach Program was established in 1997 ("Outreach to International Students and Scholars Using the World Wide Web," no. 370). Once the website was developed, its URL was widely publicized on campus via e-mail and traditional printed sources. However, as Jennifer McClure and Mangala Krishnamurthy have pointed out ("Translating the Libraries: A Multilingual Information Page for International Students," no. 366), these pages are most effective in the context of a larger program of outreach efforts; in addition to maintaining their ambitious multilingual web-based information page, the University of Alabama Libraries continued to emphasize more personalized encounters with international students. These included sponsoring one of the international center's weekly coffee hours for international students each term, thus allowing librarians to meet with students in a casual setting; maintaining two televisions, with programming in Mandarin, Japanese, and South Asian languages as well as international soccer programming; having the libraries' liaison for international students meet with students at the university orientation session for international students at the beginning of the academic year; offering library tours specifically for international students; routinely offering bibliographic instruction to international students; featuring international scholars and artists in the libraries' lecture series; and mounting periodic exhibits featuring international collections and programs.

Needs analyses are particularly important when designing library outreach programs. Yolanda Cuesta and Gail McGovern pointed out ("Getting Ready to Market the Library to Culturally Diverse Communities," no. 362) that libraries often begin the marketing process by thinking about how to "get the word out." They assume that if people are not using the library it must be because librarians have not done a good enough job of telling them about the library and the services it provides. However, a more appropriate first step would be to learn about the community to be reached. This should then lead to informed decisions with respect to setting priorities and focusing marketing efforts. Cuesta and McGovern suggest that interviews with leaders of the different cultural communities and focus groups are two of the most effective ways to conduct needs assessments. While their article does not deal with the academic library environment specifically, many of the points raised are applicable in this setting.

Library Collections

In her 1988 dissertation (*Library Knowledge of International Students from Developing Countries: A Comparison of Their Perceptions with Those of Reference Libraries*, no. 214), Dania Bilal noted that the reference librarians surveyed felt that collection development efforts were unimportant to international students. However, when the students themselves were asked to identify the most important service a library can provide, they chose collection development as a top priority. This study, and a number of others (see Hodge and Ivins, "Current International Newspapers: Some Collection Management Implications," no. 157; Vocino, "International Newspapers for U.S. Academic Libraries: A Case Study," no. 163; Ziegler, "International Students and Country of Origin News," no. 164), identified foreign newspaper coverage as a particular concern. Today, online availability means that less attention needs to be paid to maintaining paper subscriptions to newspapers with all its inherent problems. However, the provision of a library web page providing quick links to a selection of international news websites and country-of-origin news sources in English would undoubtedly be welcomed by both international students and domestic students.

One of the major components of globalization in universities has been an increased focus on the internationalization of the curriculum. For libraries this means that the need for librarians to closely monitor course offerings and class outlines is more important than ever. In the past, many collection policies specified that the geographic focus would be North America and that books would be purchased for the most part from North American or European sources. However, in today's academic environment such practices need to be revised. Collection policies need to be frequently reviewed, updated, and broadened in scope to reflect new priorities in teaching and research. If topics or geographic areas of particular importance are identified, special efforts can also be made to expand relevant collections; for example, a 2005 article by Jessica Schomberg and Michelle Grace describes a special collection development project undertaken at Minnesota State University in Mankato designed to increase holdings dealing with Somalia and Somalis ("Expanding a Collection to Reflect Diverse User Populations," no. 162). The collections that result from such efforts will benefit all students and faculty.

Although escalating prices and declining budgets make it increasingly difficult for libraries to purchase non-course-related materials, a reading area with appropriate leisure reading in English or other languages for international students can often be established at relatively little cost. Library brochures prepared for international students can also highlight the locations of materials in other languages in the general collections.

Staff Development and Training

A number of writers have highlighted the vital role of library administration in fostering and supporting a positive work and study environment for minority and international library staff and students (see, for example, Miller, "Leading the Way to Diversity: The Academic Library's Role in Promoting Multiculturalism," no. 271; Buttlar, "Facilitating Cultural Diversity in College and University Libraries," no. 356; Trujillo and Weber, "Academic Library Response to Cultural Diversity: A Position Paper for the 1990s," no. 357; Welburn, "Rethinking

Theoretical Assumptions about Diversity: Challenges for College and University Library Planning," no. 358; Welch and Lam, "The Library and the Pluralistic Campus in the Year 2000: Implications for Administrators," no. 359; Gomez, "Cultural Diversity Staff Training: The Challenge," no. 390). Administrative efforts can include recruitment of minority staff members, particularly in visible positions, and instituting programs of staff training.

There are many advantages to specifically designating a multicultural librarian or a librarian responsible for work with international students. Suhasini Kumar and Raghini Suresh ("Strategies for Providing Effective Reference Services for International Adult Learners," no. 382) pointed out that an international student library liaison can gather information from the international office about incoming students, their majors, and countries from which they are coming, and serve as a liaison between the international office and library staff. He or she can provide initial library orientation and introduce students to reference librarians and subject specialists.

A librarian taking on such a role would find the 2005 article by Helen Singer from the University of Hertfordshire in Hatfield, England ("Learning and Information Services Support for International Students at the University of Hertfordshire," no. 296), of particular interest. Singer describes her own appointment as an international student liaison at the university library in 2004, steps undertaken to prepare for the role, and the work in which she was involved during her first six months on the job. A similar article written in 2006 by Caroline Gale ("Serving Them Right? How Libraries Can Enhance the Learning Experience of International Students: A Case Study from the University of Exeter," no. 226) describes that author's experiences at her institution.

Even if there is a specific liaison appointed for international students, the literature emphasizes the importance of striving to create a multiculturally diverse staff in the library and to train all staff to be sensitive to the needs of users from different cultural backgrounds. General training is especially important for libraries lacking the staff numbers and budget for specialized library instruction for international students. There are many approaches to staff development. Staff can be assigned relevant readings, listen to presentations by authorities on cross-cultural communication, view audio-visual materials, participate in sensitivity training exercises, work alongside international students on committees, and meet to discuss concerns. They can attend functions organized or attended by international students. Education in cultural awareness should be a requirement, not a voluntary activity, and it should involve employees at all levels within the library. It should also be ongoing.

A pioneering program designed to train staff to teach international students to use the library and to prepare library staff to communicate effectively with these students was introduced at the University of Arizona library in the mid-1980s (see Greenfield, "Training Library Staff to Reach and Teach International Students," no. 391; Greenfield, Johnston, and Williams, "Educating the World:

Training Library Staff to Communicate Effectively with International Students," no. 392). The program involved an intensive one-day training session developed through the cooperative efforts of the library instruction department, the university's Center for English as a Second Language, and the international student office. Although the workshop described in the literature took place in 1986, the basic approach is still relevant. Specific goals of the program were to have participants experience some of the pressures inherent in trying to understand concepts and words in a second language; to encourage participants to feel some of the emotions of culture shock; to lead participants into an awareness of their own cultural assumptions and interpretations; to show participants some typical cultural differences and some effective ways to handle intercultural communication; and to demonstrate how to be effective when dealing with students from other cultures, especially in instructional settings. Participants were asked to read in advance two articles on cultural differences and intercultural adjustment, and a reading list of additional articles was provided. At the workshop staff members were asked to take part in a role play, pretending they were graduate students from a developing country in their first semester at the university. The session began with the showing of a twelve-minute videotape introducing the policies and procedures of the Interlibrary Loan Department. It was delivered in Spanish by a native Mexican. English words and library terms were interspersed throughout the lecture so that native English speakers were able to understand part of what was being said. The speaker was instructed to use the pace, vocabulary, and content she would normally use when addressing a Spanish-speaking graduate class. Following the videotape viewing, participants were given a quiz in English on what they had learned and took part in a discussion of issues raised. The next segment of the workshop involved a cross-cultural simulation game entitled BaFá BaFá (more information below), which allowed participants to explore the emotions of culture shock. Discussion following the exercise showed that each of the two cultural groups involved (the Alpha Culture and the Beta Culture) had begun to form stereotypes about the contrasting culture and each group became increasingly critical of the values of the other. Next an expert in international teaching and cross-cultural communication addressed participants and outlined theory and practices in this field. Problems related to libraries and differences in library systems in different countries were also addressed. This was followed by a segment in which videos of library-related scenarios—an American student and an international student approaching the information desk—were shown and differences in the two interactions were compared and discussed. In the final segment of the workshop, videotapes of two sample instructional sessions were shown, both covering the same topic but with one designed for American students and one for international students. The texts of the sessions were distributed as a handout, with point-by-point analysis of differences between the two. Follow-up feedback indicated library staff gained an increased awareness of how they interacted with international students. As a result, instruction sessions were revised and extended. It was also noted that the cooperation necessary in planning and initiating the workshop not only improved cross-cultural understanding between students and library staff, but also increased communication between library staff and those responsible for international students on campus.

The staff development program organized by the University of Michigan Libraries in 1987 (Ball and Mahony, "Foreign Students, Libraries and Culture," no. 210) is also frequently cited in the literature. It was particularly noteworthy for the way in which it dealt with the issue of stereotyping. The four-hour workshop was designed with the goals of learning to differentiate between cultural and individual behavior patterns, heightening sensitivity to problems facing international students, and learning to communicate more effectively with international student populations. The videotape created at the University of Arizona (above) was utilized, but instead of the BaFá BaFá exercise, participants were divided into five small groups, representing East Asian, Indian, Middle Eastern, Southern European, and American cultures. Group members were then asked to identify stereotypes applicable to their assigned culture based on lists of cultural and linguistic attributes. The results not only sensitized participants to their own internal biases, but also taught them to objectively assess cross-cultural situations by analyzing behavior and distinguishing cultural cues from individual traits. The session also included discussion of general cultural traits and of how libraries reflect their cultural contexts. Participants' evaluations felt the workshop was successful in broadening their understanding of international students' perspectives. However, the authors of the report suggested that theirs was only one of a number of approaches that could be used to sensitize library staff; they noted that a workshop with international students describing their experiences firsthand would also help raise consciousness.

The simulation exercise BaFá BaFá, which formed a part of the University of Arizona staff training, was initially designed in the 1970s for the U.S. Navy as a training tool for overseas assignments. It is still widely used in various educational, health, and governmental agencies (see Shirts, *BaFà BaFà: A Cross Culture Simulation*, no. 403). In the late 1990s two librarians with many years of international experience—Wendy White, director of the Division for International Organizations and Academy Cooperation at the National Research Council (U.S.), and Gail Wadsworth, a U.S. Peace Corps administrator—created the game *Pamoja* (the Swahili word for "together"), which was designed specifically for cross-cultural training of librarians and teachers. The game is based on the premise that different cultures value and share knowledge in different ways. Both culture and policy influence access to information, and information resources are not equitably distributed around the world, or even within countries. Game players learn about the facts and characteristics of each other's cultures and raise money to build information centers. Participants debrief by discussing their countries' cultural characteristics. A variety of topics can be considered, including cross-cultural relations, sustainable library development, cooperation and competition, teamwork, negotiation, and equitable access to information. (See Sapon-White, "Pamoja: Learning about International Library Issues through a Simulation Game," no. 400.)

Many university libraries have created staff development programs to assist library staff working with international students who are library users. It is also becoming increasingly important for libraries to provide cross-cultural training to librarians who supervise student employees. Heather Blenkinsopp ("Communicating across Cultures for Reference Librarians Who Supervise," no. 372) noted that as both student and employee populations become more culturally diverse, librarians need to increase their supervisory communication skills to effectively manage their departments. Jane McGurn Kathman and Michael D. Kathman ("What Difference Does Diversity Make in Managing Student Employees?" no. 394) discussed the opportunities and challenges of working with the new generation of student workers. The opportunities include employees who can serve as sources of information and who can contribute their perspectives about what might make the library more inclusive in the types of services it offers. The challenges are that library staff must rethink the way they select, train, supervise, and evaluate a more diverse workforce.

While many of the articles dealing with student employee diversity focus on ethnic minority students who are permanent residents of North America, Harriett M. Pastor and Lia S. Hemphill discussed international student employees more specifically, and the way in which academic libraries are in a unique position to help these students in the acculturation process ("Acculturation of the International Student Employee in Urban University Libraries," no. 398). The results of two surveys, one of librarians who had supervised international student employees and one of international students who had worked in libraries, showed that the library served as a learning center for both the students and library staff. Library work provided an opportunity for students to observe North American learning styles, humor, cultural practices, and language use, and to hone both their listening and communication skills, while librarians gained a greater understanding of other cultures.

Staff Exchanges and International Visits

One of the more interesting avenues for staff development is participation in international visits or librarian exchanges. The practice of job exchange can be traced back many decades. While the vast majority of articles listed in the Staff Exchanges/International Visits section of the bibliography date from the late 1980s to the present, the benefits of broadening one's professional horizons was advocated in library literature as early as the 1940s. Florence Downs, an assistant at the Bloomfield, New Jersey, Public Library noted in 1941 ("Exchange Positions," no. 433, p. 648):

An exodus of writers from America to France took place in the 1920's. Such men as Louis Bromfield and Glenway Wescott expatriated themselves because they felt that the familiar world would become more surely theirs to write about in unfamiliar surroundings. The scenes we are living in the midst of are the most difficult to visualize adequately, or in fact to evaluate at all.

The author then goes on to apply these concepts to librarians:

What would librarians see of our professions and our jobs if they were a thousand miles away from them? Would the routine and procedure seem as necessary to us as they do when we are in the midst of them?

It is of course impossible for most of us to get that perspective, even if there were a France these days to go to. But we can get the same feeling of remoteness by changing positions, the Northerner going South, the Easterner West and so on.

If we go a little distance from home then, we see new worlds, professional and physical. And this is good for us. It is the easiest thing in the world to begin to think our way of doing a thing is the only way to do it, whether it's a case of eating baked beans for supper every Saturday night or using pink book cards for seven-day books and blue cards for two-week books.

Learning to live with a new set of staff members is equally tonic, especially if they have a different set of values and interests from those we have been used to. Getting used to colloquialisms and deleting them from our own speech, eating lunch opposite new faces, and walking fresh ways all enrich a personality as only new experiences can do.

But how is this to be done? Teachers can exchange with one another without much difficulty because under certification they and their positions are as neatly labeled as the bottles in a pharmaceutical laboratory. But librarians are not so neatly labeled, as yet, largely because our backgrounds have not solidified into a real professional form, as have the teachers'. However, once we feel that exchanges are necessary to the health of the body politic and of the library profession, nothing will long stand in our way.

Exchanging positions was not seen to be without challenges. Margery Bedinger, head of the Science and Engineering Department of Denver (Colorado) Public Library, commented in a 1953 article "An Exchange Year Abroad" (no. 410, p. 285):

The thought of an exchange year in a foreign country is both stimulating and thrilling. The natural impulse of the adventurous soul, and such an experience is only for the adventurous, is to soar into that delightful land where dreams come true. And your dreams will materialize, but perhaps not quite as you pictured them. If you realize this and are aware of the less glamorous side of the picture before you go, you will be better prepared to cope with the difficult elements in the situation, and the adjustments you will have to make will be easier. You will realize that to travel in a foreign country is one thing; to live there, quite another; and to hold down a job, still a different matter. The traveler is on holiday, his outlook carefree and rose-colored. He protects himself from discomfort by staying in the best hotels, and if annoyance occurs, well, it is all a lark anyway. But when you live in a country, you get right down to conditions, good and bad. The glamor approach is replaced by the monotony of every-day experience, and if you add work, then the difficulties and irritations attendant on any job arise, necessitating an added set of adjustments.

Bedinger goes on to discuss necessary accommodations in the areas of climate, medical care, and diet. She notes travel and communication may not be as convenient as it is at home, and "strange methods of speech (even in English language countries)" and varying customs are to be expected. She also goes on at some length warning about prejudice against Americans in some countries.

While both Downs and Bedinger highlight benefits of exchanges for the participants, it was also recognized early that the goal of exchanging jobs was not solely personal growth and enrichment. Grinton I. Will, a Yonkers, New York, librarian, noted in a 1940 article ("When Assistants Exchange Positions," no. 563, p. 11):

> Any justification of exchanges must be made on the grounds that this plan for in-service training is designed to improve library service. The purpose is to give individuals in library service new, and broader experience than they would enjoy if limited to contacts made only through actual employment. Individuals profit by exchanges, but the vital point is that the libraries involved benefit and individual improvement is translated into broader terms of better library service for the communities in which exchanges have taken place.
>
> An exchange which results in Jane Doe of an eastern library going west, discovering how people live and think there, enjoying the magnificent scenery, seeing their fine paintings, etc., has definitely contributed to Miss Doe's cultural assets. That is not enough. She must bring back something that will make her library more effective in serving its public and she must have contributed something of recognized value to the service of the western library. A worthwhile exchange benefits the library, the individual, the public, and the profession.

An examination of more recent literature on librarians and international travel shows that, for the most part, the themes expressed in early works have remained consistent: though not without its difficulties, international exposure both broadens personal horizons and serves to enhance library service to the clientele of the libraries in which participants work. In a presentation to the 71st IFLA General Conference and Council held in Oslo, Norway, in 2005, Sidsel Hindal, an advisor at the Norwegian Archive, Library, and Museum Authority, highlighted the benefits of international involvement, based on his personal experiences over the previous five years ("Experiences of Job Exchange," no. 461). These included:

- inspiration—this is twofold, leading to both an increase in personal motivation to do better on the job and a desire for enhanced knowledge to keep abreast of the field and to improve one's institutional activities and outcomes;

- network building—the globalized world constantly requires a higher degree of networking and cooperation, but communication through the Internet and by telephone can never replace the value of meeting people face to face;
- knowledge sharing—by sharing knowledge and experiences we are able to learn from others' mistakes and build on an existing foundation when developing our institutions' services;
- capacity building—successful international cooperation builds on mutual understanding of the existence of different values, solutions, cultures, and so forth, and job exchange is an important means of increasing this kind of understanding;
- personal development—working your way through various unknown systems, both at work and in the society as a whole is on one hand often very frustrating, but on the other hand valuable and helpful in knowing how to tackle other assignments.

Hindal concluded his talk by urging librarians to become aware of the possibilities with respect to international visits and exchanges and then to take advantage of them.

A survey of the library literature suggests a variety of options available to librarians seeking "international experiences." Some of these are considered below.

"Library Tourists"

Some articles were produced by librarians who chose to undertake informal visits to libraries while on vacation or short-term stays in other countries. For example, an Arabic cataloger at Portland State University in Oregon wrote of a visit to the Interuniversity Library of Oriental Languages in Paris (Kern, "East Meets West in Paris," no. 477), while two other Oregon librarians reported on their tour of the library at the National Library of France in Paris (Oberlander and Oberlander, "Books under Glass: The Bibliothèque Nationale de France," no. 509). While such visits may be of more personal than professional interest, they can also provide insights into other ways of doing things in libraries and, in some cases, into other cultures. I recently visited the National Library of Bermuda, a small, two-story building that serves as the only public lending library for the island. I came away with a greater appreciation for the confusion of international students from small countries where library resources are limited when they are confronted by the size and complexity of libraries in North American institutes of higher education.

Library Field Trips or Study Tours

Many international visits have been undertaken specifically to study library conditions in other countries. In many cases these were group tours organized under the auspices of organizations within the host countries, such as the British Council, which arranged tours of libraries in Northern Ireland for fourteen American librarians (Snoeyenbos and Sharma, "American Librarians Visit Northern Ireland," no. 544) and for twelve librarians and an archivist (McBride, "A Virginia Librarian in Ulster," no. 494), or the China National Publishing Industry Trading Corporation, which hosted a group of librarians involved in Asian studies in a tour of the People's Republic of China ("North American Librarians Delegation to the People's Republic of China," no. 507). In some cases, tours resulted from partnership arrangements between library organizations, such as that between the Oregon State Library Foundation and the Fujian Provincial Library in China (Greey and Wang, "The Oregon Fujian Library Connection," no. 449; Siegel, "Horner Library Staff Exchange Still Going Strong," no. 535; Shaoning and Zhiminmg, "Libraries in Oregon, USA," no. 536). Some tours were also organized by the participants themselves; for example, in 1991 a group of five American library directors hosted six library directors from China, with a follow-up three-week visit to China by the U.S. administrators (Miller and Sessions, "A Visit to Academic Libraries in China," no. 498; Rader, "The Ohio-China Connection," no. 522).

Individuals have also arranged tours of foreign libraries, often in conjunction with sabbatical or leave projects. A catalog librarian at Brigham Young University in Provo, Utah, reported on a six-month stay in Australia, where he studied procedures and policies for automated shared cataloging and learned to use Australian legal materials; he spent considerable time at the libraries of Monash and Melbourne Universities in Melbourne, the University of New South Wales and Macquarie University in Sydney, and the National Library of Australia in Canberra (Conklin, "Living and Working in Australia," no. 423). A business reference librarian at the University of Missouri, Kansas City went to Israel to continue graduate studies in Jewish history and took the opportunity while there to study library orientation programs at seven Israeli universities (Graubart, "Orientation Sessions in Israeli Academic Libraries," no. 448).

Some library tours have taken place under the auspices of groups such as the Fulbright Senior Specialists Program. The literature includes accounts of the two-week visit to Tbilisi, Georgia, in the former Soviet Union by a library science professor at Mount Holyoke College in South Hadley, Massachusetts, during which she visited a number of libraries and explored opportunities for future cooperative activities (Intner, "Visiting Libraries in the Republic of Georgia," no. 469), and the four-month visit to the Management Library at Cranfield Institute of Technology in Cranfield, England, by a Pennsylvania State University business librarian, during which he carried out a research project on academic library services to small businesses (Westerman, "The Librarian as Fulbright Scholar," no. 562). Other study visits have been sponsored by universities as a result of partnership arrangements with overseas institutions. This was the case when I myself spent two weeks as a visiting librarian at Philipps University in Marburg,

Germany, in 2003, touring various libraries in the Marburg university system and observing operations.

Librarians have also undertaken "working field trips." For example, the library director at Prescott College in Prescott, Arizona, went to Kenya to assist students and faculty from the college who were engaged in field research on conservation (Chalfoun, "Beyond the Border: Research in Maasailand," no. 418); and two librarians, one from the University of Georgia School of Law in Athens, Georgia, and the other from Universidad del Salvador, Buenos Aires, visited each other's libraries and worked together on projects related to curriculum development in the area of alternative dispute resolution (Burnett and Martino, "The Adventures of Two Librarians in Buenos Aires, Argentina, and Athens, Georgia, U.S.A.," no. 417).

Job Exchanges

The majority of reports on international visits in the library literature describe job exchanges, which involved an exchange of duties between staff members from two institutions. Most accounts consist of brief descriptions of the participants' activities during their time abroad; see, for example, Barr, "Discovering Columbus," no. 408; Brownbridge, "To Peru on Exchange," no. 415; Buckle, "A Fair Exchange Was No Robbery," no. 416; Daniels, "Living and Working in Switzerland," no. 427; Doksansky, "Bamberg to Brown: A Library Exchange," no. 429; Dowling, "The Exchange Experience: A British Perspective," no. 432; Flake, "A Transcontinental Job Exchange," no. 440; Frail and St-Louis, "Des montagnes rocheuses au Saint-Laurent: L'expérience d'une bibliothécaire albertaine au Québec," no. 442; Griffin, "The Exchange Experience: An American Perspective," no. 450; Hampel, "The Riverside Exchange," no. 454; Hensley and Pritchard, "California to Cardiff: Cardiff to California—A Success Story," no. 460; Hooker, "Luton to Washington, D.C.—Another Success Story," no. 463; Hutchinson, "The Regensburg Exchange," no. 465; Keane, "Need a Change? Try an Exchange," no. 475; Knobloch, "British–U.S. Job Exchange," no. 484; Laundy, "Briefly Stepping into Another's Shoes," no. 486; Lees, "From King's to North Rhine-Westphalia: An Exchange through LIBEX," no. 488; McDermand and Paul, "Job Exchange: Two Perspectives. A Self-Interview," no. 497; Mood, "An Exchange in England," no. 500; Morton, "Three Summers in a Row: A Work Exchange to Australia during the English Winter," no. 501; Neff, "La Bibliothéconomie en France: An Exchange Librarian's Report," no. 505; Peters, Rader, and Smith, "The Cologne-Cleveland Librarian Exchange," no. 515; Picot, "Stage dans des bibliothèques," no. 516; Stanley and Cooper, "Swapping Loughborough for California," no. 547; Tarr and Kotasek, "Exchange of Librarians between the 'City of Brotherly Love' and the 'Land Down Under,'" no. 550; Till, "Muffins, Mountains, and Multilingual Biblioservice," no. 552; Tracy, "The Down Under Experience: A Cataloguer's Adventures in Australia," no. 555; Varley, "An

English Art Librarian in Paris: A Report and Diary," no. 557; Worley, "Hastings Exchange," no. 566; Wright, "A Library Job Exchange," no. 567; Yackle, "Living and Working in Germany," no. 570; Yealy, "Springtime in Germany," no. 571. These articles offer a mixture of personal and professional observations, including commentary on differences between living and working in the home and host environments.

Some articles go into more detail regarding the practical arrangements for setting up exchanges, for example: Cran, "Exchanging Places: Organizing an Overseas Job Swap," no. 426; Fardon, "Negotiating New Horizons: The Job Exchange Alternative," no. 438; Hanson, "The Mechanics of International Job Exchanges," no. 457; Keane, "Library Exchanges in the UK: Considerations When Arranging International Exchanges," no. 474; Kear, "International Librarianship: Getting There from Here," no. 476; McChesney, "Trading Places: Planning an International Job Exchange," no. 495; Williamson, "Going International: Librarians' Preparation Guide for a Work Experience/Job Exchange Abroad," no. 564; Williamson, "Guidelines for Planning an Exchange," no. 565. These articles discuss such issues as approaching your employer to gain support for an exchange; finding an exchange partner; general preparations for going abroad; passports and other official documentation required, such as visas or work permits; financial considerations; maintenance of insurance, health, and other benefits; living arrangements; transportation concerns; medical coverage; insurance; communications; concerns with respect to accompanying family members (for example, schooling); and tax planning.

In 1992, Tony Kidd, a librarian at Glasgow University Library, and Karen Roughton, a librarian at Iowa State University, undertook questionnaire surveys of academic library directors and of staff who had participated in exchanges (see "International Library Staff Exchanges: How Do You Organize Them and Do They Do Any Good?" no. 478 and "International Staff Exchanges for Academic Libraries," no. 479). Sixty administrators and twenty-seven staff members from libraries in the United Kingdom and Ireland and sixty administrators and thirteen staff from libraries in the United States and Canada responded. The results suggested that most library exchanges at that time had taken place between English-speaking countries. Staff traveled to a wide variety of institutions, from large universities to community colleges. Language was an important consideration for most staff participating in exchanges; most opted to experience the "less overwhelming difficulties in culture, society, and economic conditions" among the United States, the United Kingdom, Ireland, Canada, and Australia. In terms of length, exchanges varied from one month (these exchanges were more in the nature of study visits than actual work exchanges, since the time was inadequate for participants to carry out jobs in the other library) to a year. In some cases exchanges were simultaneous, with exchange partners visiting the partner institution during the same time period, while in others visits took place at different times. It was noted that most exchange partners on both sides of the Atlantic were in their thirties. Few exchanges, especially those from Britain, took place under the auspices of official university programs; the majority originated from personal contact, though organizations such as LIBEX and ACRL facilitated some. In most cases, survey respondents retained their full salary from their home institutions, and they were able to exchange accommodations.

While more up-to-date survey information on library exchanges is not available, a review of the literature suggests that the growing interest in internationalization has led to increases in both the number of library exchanges with non-English-speaking countries and university sponsorship of exchanges and international travel for academic staff.

There are various sources available to librarians interested in participating in international exchanges or working in foreign countries. A first step would be to consult with the international and/or research offices at their home institutions for listings of potential opportunities. Some library schools include international listings in their placement websites, and job advertisements sometimes appear in library and academic publications or websites. There are also various organizations that facilitate librarian exchanges. These include:

- the American Library Association International Relations Round Table International Exchanges Committee (no. 574) — information can also be found on the ALA website on the International Relations Office web page under the Awards, Grants and Exchanges link;
- LIBEX International Library and Information Job Exchange, administered by the Chartered Institute of Library and Information Professionals (United Kingdom) (no. 575);
- Deutscher Akademischer Austausch Dients/German Academic Exchange Service (DAAD). (no. 576);
- Fulbright Specialists Program, administered by the Council for the International Exchange of Scholars based in Washington, D.C., and the Canada–U.S. Fulbright Program (no. 577);
- International Federation of Library Associations and Institutions (IFLA) (no. 581);
- International Research and Exchanges Board (IREX) (no. 584);
- Shastri Indo-Canadian Institute (no. 586).

Subject-based library associations may also provide potential contacts and sources of information, for example, the American Association of Law Libraries (AALL) and the British and Irish Association of Law Librarians (BIALL) have been particularly active in promoting exchanges.

Formal Partnerships between Libraries or Academic Institutions

Many library exchanges and international visits take place under the auspices of formal partnerships between universities or between academic libraries. These types of arrangements, which often take place between libraries in developed and developing countries, may also include the exchange of library materials.

A document entitled *Guidelines on Library Twinning* (no. 321) was prepared in 1994 for UNESCO, under contract with the International Federation of Library Associations (IFLA). In the introduction it is noted that while some libraries had had twinning relationships for many years, the practice was still uncommon. The guidelines were designed to provide inspiration and assistance to those interested in setting up twinning projects. In 1996, IFLA set up its Library Twinning database (see Connolly, "Is There a Need for a Library Twinning Focal Point? The IFLA Twinning Project and Beyond," no. 320). While other organizations had previously worked in the area of library twinning, this was the first established focal point to which libraries could turn when seeking twinning partners. The aim of the project was to "introduce" potential partners, but it was then up to the libraries themselves to establish and develop a relationship. A database was created to provide information on types of libraries, size of collections, number of staff, benefits sought from a partnership, and benefits offered a partner. These benefits included such things as cultural awareness, exchange of ideas on library practice, exchange of publications or catalog records, development of programs, and exchange of expertise. While there was a great deal of enthusiasm for building partnerships between libraries, the ideas behind library twinning were not always easy to put into practice, and the IFLA Twinning Database was closed down in 2000.

However, a number of successful partnership programs have been set up independently by universities and other library organizations. Many of these partnerships date back several decades. Kent State University in Kent, Ohio, began a formal exchange program with Aristotle University in Thessaloniki, Greece, in 1985, and the university libraries have subsequently played an important role in the project (see Davis, "Kent State University, Kent, Ohio, and Aristotle University, Thessaloniki, Greece: An Exchange Program," no. 428; Tolliver, "International Interlibrary Cooperation: Exchanging Goals, Values, and Culture," no. 554). Kent State Library staff have become involved in such activities as the physical reorganization of collections and cataloging of the English Department Library at Aristotle University, the development of collections and acquisitions policies, library automation and systems development, library instruction, and development of the role of the central library. Staff from Greece have participated in practicum experiences in Ohio (see Salaba, "A Greek Librarian in America: Personal Reflections on an Eight-Month Practicum at the Kent State University Libraries," no. 528). In the early 1990s a twinning libraries experiment was set up between the Vassar College Libraries in Poughkeepsie, New York, and the All Russia State Library for Foreign Literature in Moscow. Activities undertaken included site visits; scrutinizing various areas of practice and service for further collaboration; and developing specific project proposals in the areas of acquisitions, collection development, web projects, library orientation, exhibits, and librarian and faculty visits (see Sinitsyna and Hill, "Moscow-Poughkeepsie: Report on a Twinning Libraries Experiment," no. 542).

The literature suggests that an increasing number of such formalized programs are being arranged. Recent examples include:

- a three-year partnership (1999–2002) between the libraries at West Virginia State University in Charleston and the Université Nationale du Bénin in Benin, West Africa, aimed at promoting leadership development, sharing technology, engaging in cultural exchange, creating a public archive for Benin, and establishing a selective depository of Benin government publications in the United States. Staff exchange visits between the two libraries were also undertaken (Natsis, "Bridging the Technological, Language, and Cultural Gap: Partnering with an Academic Library in Francophone Africa," no. 504; Sharma and Bess, "West Virginia to West Africa and Back: An International Collaboration," no. 538);
- a partnership between the University of Tennessee Libraries and Makerere University Libraries in Kampala, Uganda, begun in 2001 has resulted in staff exchanges in which librarians taught seminars on various library-related issues, development of interlibrary loan services, and the identification of digitization projects (Atkins, Smith, and Dewey, "From the Great Smokies to the Mountains of the Moon: U.S. and Ugandan Librarians Collaborate in a Digital World," no. 406);
- the ABLE Project (American/Bulgarian Library Exchange) set up in 2002 and sponsored by the Colorado Association of Libraries and the Iowa Resources for International Service has brought Bulgarian librarians to the United States for training and taken American librarians to Bulgaria to assist in setting up Community Information Centers (Bolt, "The ABLE Project: American/Bulgarian Library Exchange," no. 412);
- the partnership set up in 2005 between a Maryland university and a university in Monterrey, Mexico, has included library exchanges and discussion of such issues as space planning, security, interlibrary loan collaborations, marketing of library services, and the subject liaison system (Griner, Herron, and Pedersoli, "Sister Libraries Partners: Tecnologico de Monterrey, Mexico and University of Maryland–College Park," no. 452);
- the program between librarians at the Appalachian State University in Boone, North Carolina, and Fudan University Library in Shanghai, China, aimed at facilitating information sharing on culture and on library issues; this arrangement, begun in August 2009 and scheduled to continue for a minimum of four years, will allow a librarian from each university to be in residence at the partner university for one to six months per year ("Fudan-Appalachian Library Exchange Program," no. 444).

Library Consultancy

The history of international library consultancy can be traced back many years. In his 1979 article "The Overseas Library Consultant" (no. 512), Stephen Parker noted that the use of foreign librarians as consultants on a regular basis was first undertaken in the years between the two world wars by the Carnegie Corporation of New York, which sent a number of British and American librarians on advisory missions to Africa, the West Indies, Australia, and New Zealand in connection with its program of aid to overseas library development. This program continued on a reduced scale after World War II, when it was gradually overtaken in importance by the work of other agencies such as the British Council, U.S. government aid agencies, and the Specialized Agencies of the United Nations, in particular, by UNESCO.

Library consultants have taken on a wide variety of projects:

- a music librarian from the University of Richmond in Virginia spent three months at Bilkent University in Turkey where she examined the library's music collections and services and recommended improvements (Hall, "A Virginia Librarian in Turkey," no. 453);
- the head of cataloging at the University of Iowa in Iowa City spent a year at the University of North Sumatra in Medan, Indonesia, where she served as a library specialist on a development team set up to upgrade academic programs, curriculum, management, library services, and physical facilities at the university (Lorkovic, "Library Consultant in Indonesia," no. 490);
- a team of four librarians from Indiana University in Bloomington worked over the course of a year as consultants for a project of library development at the University of Indonesia in Jakarta as it prepared to move to a new campus; they assisted in the design of a library master plan, designed an automated library system, held regular discussions with relevant parties, and drew up a final report (Snyder, Griffin, Singer, and Beckman, "The Team Approach to Library Consulting in a Developing Country," no. 546).

In the past, many library consultants received support for projects from the Library Fellows program, funded by the United States Information Agency and administered by the American Library Association:

- a documents/reference librarian at the College of Wooster, Ohio, spent nine months at the University of Namibia in Windhoek, where she worked to establish procedures and guidelines for a national bibliography based on a legal deposit collection and trained staff to continue the bibliography (Bell, "When the Rains Came to Namibia," no. 411).
- a reference librarian at the University of Arizona College of Law Library in Tucson spent ten months in Ghana, where she provided law librarianship training (Elliott, "A Library Fellow in Equatorial West Africa," no. 436);
- a librarian from the University of California in Oakland taught fundamental library science to the staff of the Tibet Autonomous Region Library in Lhasa for nine months (Hutton, "High-Altitude Librarianship: The Adventures of

an ALA Fellow in Tibet," no. 466; Hutton, "How I Came to Be in Tibet," no. 467);

- a librarian at Rice University in Houston, Texas, worked at the National Central Library in Taipei, Taiwan, assisting staff in developing and organizing their U.S. government publications and providing staff training on the management and use of government documents (Kile, "The Library/Book Fellow Program—A Report," no. 480);
- a doctoral student in library and information studies at Texas Woman's University in Denton spent three and a half months in Estonia presenting training workshops, lecturing on librarianship and library education in the United States and on the role of the public library in a democracy, and working as a consultant in various library departments on library automation and workflow (Little, "Estonia Journal: An ALA Fellow in Tallinn," no. 489);
- the manager of cataloging at St. Louis Public Library spent eleven months at the University of Malawi helping initiate the automation of cataloging, training staff, and advising on issues of workflow and computer room arrangements (Nystrom, "What's It Like Being a Librarian in Africa?" no. 508);
- a social sciences librarian from Portland State University in Oregon worked at the American Studies Research Centre at Osmania University in Hyderabad, India, where her projects included assessing the social sciences collection and making recommendations for purchases to bring it up to the graduate level (Powell, "A Librarian's Passage to India," no. 518);
- a library professor at the University of Vermont in Burlington helped develop a strategic long-range plan for the National Library of Latvia in Riga (Saule, "Back to the Future," no. 529).

The Library Fellows Program, which began in 1986, sponsored 147 Fellows during the ten years in which it was in operation, but it was disbanded due to lack of funding in 1997.

Volunteer Work

Librarians can also participate in international development projects by volunteering at libraries in developing countries. Although written in 1989, Robert Tabachnick's article "Librarians Can Play a Part in Overseas Development Projects" (no. 549) still provides interesting reading. He provides an overview of changes in developing countries since they achieved independence in the years following World War II and into the 1950s and 1960s, noting that one of the most significant changes was the shift in relationship between the former "receiving" countries and the former "donors." Grants for development work in the previous twenty or thirty years put the projects largely under the control of the grantor, who tended to be the judge of what should be supported and how the money would be spent. However, there was a change in focus beginning in the 1980s, with host countries and host institutions exercising much more control over project decisions. This has led to a changed view of volunteer consultants, who are now considered colleague-advisors rather than mentor-controllers. It has also been recognized that indigenous solutions may be more sensitive to local conditions and more appropriate than solutions proposed at a distance.

North American librarians who choose to do volunteer work in developing countries often work as a team with librarians from countries with fewer resources and who face different kinds of challenges. While this type of international experience is not for everyone, it can be a rewarding and life-changing experience.

In the 1990s and early 2000s library-related voluntarism was facilitated by the World Library Partnership (WLP), a nonprofit organization whose mission was to advocate for sustainable, community-based libraries in developing areas of the world. Volunteers lived in local communities and worked with local librarians providing assistance and training (see Hytnen, "Toward Sustainable Library Development: The Inform the World Librarian Volunteer Program," no. 468; Mizzy, "World Library Partnership," no. 499). Unfortunately, the WLP organization suspended operations in 2004 due to a lack of funding. However, similar kinds of volunteer opportunities are available through various faith-based and governmental or nongovernmental international aid organizations.

GLOBALIZATION AND LIBRARIES

Most of the literature dealing with international students and libraries takes a practical approach, describing problems and issues and outlining ways of addressing them. However, in the past decade more theoretical literature has begun to appear, much of it emanating from Australia or based on the Australian experience. As noted previously, Australia has one of the highest percentages of international students of any country in the world.

In her 2001 Ph.D. dissertation completed at Monash University in Melbourne (*Internationalisation of the University: Implications for the Academic Library*, no. 327), Carolyn McSwiney explored the social and cultural changes associated with the internationalization of the university and the academic library. She noted that these changes have an impact on the library user group and on the use and provision of information resources made accessible through the library. They call into question the perceived role of the library and add another dimension to policy and planning issues for library management. In a 2002 paper presented at the 68th IFLA Council and General Conference ("Cultural Implications of a Global Context: The Need for the Reference Librarian to Ask Again 'Who Is My

Client?'" no. 325), McSwiney summarized many of the issues discussed in her dissertation. She commented:

> Globalization touches on the thoughts, ideas, and processes that affect our everyday lives. The media more often links the changes associated with globalization with power plays between nations, with trade advantages and exploitation leading to a widening gap between the rich and poor, and with the growing dominance of the economically advantaged. However, the effects of the gathering momentum of globalization can also be felt across areas of the social domain including the environment, popular culture, and the migration of peoples and communication. In this sense it can be regarded constructively as a set of processes that can energize much of our thinking and professional practice.
>
> Technological innovation has accompanied, and been integral to changes in global concepts, and the transformation it has effected is fundamental to the management and exchange of information. The interconnectedness that has resulted, and an accompanying sense of constant and rapid change is particularly characteristic of the workplace of the librarian and knowledge manager. Thus taken in its broader sociological context, globalization can be seen as a source of energy for re-thinking many of the professional assumptions we make in the library/information work environment. At the level of the library user group, the cultural changes it has brought call for a review of assumptions relating to issues such as cross-cultural communication, patterns of information-seeking, and approaches to learning. (pp. 2–3)

Drawing on the thought of sociologist Anthony Giddens, McSwiney then suggested that developments in systems of communication and the transfer of information were the prime motivators of the globalization movement. These developments could be linked in pragmatic library terms not only to the quantity of information available, the development of technology, and the impact of the web and the Internet, but could also account for the changing profile of the library user. Today's users bring with them a body of beliefs and social forms that are often quite foreign to librarians, and responding to the differential needs of these users in a climate of global change and diversity requires new skills and heightened sensitivity. McSwiney concluded,

> By being pro-active in identifying and implementing research initiatives, by designing staff development programs with cultural awareness as their focus, and by investing funds and human resources in library education and information literacy programs designed to address the differential needs relating to cultural backgrounds, the library profession can add an important dimension to its research base and its literature. (p. 7)

At the same time, and on a more practical level, "the cultural implications of this context call for a shift from the comfort of routine and ritualised services to a level of cultural exchange that is energizing and enriching for librarian and client alike" (p. 7).

Many of McSwiney's ideas were developed by Linda K. W. Becker, the former director of libraries at Bunker Hill Community College in Boston, Massachusetts. Her 2005 Ed.D. dissertation completed at the University of Massachusetts focused on the successful pattern for internationalization emerging in Australian academic libraries (*Globalization and Structural Change: Internationalization and the Role of Librarians in Australian Universities*, no. 317). While McSwiney's study had focused on the way in which social and cultural change impact library users, Becker's study examined strategies employed by librarians in internationalizing their practice and perspective in the library, the university, and within higher education. Her research included a survey of thirty-six university librarians and extensive case studies at two public universities, a regional mid-sized university located in a coastal city and a major university located in its state capital. She reported on her findings in a series of three articles published in the journal *Australian Academic and Research Libraries* in 2006 ("Globalisation and Changing Practices for Academic Librarians in Australia: A Literature Review," no. 315; "Internationalisation: Australian Librarians and Expanding Roles in Higher Education," no. 318; "Globalisation and Internationalisation: Models and Patterns for Change for Australian Academic Librarians," no. 316). In these articles Becker noted that in the age of the Internet, the knowledge society is linked with globalization and provides the framework for the modern university. She went on to explore such questions as: Are librarians' activities important only in library terms, or do they have an impact on other parts of the university? Where do librarians fit into the wider institutional context? What is the role of librarians in the internationalization of higher education in general?

A number of issues are highlighted in Becker's discussion. She emphasized the importance of having the library participate in university strategic planning. Librarians must be proactive and not wait to be invited to join the process. Within the library itself, strategic planning should begin with determining guiding values and goals. This process should be followed by discussion of how these values and goals fit into the university's vision and structure. To be effective any models for change adopted in the library should be consistent with the model for change adopted by the parent institution. These models may vary from university to university; some institutions, for example, focus on quality assurance and customer service while others are developing a corporate model that emphasizes entrepreneurial initiatives. The university librarian and other administrative librarians should logically provide the leadership for instituting strategic planning for change, and they should present a consistent vision over time, since changing the practice and perspective of a library is a long-term project. The library should establish a budget for international activities in order to fund proposals that further the aims of both the library and the university.

Librarians are also advised to become proactive in seeking to join both administrative and academic groups working to internationalize the university as a whole. These can include committees considering a variety of issues, including teaching and learning, research, community service, and the use of information technology. In addition librarians can take advantage of collaborative opportunities outside of formalized committees by building partnerships across the campus, in the community, and in international settings. For example, librarians should be encouraged to present the results of their research in international forums or to become involved in cooperative work with colleagues around the world. Such efforts demonstrate to the university that the library is already a stakeholder in the globalization process and that it is aware of the challenges of internationalization.

Research by librarians such as McSwiney and Becker raise many important issues regarding librarians and their relationship to the globalization of academia. At this point many of the questions they raise remain unanswered and there is a need for further study to expand understanding of the process and outcomes of internationalization and its implications for the academic library. Fortunately, increasing numbers of library schools are introducing courses on global librarianship, and Wayne State University in Detroit, Michigan, recently announced plans to launch a specialized program designed "to prepare the new generation of global librarians for the 21st century." Goals of this proposed program include exposing students to various aspects of the field; helping students understand and appreciate cultural differences and values other than those of North America; preparing students to work in libraries serving international patrons, in international organizations, and in other countries; and preparing students working in North America to understand, debate, and solve problems pertaining to library service to multiethnic, multilingual, and multicultural groups. (For more information about Wayne State's International and Comparative Librarianship Program, see the spring 2007 issue of *Connections*, WSU's Library and Information Science Program newsletter, p. 2.)

CONCLUDING REMARKS

In 2007, the SCONUL Access Group, a committee of the Society of College, National, and University Libraries in Great Britain, undertook a research study aimed at determining how university libraries in the United Kingdom could best support international students (see Bent, Scopes, and Senior, "Discrete Library Services for International Students: How Can Exclusivity Lead to Inclusivity?" no. 212). This research examined issues surrounding the debate over exclusivity versus inclusivity, that is, development of specialized programs for international students versus integration into the mainstream. It included descriptions of techniques libraries were currently employing, feedback from international students about their priorities for library support, comparison of how student views matched library staff perceptions, and discussion of groups with which libraries need to collaborate to improve service provision. Data was derived from a literature review; a survey of SCONUL member institutions (fifty responses); a web survey of most UK library and institutional websites; a web survey of a sample of international institutional and library websites in Australia, New Zealand, and North America; focus groups with international students; surveys and interviews with international students; and institutional visits overseas. Information was collected on designated staff support for international students, staff development, library web pages, publications, services provided, and emerging themes. The outcome was a set of guidelines published in 2008. This document, entitled *Library Services for International Students* (no. 298), was designed to be a practical tool for library practitioners, providing them with a comprehensive overview of issues as seen both by their peers and by students, along with suggested solutions and best practices case studies. Appendices include a summary of the survey and its results; strategy document examples; links to selected library websites reflecting good practice; links to sample glossaries of library terms; links to selected websites on academic writing skills, useful for those developing instruction programs; sample job descriptions for international support librarians; a listing of companies offering staff training on international issues; a listing of "good ideas and special touches" that can be used in marketing to and working with international students; and a checklist of seventeen key concepts for consideration by strategists and practitioners. The SCONUL research provides an up-to-date and extremely useful starting point for libraries seeking to understand and improve services to international students.

It should also be noted that many of the recommendations made in the SCONUL report and other library literature dealing with international students are equally applicable to domestic students. Developing jargon-free library presentations and publications, providing service that actively seeks to determine and respond to the needs of users, training staff to be culturally sensitive, engaging in strategic planning within the library, working with university administrations toward achieving broader institutional goals, and making an effort to reflect the diversity and multiculturalism of the academic world today can benefit all library users, not just those who come to universities from other countries.

The annotated bibliography that follows contains 591 entries. Chronologically, these works cover a time span from 1940 to 2008. The bibliography is divided into eighteen sections. Works were placed in the category considered most descriptive of the content, with cross-references to other relevant sections. An author index and a detailed subject index are included. The language in which the work is written is that of the title, but all abstracts are in English. URLs are included for works that were retrieved electronically.

In terms of content, the bibliography focuses on literature dealing with international students in academic libraries, though some articles dealing with minority students living in North America were included if the material was relevant and adaptable for use with students who come to North America specifically to study at the university level. Also included are some recent general articles on cross-cultural issues such as learning styles of international students and cross-cultural communication, even though these articles do not focus specifically on academic library settings. Other related literature, such as material on web page usability testing in global contexts, was also included selectively. However, articles discussing international library school students and the hiring of minority librarians to create more diverse workforces were not included.

document no. ED284580 (1987). 16 p. http://www.eric.ed.gov/ERICDocs/data/ericdocs2sql/content_storage_01/0000019b/80/16/25/41.pdf (August 7, 2008).

Describes the bibliographic instruction program at the University of Illinois, Urbana–Champaign Undergraduate Library for students in freshman rhetoric, English, or English-as-a-second-language courses. It consists of eleven different programs and ten distinct components, each developed for a specific student group. Paper describes in detail the program offered for the basic writer, Pre-Research Skills Instruction (PRSI). Appendices include "Keystones of Bibliographic Information: Hierarchical Structure of Information," listing of research topics, subject bibliography, bibliographic instruction checklist for the classroom teacher, and seven-item bibliography of material related to librarian–English instructor cooperation.

9. Amsberry, Dawn. "Talking the talk: Library classroom communication and international students." *The Journal of International Librarianship* 34, no. 4 (2008): 354–57.

Reviews literature on classroom communication from both the second language acquisition and library fields, then suggests ways in which second language acquisition research can be applied to communication with international students in library instruction classrooms. Considers such issues as pronunciation, grammar, vocabulary, use of jargon, idioms, and cultural references.

10. Anderson, Anne. *ESL library assignments and resources for ESL students.* http://www.nvcc.edu/library/esl/eslresources.htm (April 15, 2008).

Website developed at Northern Virginia Community College. Includes sample English-as-a-second-language assignments and handouts and exercises used by librarians in library sessions for ESL students. Material could be adapted for use with international students.

11. Anderson, James A., and Maurianne Adams. "Acknowledging the learning styles of diverse student populations: Implications for instructional design." 19–33 in *Teaching for diversity: New directions for teaching and learning* 49, edited by Laura L. B. Border and Nancy Van Note Chism. San Francisco: Jossey-Bass, 1992.

Examines how to take student learning styles into account when designing instruction. Discusses learning styles and cultural diversity, teaching styles and strategies, and ways to design flexible and responsive instruction. Material is not library-specific, but useful for those providing bibliographic instruction.

12. Arkoudis, Sophie. *Teaching international students: Strategies to enhance learning.* Melbourne: Centre for the Study of Higher Education, University of Melbourne, 2006. http://www.cshe.unimelb.edu.au/pdfs/international.pdf (July 21, 2008).

Handbook offering practical suggestions for teaching international students at the University of Melbourne, Australia. Focuses on internationalizing the curriculum, making lectures accessible, encouraging participation in small group work, adopting an educative approach to plagiarism, supporting students in developing critical thinking skills, explaining assessment expectations. Designed for teaching faculty, but many ideas adaptable for bibliographic instruction in the library.

13. Badke, William B. "International students: Information literacy or academic literacy?" *Academic Exchange Quarterly* 6, no. 4 (2002): 60–66.

Discusses challenges faced by international students and proposes a move beyond teaching information literacy to teaching a broader "academic literacy." Outlines the structure of Western academic culture, with particular emphasis on research and writing, then lists five requirements for helping international students understand and thrive in the Western approach to education. Also refers to his website developed to introduce international students to writing research essays (http://www.acts.twu.ca/lbr/research_essays.htm).

14. Bagnole, John W., and John W. Miller. "An interactive information literacy course for international students: A practical blueprint for ESL learners." *Teaching English as a Second or Foreign Language* 6, no. 4 (2003). http://tesl-ej.org/ej24/a1.html (July 24, 2008).

Describes the creation of a university-based English for Academic Purposes (EAP) course. Discusses syllabus design, activities, and challenges and triumphs met during course development, which was undertaken as part of the Ohio Program of Intensive English (OPIE) at Ohio University in Athens, Ohio. Written for English-as-a-second-language teachers but provides useful teaching suggestions for library instructors.

15. Ballard, Brigid. *Helping students from non-English-speaking backgrounds to learn more effectively.* Melbourne: Royal Melbourne Institute of Technology Educational Research and Development Unit, 1991. 12 p.

Discusses differences in learning styles of international students that lead to difficulties in the university environment. Compares and contrasts stages of learning in Asia and Australia and offers examples of how things can go wrong. Recommends ways teaching staff can raise their awareness of cultural differences.

16. Ballard, Brigid. "Overseas students and Australian academics: Learning and teaching styles." 87–98 in *Overseas students in Australia: Policy and practice*, edited by Bruce Williams. Canberra, ACT: IDP Education Australia, 1989.

Emphasizes the need for those teaching overseas students to be aware of their learning difficulties. Also considers issue of plagiarism and differences in reading methods that may lead to frustration and underuse of library facilities.

17. Ballard, Brigid. "Sink or swim: In class or at home." 41–47 in *Overseas students, educational opportunity and challenge*, edited by Ronald Kentish Browne and E. C. Dale. Curtin, ACT: Australian College of Education, 1990.

Brief summary of support services available to overseas students, with comments on their responses. Points out cultural differences and emphasizes the need for re-evaluating teaching methods to address them.

18. Ballard, Brigid, and John Clancy. *Teaching students from overseas: A brief guide for lecturers and teachers.* Melbourne: Longman Cheshire, 1991. x, 100 p.

Guide for teachers at the university level offering practical suggestions for approaching learning and communication difficulties of many overseas students. Written from an Australian perspective.

19. Ballard, Brigid, and John Clancy. *Teaching international students: A brief guide for lecturers and supervisors.* Canberra, ACT: IDP Education Australia, 1997. ix, 96 p.

Updated version of no. 18. Focus is on Asian students, who make up a large percentage of the international students in Australia.

20. Baron, Sara, and Alexia Strout-Dapaz. "Communicating with and empowering international students with a library skills set." *Reference Services Review* 29, no. 4 (2001): 314–26.

Based on data collected by librarians and staff of international student offices in 123 colleges and universities in the southern United States. Outlines difficulties experienced by international students, then recommends a model for library skills training that integrates the ACRL Information Literacy Competency Standards within the framework of communication, education, and cultural adjustments of international students. Includes a list of pedagogical suggestions drawn from works published between 1993 and 2000.

21. Battle, Joel C. *The effect of information literacy instruction on library anxiety among international students.* Ph.D. dissertation, University of North Texas, 2004. UMI no. 3126554. vi, 143 p. Full-text in *Dissertations and Theses* database.

Explores issues regarding information literacy instruction and both general anxiety and specific library anxiety. The sixty study participants were international students enrolled in an English for Speakers of Other Languages (ESOL) program at Richland College in Dallas, Texas. The experimental group attended several library instruction classes while the control group worked in the library on an assignment but did not receive formal instruction. Results indicated library instruction reduced both general and library anxiety. Appendices include: Library Anxiety Scale, demographic information form, sample lesson plan, and evaluation questionnaire.

22. Beck, Susan E. *The role of library instruction in the Ohio program of intensive English in reaction to students needs.* M.A. thesis, Ohio University, 1990. x, 154 p.

Questionnaires were administered to Ohio Program of Intensive English (OPIE) faculty and former students to determine how library instruction was implemented in the program and if research assignments differed from those given after OPIE students matriculated into other academic classes. Also examined whether students felt prepared to handle research assignments and compared preparation levels between students studying social sciences and other disciplines.

23. Beristain, Maureen Fanning. *A survey of primary bibliographic instruction methods and aids currently used in selected Canadian academic libraries.* ERIC document no. ED264892, 1985. [xi], 95 p. http://www.eric.ed.gov/ERIC Docs/data/ericdocs2sql/content_storage_01/0000019b/80/2f/0c/7e.pdf (August 8, 2008)

Aims to identify: the current state of bibliographic instruction; programs or special services offered for foreign students; changes or developments that took place in bibliographic instruction methodologies or use of instructional aids since 1976; and trends predicted during the next three years. Data was collected through a questionnaire survey mailed to thirty-eight libraries in two categories: universities and colleges, and community colleges (twenty-nine responses). Report includes: historical background, outline of the purpose of the study, and an explanation of project objectives, limitations, and definitions; review of related literature; description of research procedures, including study and instrument design and the surveyed population; project findings in a number of areas, including bibliographic instruction programs offered, instructors, publicity, methods, aids, and future trends; comparison of project findings with those of a similar survey conducted by Sheila Laidlaw in 1977; and conclusions. Foreign students were not distinguished from other students in the institutions surveyed, but it is noted that only one institution offered bibliographic instruction in a language other than English or French, and that foreign students received almost no special instruction despite their special needs identified in the literature. Questionnaires for both the 1977 and the current study are appended.

24. Biggs, John B. "Teaching across and within cultures: The issue of international students." 1–22 in *Teaching in higher education: Advancing international perspectives: Proceedings of the Higher Education Research & Development Society of Australasia Conference, Adelaide, South Australia, 8–11 July 1997 (Special issue),* edited by Rosalind Murray-Harvey and Halia C. Silins. Adelaide: Higher Education Research and Development Society of Australasia, 1997.

Introductory essay in a collection of pre-conference papers outlining basic issues that arise in teaching international students in the Australasian academic environment. Focuses on language and cultural needs of Asia-Pacific region students and teaching styles in a multicultural environment. Notes that "difference does not mean deficiency" and that both teachers and students need to be aware of the cultural assumptions and attitudes that underlie instruction (e.g., differing approaches in Eastern and Western thought on the concept of critical thinking).

25. Bilal, Dania M. "International students' acquisition of library research skills: Relationship with English language proficiency." *The Reference Librarian* 24 (1989): 129–45.

Reports on an experimental study involving thirteen students at the Center for Intensive English Studies at Florida State University in Tallahassee. Seven students took part in a seven-week bibliographic instruction course. Pre- and post-tests were administered to both experimental and control groups. Results showed a moderate correlation between students' exit Test of English as a Foreign Language (TOEFL) scores and their post-test library skills scores. Lack of command of the English language, lack of self-sufficiency, and absence of the conceptual awareness of library research were major obstacles to comprehension of material.

26. Boers, Greta G. "Designing a library instruction program for international students." *Georgia Librarian* 31 (1994): 92–95.

Briefly discusses the debate regarding the creation of special library instruction programs for international students and highlights successful programs in the literature. Characteristics of the latter include an encouraging attitude, avoidance of stereotyping, watching what is said, offering staff development and sensitivity training, teaching small classes, simplifying information presented, using handouts, offering library orientation at the beginning of semesters, and offering instruction in native languages. Concludes with recommendations for measuring success.

27. Bowley, Barbara, and Lynn Whitnall Meng. "Information literacy for ESL students: Retooling instructional models to accommodate diversity." 403–7 in *Continuity and transformation: The promise of confluence: Proceedings of the 7th National Conference of the Association of College and Research Libraries, Pittsburgh, Pennsylvania, March 29–April 1, 1995*, edited by Richard AmRhein. Chicago: Association of Research Libraries, 1995.

Discusses the development of an instructional model designed to meet the needs of English-as-a-second-language students, who demonstrate a variety of information skills levels, intellectual backgrounds, and language abilities. *See also* no. 28.

28. Bowley, Barbara, and Lynn Meng. "Library skills for ESL students." *Community College Journal* 64, no. 5 (1994): 13–14.

Discusses the development of a new library instruction program for students whose first language is not English, noting points most crucial to the program's success: awareness of cultural differences, knowledge of language skills levels, targeted collection development, use of instructional methods and design, imaginative assignment design, and faculty-library partnerships. *See also* no. 27.

29. Braaksma, Betty, Kathy Drewes, George Siemens, and Peter Tittenberger. "Building a virtual learning commons: What do YOU want to do?" Paper presented

at the World Library and Information Congress: 73rd IFLA General Conference and Council, Durban, South Africa, August 2007. http://www.ifla.org/IV/ifla73/papers/133-Braaksma-en.pdf (August 15, 2008).

Discusses an online tutorial to support the development of international students' information literacy skills. The project, which was developed in 2006 through the efforts of the Libraries and the Learning Technologies Centre at the University of Manitoba in Winnipeg, addressed a broad range of topics, including the enhancement of social and cultural skills in addition to information-seeking skills. Web 2.0 functionality was incorporated in order to allow students to interact outside the classroom. The final product was placed in the university's Virtual Learning Commons, a webspace designed to be a central location for online learning and discussion.

30. Brock, Barbara. "Library skills for international students: From theory to practice." 111–17 in *Bibliographic instruction and the learning process: Theory, style, and motivation: Papers presented at the Twelfth Annual Library Instruction Conference, held at Eastern Michigan University, May 6–7, 1982*, edited by Carolyn A. Kirkendall. Ann Arbor, MI: Pierian Press, 1984.

Reviews natural and controlled-language challenges that prevent international students from accessing information, then discusses the development and implementation of a four-hour credit course at the University of Toledo in Toledo, Ohio, designed to meet these challenges. Main goals of the program were to teach students to understand classification systems, read call numbers and card catalog entries, and navigate journal indexes. Material is dated. *See also* no. 31.

31. Brock, Barbara, and Peter Archer. "Library search strategies for international students: A practical experience." *TESOL Newsletter* 16, no. 2 (1982): 15–16.

Discusses "Library Research Strategies," a four-week credit course offered at the University of Toledo in Ohio that aimed to support students in their transition to becoming independent learners and effective researchers. Focus was on linguistics, including converting natural language to control language, hierarchy, and syntax. The course introduced various library formats, provided a walking tour to show library locations of materials, and trained students to systematically gather information on a particular topic. Article also outlines course testing and assessment and the impact of the course on student research skills and confidence. *See also* no. 30.

32. Brown, Ben. "Getting it together: Tactics for reducing verbal miscommunication between native English-speaking instructors and non-native English-speaking students." *Journal on Excellence in College Teaching* 10, no. 3 (1999): 69–91.

Outlines problems faced by non-native speakers of English and offers suggestions to avoid or reduce miscommunication. These include: being patient, emphasizing vowel sounds, avoiding overenunciation, utilizing phenomenological bracketing, minimizing the use of metaphors and idioms, and avoiding the use of intonation to convey meaning. Suggestions are based on an ethnographic study conducted by the author in South Korea.

33. Cable, John N. "Foreign students in the United States." *Improving College and University Teaching* 22 (1974): 40–41.

Brief article discussing international students at American universities. Considers the students' diversity of backgrounds and problems encountered, and highlights the need for instructors to be aware of these issues. Offers suggestions to facilitate instruction. Does not deal with library issues specifically.

34. Carder, Linda, Carl Pracht, and Robert Willingham. "Reaching the whole population: Adaptive techniques for reaching students who fall through the cracks." 67–75 in *Programs that work: Papers and sessions material presented at the Twenty-fourth National LOEX Library Instruction Conference held in Denton, Texas, 16–18 May 1996*, edited by Linda Shirato. Ann Arbor, MI: Pierian Press, 1997.

Discusses library orientation at Southeast Missouri State University in Cape Girardeau, with emphasis on needs of three special needs groups: nontraditional students, international students, and hearing-impaired students. Second segment outlines Hersey's Situational Leadership Model and how it can be used to provide a framework for determining the students' levels of experience and ability.

35. Carroll, Jude. *Suggestions for teaching international students more effectively.* Oxford Centre for Staff and Learning Development Learning and Teaching Briefing Papers series, 2002. http://www.brookes.ac.uk/services/ocsd/2_learntch/briefing_papers/international_students.pdf (July 21, 2008).

Guidelines developed for faculty at the Oxford Centre for Staff and Learning Development in England offering teaching suggestions for international students. Includes suggestions on being explicit, lightening the cognitive load, speaking in class, teaching "Western" academic skills, and group work.

36. Carroll, Jude, and Janette Ryan (eds). *Teaching international students: Improving learning for all.* London: Routledge, 2005. xii, 155 p.

Collection of essays for teachers of international students. Includes chapters on gathering cultural knowledge, strategies for becoming more explicit, building intercultural competencies, and improving teaching and learning practices for international students.

37. Chan, Sally. "The Chinese learner: A question of style." *Education and Training* 41, no. 6/7 (1999): 294–305.

Examines how cultural values and beliefs shape learning styles and classroom behavior of Chinese students. Discusses issues such as Chinese students' preference for repetitive learning and concrete examples, a lack of abstract or creative thinking, and the need to compromise in group situations. Suggests that understanding and appreciation of different approaches to learning can help design better educational programs for Chinese students.

38. Chin, Susan Ho. "Collaborative library research: A learning process for ESL students." *Teaching English in the Two-Year College* 21, no. 1 (1994): 47–52.

Discusses the need for English-as-a-second-language instructors to collaborate with academic librarians. Provides guidelines for creating appropriate bibliographic instruction sessions, along with a list of library-related handouts. Also outlines the author's collaborative approach, which highlights cooperative learning, a mini research project, and a research project that takes place within the library and encourages ESL student interaction with librarians and library staff. Written by an ESL instructor and aimed mainly at teaching ESL students, but provides useful ideas for teaching international students.

39. Chin, Susan Ho, and Caroline Blumenthal. *Bibliographic instruction for "real world" reading.* ERIC document no. ED323758, 1989. 20 p.

Argues that English-as-a-second-language (ESL) educators cannot prepare students for mainstreaming in American colleges and universities if the students are limited to ESL textbooks. When teachers assign library projects, they generally neglect the vital area of bibliographic instruction because they assume that the foreign student has basic library knowledge, an assumption that is often not true. Describes a small-group project in a high intermediate/low advanced level reading class that demonstrates how students can profit from bibliographic instruction by participating in a guided research assignment. The advantages to English-as-a-second-language students of being assigned a library project in a reading class instead of in a writing class are also explained. Aimed mainly at students in ESL classes rather than international students specifically.

40. Coleman, Susan. " International students in the classroom: A resource and an opportunity." *International Education* 26, no. 2 (1997): 52–61.

Provides general background on international students in American higher education, then discusses problems and pressures these students face. Also considers language issues, teaching strategies, and international students as resources in the classroom. Written for academic faculty, but information is relevant for library instructors.

41. Conteh-Morgan, Miriam. "Connecting the dots: Limited English proficiency, second language learning theories, and information literacy instruction." *The Journal of Academic Librarianship* 28, no.4 (2002): 191–96.

Reviews the application of two English-as-a-second-language (ESL) theories—Innatist and Interactionist—and discusses how they can be applied to information literacy instruction. This can be done by integrating five factors linguists believe influence language learning: social context, learner characteristics, learning conditions, learning process, and learning outcomes. Includes a checklist for course instruction and preparation. Focus is on ESL instruction, but provides useful information for those teaching international students.

42. Conteh-Morgan, Miriam E. "Empowering ESL students: A new model for information literacy instruction." *Research Strategies* 18, no. 1 (2001): 29–38.

Suggests a new kind of collaboration between librarians and English-as-a-second-language instructors and proposes a model in which information literacy and ESL concepts and objectives are matched. The resulting course would be integrated into the ESL curriculum and taught by the ESL instructor. Benefits of this approach would include opportunities for more sustained learning in the learner-centered, low-anxiety environment of an ESL classroom. Sample lesson plans are appended. Written for ESL instructors, but provides useful information for teachers of international students.

43. Conteh-Morgan, Miriam. "Journey with new maps: Adjusting mental models and rethinking instruction to language minority students." 257–66 in *Learning to make a difference: Proceedings of the Eleventh National Conference of the Association of College and Research Libraries, April 10–13, 2004, Charlotte, North Carolina,* edited by Hugh Thompson. http://www.ala.org/ala/acrl/acrlevents/contehmorgan.PDF (August 6, 2008).

Explores the ways in which librarians' understanding of international students can influence the library services offered to them. Argues that literature regarding international student and information literacy instruction compounds student challenges by presenting librarians with a one-dimensional "problem" to be solved by their own inferences about the learning abilities and educational levels of this group. Although librarians tend to associate language and technology barriers with international students, such associations may not accurately reflect the demographics of today's international students. Proposes new mental models that reinvent teaching and learning through continuous professional development, self-awareness of framing educational deviations as negative, and cultural sensitivity checks.

44. Cope, Johnnye, and Evelyn Black. "New library orientation for international students." *College Teaching* 33 (1985): 159–62.

Documents the evolution of the library instruction program for international students at North Texas State University in Denton, which is taught cooperatively by librarians and English-as-a-second-language teachers. The program, which is designed for students enrolled in a non-credit English course prior to university admission, emphasizes both cognitive and attitudinal learning and development.

45. Correll, Lou P. *Attitudes of international students in regard to library skills development in the academic setting.* ERIC document no. ED235810, 1983. 70 p.

Presents results of a study at East Texas State University in Commerce, Texas, that examined attitudes of twenty-eight international students regarding the importance and usefulness of a three-hour credit library instruction course. Results indicated all students agreed library skills instruction was a good way to learn to use the library. Students had positive attitudes regarding their understanding and use of library services and materials, except for government documents. Outlines fourteen conclusions. List of resources covered in the course, sample survey instruments, and tables of survey results appended. *See also* no. 46.

46. Correll, Lou P., and Robin Brooks. "The international student and use of the library in graduate study." *International Journal of Instructional Media* 11, no. 3 (1983/84): 205–8.

Describes class objectives and students' attitudes regarding the necessity and usefulness of a three-hour credit course on library use given at East Texas State University in Commerce, Texas. Also provides abbreviated data analysis of a larger study (see no. 45).

47. Dame, Melvina Azar. "Teaching library skills and content to linguistically diverse students: The role of advance organizers and visual resources." *MultiCultural Review* 4, no. 4 (1995): 40–44.

Written for school library media specialists, but applicable to college and university instruction programs. Provides concrete suggestions to assist in activating relevant background knowledge in order to enhance classroom content learning. Focus is on use of visual aids.

48. Davis, Harry O. "Map librarians, the international student, and ESL: Opportunity and challenge." *Bulletin (Special Libraries Association Geography and Map Division)* 169 (1992): 17–28.

Proposes that English-as-a-second-language instructors integrate maps into their courses to facilitate discussion. Offers recommendations on map usage and presentation to international students. Discusses varying methodologies for incorporating maps and the use of games and simulation for hands-on experiences.

49. Deckert, Glenn D. "Perspectives on plagiarism from ESL students in Hong Kong." *Journal of Second Language Writing* 2, no. 3 (1993): 131–48.

A survey of 170 first-year and 41 third-year Chinese students in a Hong Kong college aimed to uncover attitudes toward plagiarism. Results showed these students had little familiarity with the Western notion of plagiarism and poor ability to recognize it. Concluded that students needed explicit orientation and training on how to avoid plagiarism when writing in a Western academic community.

50. DiMartino, Diane, and Lucinda R. Zoe. "International students and the library: New tools, new users, and new instruction." 17–43 in *Teaching the new library to today's users: Reaching international, minority, senior citizens, gay/lesbian, first generation, at-risk, graduate and returning students, and distance learners*, edited by Trudi E. Jacobson and Helene C. Williams. New York: Neal Schuman, 2000.

Provides an overview of issues related to library instruction for international students. Discusses cultural differences in learning styles, language issues and their implications in the classroom, challenges international students face in using library services and tools, and issues surrounding computer literacy (databases, search engines, computer interfaces). Suggests instructional approaches to address concerns.

51. Downing, Karen E. "Instruction in a multicultural setting: Teaching and learning with students of color." 47–70 in *Teaching the new library to today's users: Reaching international, minority, senior citizens, gay/lesbian, first generation, at-risk, graduate and returning students, and distance learners*, edited by Trudi E. Jacobson and Helene C. Williams. New York: Neal Schuman, 2000.

Addresses frameworks and strategies for increasing the effectiveness of cross-cultural library instruction. Discusses interracial communication, learning styles, use of multicultural examples in teaching, and affective considerations. Emphasizes the importance of peer teachers and outreach to multicultural campus units and professors.

52. Downing, Karen E., and Joseph Diaz. "Instruction in a multicultural/multiracial environment." 37–45 in *Learning to teach: Workshops on Instruction*, edited by the Learning to Teach Task Force. Chicago: American Library Association, 1993.

Discusses a teaching module designed to move instruction librarians from teaching in a homogeneous to a diverse learning environment. Provides pointers and group exercises on cross-cultural communication, interacting with students, and recognizing unique learning and emotional issues faced by multicultural students. Also discusses bias and perspective in learning materials, difficulties with controlled vocabulary, and strategies for keeping students' interested (pre-class contact with instructors, active learning, involvement of multicultural staff, using alternative and multicultural resources). Emphasizes the importance of peer teachers and outreach to multicultural populations.

53. Dunbar, H. Minnie. *Bibliographic instruction for freshman students at Florida International University*. ERIC document no. ED270106, 1986. 8 p.

Outline of a presentation made to the National Conference on the Freshman Year Experience (Columbia, South Carolina, February 18, 1986). Includes a brief account of the conception, initiation, and implementation of a bibliographic instruction program to serve all freshman students, including such special populations as international and minority freshmen; outline of the general characteristics of each category of students, the type of services and skills they require, and the methods used to organize and deliver information to them; description of the functions of librarians in bridging the gap between the students, academic departments, and the library; and discussion of the role of the librarian in helping students develop skills for acquiring, processing, and using information independently. Program described began in 1983. General focus of the instruction is a guided tour of the library and coverage of basic library tools.

54. Ender, S. C., and F. B. Newton. *Students helping students: A guide for peer educators on college campuses*. San Francisco, CA: Jossey-Bass, 2000. xvii, 254 p.

Resource for students in training to become peer educators. Includes discussion on the impact of peers, intercultural competence when dealing with diverse populations, interpersonal communication skills, problem solving, leading groups, and using campus resources. Does not deal with international students or library resources specifically, but provides useful information for setting up a library peer training program for international students.

55. Engeldinger, Eugene A. "Bibliographic instruction for study abroad programs." *College & Research Libraries News* 46, no. 8 (1985): 395–98.

Discusses the role of academic librarians in preparing American exchange students for research in foreign libraries and the bibliographic culture shock that may occur. Considers academic goals, research and library expectations, English language holdings, access to materials, and library services and policies in the host institutions. Also useful in helping instruction librarians understand the home library environments of international students in the United States.

56. Espiñal, Isabel. "What do Latino students know anyway about information literacy?" *Versed: Bulletin of the Office of Diversity, American Library Association* (2004). http://www.ala.org/ala/diversity/versed/versedbackissues/Versed _MW04.pdf (July 21, 2008).

Urges more research and publication in the professional literature about Latinos and information literacy and discusses issues related to both Latino Studies and Spanish-speaking library users.

57. Evans, Karen. "INTERLINK© at Indiana State University: Adventures in library instruction for international students." *Indiana Libraries* 25, no. 4 (2006): 8–10.

INTERLINK Language Centers provide assistance to students in various areas, including speaking and understanding the English language, research and writing skills, an appreciation of cultural conventions, and the ability to use technology. INTERLINK Centers have been set up at four universities in the United States, including Indiana State University in Terre Haute. The INTERLINK program, which is designed to prepare international students for university work, provides library instruction at various points and a library research component for advanced level classes. Article notes challenges faced by international students: cultural differences, alphabetization, locating items in the library, variety of materials in the library, library services, library vocabulary, asking for assistance, finding government materials, and the concept of plagiarism.

58. Feldman, Dick. "The international student and course-integrated instruction: The ESL instructor's perspective." *Research Strategies* 7, no. 4 (1989): 159–66.

Presents views of the author, a lecturer in the Intensive English Program at Cornell University in Ithaca, New York, on the development and implementation of a library instruction program for international students. Reviews different assumptions and expectations, conveying library use skills, building effective staff partnerships, and librarian participation. Also considers the program's problems and progress. *See also* Ormondroyd, no. 108.

59. Garcha, Rajinder, and Patricia Yates. "Bibliographic instruction for international students in academic libraries." *Library Review* 42, no. 6 (1993): 14–22.
    Provides a brief profile of international students in the United States, then discusses the need to develop appropriate bibliographic instruction programs for this group. Discusses the impact of learning styles, previous library experiences, and problems faced by librarians, then outlines the purpose, methodology, and findings of a survey created to assess the library knowledge of international students enrolled in the American Language Institute's Intensive English program at the University of Toledo in Ohio (sixty-three participants). Results were designed to be used in developing a library instruction program to meet the students' unique needs. Includes recommendations.

60. Gilton, Donna Louise. "Culture shock in the library: Implications for information literacy instruction." *Research Strategies* 20 (2007): 424–32.
    Defines and describes culture shock and clash in general and in relation to international students. Reviews library and information science perspectives on culture shock, then offers suggestions for teaching international students in the library.

61. Gilton, Donna Louise. "A world of difference: Preparing for information literacy instruction for diverse groups." *Multicultural Review* 3, no. 3 (1994): 54–62.
    Examines culture shock and how it impacts library anxiety in international students. Discusses how a well-designed information literacy instruction program can lessen side effects. Outlines points to consider when preparing information literacy instruction for non-Caucasian students, including being aware of the role of the gatekeeper in certain cultures and adapting teaching methods.

62. Golemon, Patricia. "Intercultural classroom communication: Articles of intercultural interest." The Society for Intercultural Education and Research, n.d. http://www.sietarhouston.org/articles/articles10.htm (September 14, 2007).
    Brief overview of issues related to intercultural communication in the classroom. Notes areas where intercultural knowledge can be helpful to teachers, including concepts of time, power distribution, individuals/groups, names, truth/fairness, and phrasal verbs.

63. Goudy, Frank William, and Eugene Moushey. "Library instruction and foreign students: A survey of opinions and practices among selected libraries." 215–26 in *Library instruction and reference services*, edited by William A. Katz and Ruth A. Fraley. New York: Haworth Press, 1984. Co-published as *The Reference Librarian* 10 (1984): 215–26.
    Discusses the design of a questionnaire sent to directors at large American academic libraries (forty-four responses) and aimed at finding out the

perceived proficiency of international students' library use, whether library instruction would be helpful to them, and how the instruction could be accomplished. Survey findings showed librarians perceive foreign students have additional problems in using the library because of poor English skills, lack of adequate vocabulary, cultural differences, and a lack of library skills. The type of instruction offered international students and the degree of coordination that existed between the library and other areas of campus differed considerably. Concludes that library instruction should be more extensive than what was currently offered. Sources of additional ideas and programs are appended. *See also* Tsai, no. 134.

64. Grassian, Esther S., and Joan R. Kaplowitz. "Designing information literacy for diverse populations." 313–35 in *Information literacy instruction: Theory and practice*. New York: Neal-Schuman, 2001.

Emphasizes the importance of knowing learner populations and of recognizing differences between individual and group characteristics. Discusses socialization and acculturation issues, different populations' characteristics and variations in context factors, social interaction, separate versus connected learning, rewards and punishments, communication styles, and immediacy. Focuses on needs of adult learners, international students, and students with disabilities.

65. Graves, Gail T., and Barbara K. Adams. "Library instruction and cultural diversity: Programming in an academic library." *Mississippi Libraries* 57 (1993): 99–101.

Reports on three distinct library orientation and instruction programs offered at William Library, University of Mississippi in Oxford. Two were designed for African American and other American ethnic students and the third for international students. Notes that tour content for international student orientation is based on knowledge of academic libraries abroad and emphasis is placed on the independent use of the library.

66. Griggs, Shirley, and Rita Stafford Dunn. "Hispanic-American students and learning style." *Emergency Librarian* 23, no. 2 (1995): 11–16.

Discusses learning styles of Hispanics and provides information on topics ranging from environmental preferences (lighting, sound levels) to psychological orientations (group vs. individual work). Offers cultural insights into Hispanic groups and discusses implications for instruction. Does not deal specifically with international students.

67. Griggs, Shirley, and Rita Stafford Dunn. "Learning styles of Asian-American adolescents." *Emergency Librarian* 24, no. 1 (1996): 8–13.

Does not deal specifically with international students, but provides a useful overview of learning styles of different groups of Asian Americans. Provides information on diverse topics, from environmental preferences (lighting, sound levels) to psychological orientations (group vs. individual work).

68. Hall, Patrick Andrew. "The role of affectivity in instructing people of color." *Library Trends* 39, no. 3 (1991): 316–26.

Notes that it is important for library instructors to be familiar with the cultural experiences of their students. Discusses effective teaching as a relationship and emphasizes the necessity to establish a rapport with students through maximizing contact and taking a personal interest in them. This is especially important for non-European students, who tend to place their frame of reference in a person or group rather than in objects. Instructors need to recognize diversity within as well as between ethnic groups.

69. Helms, Cynthia Mae. "Reaching out to the international students through bibliographic instruction." 295–307 in *Library instruction revisited: Bibliographic instruction comes of age*, edited by Lynne M. Martin. New York: Haworth Press. Co-published as *The Reference Librarian* 51/52 (1995): 295–307.

Discusses outreach to international students at Andrews University in Berrien Springs, Michigan, through general instruction workshops and more specific library instruction in the university's English Language Institute (ELI) classes. Outlines guidelines for success and challenges faced, then provides observations and suggestions.

70. Hendricks, Yoshi. "The Japanese as library patrons: An intercultural perspective on information literacy." *College and Research Library News* 52, no. 4 (1991): 221–25.

Provides an overview of Japanese social and educational culture and emphasizes how culture creates specific challenges to Japanese students in American academic libraries. Discusses fears of appearing ignorant or disrespectful to persons in authority, and unfamiliarity with the American concepts of individual thought and making choices. Makes suggestions as to how academic library staff can attempt to alleviate these fears.

71. Hickok, John. "Bringing them into the community: Innovative library instructional strategies for international and ESL students." 159–67 in *Practical pedagogy for library instructors: 17 innovative strategies to improve student learning*, edited by Doug Cook and Ryan Sittler. Chicago: American Library Association, 2008.

Discusses unique challenges faced by international and English-as-a-second-language students, then describes efforts to reach and teach them undertaken at California State University, Fullerton. Strategies developed are referred to as the Three I's: Inviting, Involving, and Interfacing. Inviting involves going to the students (visiting cultural clubs, international office events, ESL classes), not waiting for them to come to the library, and making presentations relevant to their interests or home country. Involving means adopting experiential instruction. Interfacing refers to interacting with students by building on what is already known. Describes how these strategies came into play in an actual instruction session, and notes lessons learned.

72. Hockey, Julie, and Carolyn McSwiney. *Articulating students: Differential needs: An academic library's response.* ISANA (International Education Association, Australia), 2005. http://www.isana.org.au/files/20051017165347 _ArticulatingStudentsAcademicLibrary_sResponse.pdf (October 1, 2008).

Addresses the needs of a subgroup of international students, those who have completed part of their degree in their home countries. Describes a dual "pre-departure" and "on-arrival" academic library program developed to meet the needs of a group of third-year pharmacy students at the University of South Australia in Adelaide. The program resulted from four years of reflective practice initiated by a health sciences liaison librarian working with academic staff. It aims to develop the students' information literacy skills to work both independently and collaboratively to retrieve and evaluate academic information. Notes that academic, social, information literacy, and personal/professional outcomes of the program have been significant.

73. Hoffman, Irene, and Opritsa Popa. "Library orientation and instruction for international students: The University of California–Davis experience." *RQ* 25, no. 3 (1986): 356–60.

The UC Davis library created a customized instruction program, LOIIS (Library Orientation and Instruction for International Students), designed to assist international students with adjustment to the American academic environment. The program focused on small group library orientations and a librarian "on-call" service that worked in tandem with educating staff to recognize and respond to the unique needs of international student users. Article discusses how the UC Davis community accepted and supported the program and suggests parameters regarding the best environment to begin a similar program, designed for institutions with small to moderate foreign student enrollment. *See also* Popa and Hoffman, no. 118.

74. Hofstede, Geert. "Cultural differences in teaching and learning." *International Journal of Intercultural Relations* 10 (1986): 301–20.

Discusses differences in interactions between teachers and students from different cultures. Differences are listed with reference to four dimensions: Individualism vs. Collectivism; large vs. small Power Distance; strong vs. weak Uncertainty Avoidance; and Masculinity vs. Femininity. Notes that the burden of adaptation in cross-cultural learning situations should be primarily on the teachers. Many later researchers on teaching international students have drawn upon Hofstede's analytical framework.

75. Howard, Vivian F. *Orientation programs for international students at Canadian academic libraries.* M.A. dissertation, Dalhousie University, 1994. UMI no. MM05205. xiii, 223 p.

Examined the current state of orientation programs for international students at Canadian academic libraries from a variety of perspectives. Based on data from surveys sent to academic librarians and international student advisors at thirty selected Canadian universities and degree-granting colleges, and by a random sample of thirty-five international students enrolled at Dalhousie University and at the University of British Columbia. Analysis showed optional integrated orientations were the norm at the majority of libraries surveyed. Eighty percent of libraries did not offer any form of training program to acquaint library staff with the special needs of international students. At libraries that did offer separate orientations for international students, methods used in the orientation and specific library features included did not differ significantly from methods and features included in integrated orientations with two exceptions: government documents and electronic reference sources appear to be included less often than expected in separate orientations for international students. The majority of librarians surveyed indicated that they did not formally evaluate their orientations for international students nor did they maintain any liaison with university personnel responsible for the academic welfare of international students.

76. Hughes, Hilary. *Information literacy with an international focus.* Paper presented at the Second International Lifelong Learning Conference, Yeppoon, Central Queensland, Australia, 16–19 June 2002. http://lifelonglearning.cqu.edu .au/2002/index.htm (October 16, 2007).

Outlines challenges faced by international students and makes recommendations on overcoming obstacles to teaching information literacy. Discusses the ACRL Information Literacy Competency Standards (2000) and the Council of Australian University Librarians' (CAUL) Information Literacy Standards (2001) as effective and practical frameworks for information literacy education designed to meet the needs of all students, including international students.

77. Hughes, Hilary, Christine S. Bruce, and Sylvia L. Edwards. "Models for reflection and learning: A culturally inclusive response to the information literacy imbalance." 59–84 in *Change and challenge: Information literacy for the 21st century,* edited by Susie Andretta. Adelaide: Auslib Press, 2007.

Examines the apparent information literacy imbalance between many university students' well-developed digital and IT skills and less developed critical awareness skills. Notes that the adverse effect of this imbalance on learning may be intensified by students' differing cultural, linguistic, and educational experiences. Discusses the diverse learning contexts in the Australian higher education environment and cultural and linguistic influences on online information use. Outlines models for reflective information use in theory and as practiced at Queensland University of Technology in Brisbane, where the ROSS (Reflective Online Searching Skills) model was developed to foster students' skills and knowledge of online searching. Considers the use of the model with international students.

78. Hurley, Tina, Nora Hegarty, and Jennifer Bolger. "Crossing a bridge." *New Library World* 107, no. 1226/1227 (2006): 302–20.

Librarians from the Waterford Institute of Technology in Ireland discuss the complexities of creating and implementing a new information literacy course for students from China and Pakistan. Notes that students presented excellent information technology skills, but communication issues remained a barrier between instructors and students. Discusses learning outcomes, course content and delivery, student assessment, and recommendations. Appendices include: a list of information literacy standards for a bridging studies course for international students, course outline for a twelve-hour information literacy course, library tutorial evaluation form.

79. Huston, Mary M. "Instructional responses to the presence and potential of diversity: Toward expert collaboration." 79–92 in *Racial and ethnic diversity in academic libraries: Multicultural issues*, edited by Deborah A. Curry, Susan Griswold Blandy, and Lynne M. Martin. New York: Haworth Press, 1994. Co-published as *The Reference Librarian* 45/46 (1994): 79–92.

Argues that librarians must deliberately become responsive to multiculturalism, multifaceted needs (such as those of nontraditional students), and diverse learning style preferences. Describes several personal experiences that provided insights into other cultures and world views. Advocates "cognitive apprenticeship" in which thinking is cultivated by example. Considers such issues as communication competence, ethnic competence, ethnocentrism, navigating community information systems as opposed to libraries, different ways of learning, and nonverbal communication.

80. Huston, Mary M. "May I introduce you: Teaching culturally diverse end-users through everyday information seeking experiences." *Reference Services Review* 17 (1989): 7–11.

Reports on a study at Evergreen State College in Tacoma, Washington, examining information-seeking behaviors. A diverse group of sixty-five novice library users were interviewed to identify experiential strengths and to gain insight into how participants learned about computer-based systems. Thirty-nine experienced researchers were also interviewed and results compared. Concludes that effective instruction should build on the collective strengths of learners rather than on librarians' professional strengths.

81. Ishimura, Yusuke. *Information literacy in academic libraries: Assessment of Japanese students' needs for successful assignment completion in two Halifax universities*. M.L.I.S. dissertation, Dalhousie University, 2007. UMI no. MR26846. xiv, 99 p. Full text in *Dissertations and Theses* database.

Notes that previous research has shown international students have difficulties accessing, evaluating, and using information. Investigates specific difficulties and recommends types of assistance that should be provided to Japanese students. Subjects were students at two universities in Halifax, Nova Scotia: Dalhousie and Saint Mary's. Research was conducted using focus group methodology, with discussion points based on students' assignment completion processes and needs. Analysis showed that Japanese students needed language support to complete their assignments. Students showed certain information literacy skills, but there was room for improvement. Campus-wide collaboration is indispensable to reach and assist Japanese students. Appendices include copies of research instruments and sample analysis table.

82. Jackson, Rebecca. "Using library paraprofessionals to teach library skills in an EFL program." 85–89 in *Programs that work: Papers and sessions material presented at the Twenty-fourth National LOEX Library Instruction Conference held in Denton, Texas, 16–18 May 1996*, edited by Linda Shirato. Ann Arbor, MI: Pierian Press, 1997.

Discusses a program at George Washington University in Washington, D.C., in which library paraprofessionals were trained to offer bibliographic instruction to students whose first language was not English. This program has proven successful and freed librarians to spend more time on outreach within their subject areas. Includes appendices on points to remember when working with international students and on teaching tips.

83. Jacobson, Frances F. "Bibliographic instruction and international students." *Illinois Libraries* 70, no. 10 (1988): 628–33.

Discusses various factors that impact international students' adjustment to the American social and educational environment, including educational backgrounds and teaching practices in foreign countries and experiences in their home libraries. Provides an overview of learning issues faced by international students and of teaching issues that librarians and library staff should consider. Suggests that bibliographic instruction for international students is most effective when multiple approaches are employed: formal programs, peer support, library staff development.

84. Jenkins, Mercilee M. "Teaching the new majority: Guidelines for cross-cultural communication between students and faculty." *Feminist Teacher* 5, no. 1 (1990): 8–14, 46.

Presents guidelines based on information and ideas derived from interviews with seventy-seven students at San Francisco State University in California. Includes sections on classroom interaction, advising, and evaluation. Designed primarily for classroom teachers of minority students, but includes useful information for librarians who instruct students from diverse cultural backgrounds.

85. Jourdenais, Renee. *Academic library skills for the ESL student.* ERIC document no. ED376711, 1994. 10 p. http://www.eric.ed.gov/ERICDocs/data/ericdocs 2sql/content_storage_01/0000019b/80/13/6f/4b.pdf (August 1, 2008).

Syllabus for an academic library skills course for college-level English-as-a-second-language students. Designed to be incorporated into a fifteen-week program in which students were required to complete an original research paper.

Discusses the rationale for development of the syllabus and reviews the testing phase, done at the University of Florida in Gainesville. Includes two sets of student comments, the first concerning their reactions to North American university libraries in general and the second concerning perceptions of the benefits to be derived from the library skills program.

86. Kamhi-Stein, Lia D., and Alan Paul Stein. "Teaching information competency as a third language: A new model for library instruction." *Reference and User Services Quarterly* 38, no. 2 (1998): 173–79.

Describes a model of library instruction that emphasizes collaboration between English-as-a-second-language teachers and reference librarians. The principles on which the model is based were grounded in second-language teaching theories, educational research, and library instructional practices. Notes that library instruction should provide students with comprehensible input, provide students with scaffolds, be "adjuncted" to content courses, be relevant to students' academic needs, integrate information competence strategy training, and be hands-on. Discusses the application of the principles at California State University, Los Angeles and outlines the impact of the model on student learning outcomes. *See also* no. 182.

87. Kflu, Tesfa, and Mary A. Loomba. "Academic libraries and the culturally diverse student population." *College and Research Libraries News* 51, no. 6 (1990): 524–27.

Compares and differentiates educational challenges of American ethnically diverse and international students, focusing on information literacy and acclimatization to the academic library environment. Briefly outlines behaviors to avoid for each group considered.

88. Kim, Soonhyang. "Teaching international students across the curriculum: Supporting academic listening/speaking." Columbus: Ohio State University, 2007. http://ftad/osu.edu/Publications/intloral.html. (September 11, 2007).

Guidelines prepared for faculty and teaching assistants at Ohio State University in Columbus, but relevant to library instruction. Notes that note-taking and listening comprehension are often difficult for international students, that lack of a second-language self-confidence often inhibits speaking in class, and that American academic discourse patterns and instructors' expectations are not always clear or familiar.

89. Koehler, Boyd, and Kathryn Swanson. "ESL students and bibliographic instruction: Learning yet another language." *Research Strategies* 6, no. 4 (1988): 148–60.

Outlines a four-phase instruction approach that includes ability grouping, online catalog searching, and sensitivity to individual communication problems and learning styles. Discusses the course, students' unfamiliarity with libraries, initial assumptions about librarian/teacher collaboration, various pre-test and post-test phases, and results. Course was developed for use at Augsburg College in Minneapolis, Minnesota.

90. Korolev, Svetlana. "Chemical information literacy: Integration of international graduate students in the research." *Science & Technology Libraries* 19, no. 2 (2001): 35–42.

Notes that chemical information is complex and distinctive in many ways. Bibliographic instruction must be designed to make up for the information deficits of international students. Chemical information literacy programs may be implemented in a variety of ways such as summer courses, special seminars, mentoring programs, and systematic instruction.

91. Kurucz, Paul J. *How to teach international students: A practical teaching guide for universities and colleges.* Nanaimo, BC: Success Orientations, 2006. 210, viii, [3] p.

General textbook covering such topics as: reasons why international students come to "Western countries" (Canada, the United States, the United Kingdom, Western Europe, Australia, New Zealand); differences between post-secondary institutions in these Western countries; how to get international students to understand the Western educational system; successful orientation models; learning styles; assessing international students; common challenges; creating positive learning experiences and environments for international students; rewards of teaching international students.

92. Ladd, Paula D., and Ralph Ruby, Jr. "Learning style and adjustment issues of international students." *Journal of Education for Business* 74, no. 6 (1999): 363–67.

The Canfield Learning Styles Inventory was administered to thirty-five international students enrolled in an MBA program at an American state university. Results indicated that students' preferred mode of learning was direct experience, though the majority had been previously taught by the lecture method. Preferred conditions for learning were identifying and pursuing goals and having a friendly relationship with the instructor. Most expected to perform at an excellent or superior level. Ways in which instructors can build upon this knowledge of learning styles are suggested.

93. Lewis, Mary Genevieve. "Library orientation for Asian college students." *College and Research Libraries* 30 (1969): 267–72.

Considers difficulties of translating an Asian education to American academic libraries, including library perception, classification, and catalog use. Discusses a library orientation program developed at the University of Hawaii's East-West Center and presents results of sixty student interviews regarding their difficulties in using the library. Recommends offering library information in small but steady pieces and giving individual attention to these users.

94. Liestman, Daniel. "Implementing library instruction for international students." *PNLA Quarterly* 56 (1992): 11–14.

Summarizes several approaches to teaching international students how to use North American academic libraries. Discusses barriers faced by international students and highlights different materials used in library instruction, including handouts, tours, and visual presentations. Concludes with recommendations for creating and presenting library instruction courses to international students.

95. Lin, Poping. "Library instruction for culturally diverse populations: A comparative approach." *Research Strategies* 12, no. 3 (1994): 168–73.

Compares the more holistic and macroscopic world view of Chinese students and the specific mechanistic and microscopic world view of Western students, then discusses the impact of these views on each group's mode of thinking. Final section outlines the design of a library instruction workshop at Purdue University Libraries in West Lafayette, Indiana, that attempted to integrate these contrasting thinking patterns.

96. MacAdam, Barbara, and Darlene Nichols. "Peer information counseling: An academic library program for minority students." *The Journal of Academic Librarianship* 15, no. 4 (1989): 204–9.

Discusses a library-based peer counseling program staffed by minority undergraduates at the University of Michigan in Ann Arbor. Designed for minority students, particularly Blacks and Hispanics, but concept could be adapted for international students.

97. Mandernack, Scott B., Poping Lin, and David M. Hovde. "Cultural awareness and bibliographic instruction in libraries." 85–104 in *Diversity and multiculturalism in libraries*, edited by Katherine Hoover Hill. Greenwich, CT: JAI Press, 1994.

Considers the needs of an increasingly diverse library clientele on university campuses and factors to consider in providing effective instruction. These include facilities, staffing, and multicultural collections. Also discusses developing an instructional program that takes into account such issues as learning styles, language proficiency, and perceptions about the library.

98. McLean, Dulce DiDio. *Library user education for the international student: A feasibility study.* ERIC document no. ED197702, 1978. 24 p.

Discusses the development of a library skills program for international students at the University of Toledo Libraries in Ohio. Individual sections present the study framework (methodology, assumptions, purpose of study, definition of a library user education program); summary discussion of aspects to be considered in program development; international students' backgrounds, in general and at the University of Toledo; and description of the suggested user education program. An annotated list of references is appended.

99. McMillian-Nelson, Sharyl, and Marilyn Graubart. "Planning for diversity: A library instruction program for students with special needs." 91–100 in *Programs that work: Papers and sessions material presented at the Twenty-fourth National*

LOEX Library Instruction Conference held in Denton, Texas, 16–18 May 1996, edited by Linda Shirato. Ann Arbor, MI: Pierian Press, 1997.

Discusses a diversity program developed at the University of Missouri–Kansas City to work with students with special needs, here defined as international students, minority students, and students with physical disabilities. The program, which was funded by a university grant, covered sensitivity training for staff, library instruction (main focus of the article), and collection development. Includes an outline of the grant proposal and expenditures involved. An outline of library instruction sessions and sample evaluation form are appended.

100. Meng, Lynn Whitnall, and Mark Meng. *Developing library skills for ESL students.* ERIC document no. 374649, 1994. 7 p. http://www.eric.ed.gov/ERIC Docs/data/ericdocs2sql/content_storage_01/0000019b/80/13/58/54.pdf (July 24, 2008).

Discusses library use instruction designed specifically for limited-English-proficient (LEP) students and library skill activities developed for use with this population at Union County College in Elizabeth, New Jersey. Notes many students from other countries have had little or no exposure to libraries. Typical college-level library orientation lectures may be inappropriate, and even alphabetization may be unfamiliar. Recommends close collaboration of English-as-a-second-language (ESL) instructors and library professionals. Material is dated.

101. Moeckel, Nancy, and Jenny Presnell. "Recognizing, understanding, and responding: A program model of library instruction services for international students." 309–25 in *Library instruction revisited: Bibliographic instruction comes of age,* edited by Lynne M. Martin. New York: Haworth Press, 1995. Co-published as *The Reference Librarian* 51/52 (1995): 309–25.

Outlines functional and cultural barriers faced by international students, then discusses a service model that could be used to create or augment library services for this group. The model includes five programs: promotion, instruction, staff development, writing, and purchasing (collection development). Paper was based in part on data collected through a survey to determine the status of library instruction programs for international students at academic libraries in the state of Ohio (forty-eight respondents). Copy of the survey is appended.

102. Moorhead, Wendy. "Ignorance was our excuse: BI for foreign students requires a shift in cultural perspective." *College & Research Libraries News* 47, no. 9 (1986): 585–87.

Discusses problems encountered in the bibliographic instruction program for students whose first language was not English at Roosevelt University library in Chicago, Illinois. Analysis of instructors' cultural misconceptions, students' misunderstanding of the role of the academic library, and cross-cultural communication obstacles resulted in the development of a new approach to bibliographic instruction based on cultural understanding and the presentation of useful skill sets. Provides outlines for two fifty-minute library sessions.

103. Nield, Kevin. "Questioning the myth of the Chinese learner." *International Journal of Contemporary Hospitality Management* 16, no. 3 (2004): 189–96.

Considers the learning, teaching, and assessment preferences of Chinese learners. Written in the context of distance learning, but provides a helpful general overview. Based in part on a survey administered to twenty-five students at a study school in Hong Kong. Research findings are discussed in terms of curriculum content, teaching and learning strategies, role of the teacher/lecturer, assessments, and rote learning.

104. Niles, F. Sushila. "Cultural differences in learning motivation and learning strategies: A comparison of overseas and Australian students at an Australian university." *International Journal of Intercultural Relations* 19, no. 3 (1995): 369–85.

Reports on a questionnaire survey administered at the Northern Territory University in Darwin, Australia. Respondents were 136 Australian-born students and 72 overseas students. Results showed some similarities and differences between cultures in what motivates students and how they approach learning, and lent support to the argument that Asian learners are not rote learners.

105. Nilles, Mary E., and Dorothy B. Simon. "New approaches to the multilingual, multicultural students in your library." *Catholic Library World* 55 (1984): 435–38.

Discusses challenges faced by English-as-a-second-language students in libraries and advocates the need for internationalizing curricula at the college, high school, and elementary school levels and for promoting library skills as an adjunct to learning. Includes a description of the library learning modules used in conjunction with an advanced writing program at New York City Technical College and discusses problems involved in making a videotape with and for foreign students.

106. Norlin, Elaina. "University goes back to basics to reach minority students." *American Libraries* 32, no. 7 (2001): 60–63.

The author, who serves as the Peer Information Counselling Program coordinator at the University of Arizona in Tucson, discusses her role in promoting information literacy among international and minority students. Accomplishments and outcomes of the program's first year are outlined.

107. O'Hara, Molly. "Bibliographic instruction for foreign students." 230–33 in *Academic libraries: Myths and realities: Proceedings of the Third National Conference of the Association of College and Research Libraries*, edited by Susan C. Dodson and Gary L. Menges. Chicago: Association of College and Research Libraries, 1984.

Reviews issues to be addressed when developing library instruction programs for international students. Emphasizes the need for librarians to seek out and use training in cross-cultural understanding in order to create more effective bibliographic instruction programs. Notes that many teaching points librarians take for granted are based on culture (e.g., alphabetization, plagiarism, etc.). These points need to be recognized and presented according to the cultural background of students. Outlines a useful format for a bibliographic instruction session.

108. Ormondroyd, Joan. "The international student and course-integrated instruction: The librarian's perspective." *Research Strategies* 7, no. 4 (1989): 148–58.

Presents the views of the author, a librarian at Cornell University's Uris Library in Ithaca, New York, on the development and implementation of a library instruction program for international students. Four sessions covered such issues as search strategies, critical thinking, use of the card catalog, and periodical indexes. Discusses the need for program redesign, overcoming constant challenges, and the ultimate expansion of the program. Concludes with an overview of ongoing improvements within the program. *See also* Feldman, no. 58.

109. Orr, Debbie, Jacqueline Slee, and Efthimia Evryniadis. "International students and the electronic library facilities at Central Queensland University." 377–88 in *Proceedings of the Ninth Australasian Information Online & On Disc Conference and Exhibition, Sydney, 19–21 January 1999.* Sydney: Australian Library and Information Association, 1999.

Outlines results of a study of the information literacy needs of international students at the Sydney (Australia) International Campus of Central Queensland University. Provides background on the CQU-SIC electronic library and international students reactions. A questionnaire survey was administered (sixty-six respondents). While the majority of respondents (52 percent) were frequent library users, only 8 percent were satisfied with information received at the library. Only 66 percent chose to attend library tutorials, though most students seemed unaware of the range of available library services and facilities. Results were analyzed and new strategies developed for library instruction programs.

110. Osa, Justina O. "Teaching international students to access and use library resources." 156–64 in *Teaching information literacy skills to social sciences students and practitioners: A casebook of applications*, edited by Douglas Cook and Natasha Cooper. Chicago: Association of College and Research Libraries, 2006.

Describes Pennsylvania State University's Humphrey Fellowship Program, a one-year non-degree program of combined academic and professional development opportunities for mid-career professionals from Africa, Asia, Latin America, the Caribbean, and the Middle East. Article discusses the process of designing an appropriate orientation session to prepare the fellows to use the library, conduct of the session, and lessons learned as a result.

111. Osborne, Nancy Seale, and Cecilia Poon. "Serving diverse library populations through the Specialized Instructional Services concept." 285–94 in *Library instruction revisited: Bibliographic instruction comes of age*, edited by Lynne M. Martin. New York: Haworth Press, 1995. Co-published as *The Reference Librarian* 51/52 (1995): 285–94.

Outlines the State University of New York at Oswego library's Specialized Instructional Services initiative, which focuses on cultural diversity. Provides background on the program, its evolution and current focus, successful initiatives, and future directions. Suggested strategies include communicating with cultural diversity groups on campus, having personnel dedicated to working with diverse populations, creating displays of culturally diverse library materials, allowing students to create displays for the library, encouraging students to recommend materials for purchase, hosting brown bag discussions with students, and developing culturally sensitive library staff.

112. Owens, Alison. "'Fitting in' in a 'stand out' culture: An examination of the interplay of collectivist and individualist cultural frameworks in the Australian university classroom." *Studies in Learning, Evaluation, Innovation and Development* 5, no. 1 (2008): 70–80.

Notes that Australian university students originate from diverse cultural backgrounds, many of which are defined as collectivist communities. This often results in a values clash with the individualist Australian culture. Paper examines cross-cultural perceptions about student motivations for study and perceptions about classroom behavior within collectivist/individualist frameworks, then discusses the best pedagogical principles and practices for working within academic environments where these differing values systems are evident.

113. Park, Clara C. "Learning style preferences of southeast Asian students." *Urban Education* 35, no. 3 (2000): 245–68.

Focus is on high school students, but provides a useful description of differences between the experiences and approaches to learning of Southeast Asian students (Cambodian, Hmong, Lao, and Vietnamese) and those of East Asian students (Chinese, Japanese). Summarizes multiple studies on learning styles of Southeast Asian students and offers suggestions for instructional activities.

114. Parker, D. Randall. *Teaching, learning, and working with international students: A case study.* Paper presented at the Annual Meeting of the Mid-South Educational Research Association, Point Clear, Alabama, 17–19 November 1999. ERIC document no. ED438756, 1999. 16 p.

Report of a program for Taiwanese students at Louisiana Tech University in Ruston. Data was gathered from literature on international education, interviews with Taiwanese graduate students in the program, observations of classes, personal reflections of the researcher, and interviews with participating faculty. Challenges for teachers included coping with students' culture shock and language limitations, determining students' experiential base, and helping students adjust to the academic environment and requirements of an American university. Students had to cope with concepts of individualism versus collaboration (students tended to be competitive and have difficulty engaging in collaborative learning activities), equality and informality (many found the informal academic setting unsettling and were uncomfortable asking repeated questions), different reasoning styles (students tended to be task oriented, an approach not conducive to the development of critical thinking), time versus process orientation (students found techniques such as discovery learning inappropriate), and plagiarism. Results of the experience included the building of cross-cultural awareness and the development of greater cultural and global understanding among faculty and students, as well as the improvement of communication and socialization skills of faculty and students.

115. Pearce, Robert. "The overseas student and library use: A case for special treatment." 45–52 in *Proceedings of the Second International Conference on Library User Education*, Keble College, Oxford, 7–10 July 1981, edited by P. Fox. Loughborough: INFUSE, 1981.

   Discusses problems faced by international students in Britain (language skills, cultural thought patterns, study modes, diverse educational backgrounds) and highlights programs developed in various academic libraries in the United Kingdom. Concludes with a list of practical suggestions for assisting overseas students in library use, focusing in particular on situations where there are no specialized orientation sessions for these students.

116. Pearson, Richard C., and Rex Fransden. "Library instruction in a multicultural setting." *Hawaii Library Association Journal* 40 (1983): 33–36.

   Briefly outlines learning styles of different groups of international students and discusses how to develop appropriate instruction. Based on the authors' experience at Brigham Young University–Hawaii Campus in Laie, Hawaii.

117. Peck, Shirley S. "International students and the research process." 89–105 in *Understanding the international student*, edited by Septimus M. Kaikai and Regina E. Kaikai. New York: McGraw Hill, 1992.

   Provides background on foreign student enrollment in the United States, then discusses the kind of education international students received in their homelands, cultural barriers to research (language, the norm of communalism), and international students' knowledge of libraries. Suggests ways in which teachers can assist international students with adjusting to the American concept of the research method.

118. Popa, Opritsa, and Irene Hoffman. "THE LOIIS program: Final report." 94–106 in *Bibliographic instruction in ARL libraries*, edited by Carol F. Ahmad. Washington, DC: Association of Research Libraries, 1986.

   Describes the purpose and development of the Library Orientation and Instruction for International Students (LOIIS) Program at the University of California–Davis.

Includes program materials, evaluation questionnaires, and a short summary of completed questionnaires. See also Hoffman and Popa, no. 73.

119. Pracht, Carl Joseph. *Library skills for ESL students.* ERIC document no. ED335051, 1991. 86 p.

Teacher's manual for use with a course developed for international students at Southeast Missouri State University in Cape Girardeau. Includes curriculum guide, syllabus, lesson plans, tests, quizzes, and exercises. Course is designed to reinforce library skills in the use of the card catalog, indexes, abstracts, reference materials, and government documents. Material is dated but outlines are useful.

120. Rao, Zhenhui. "Bridging the gap between teaching and learning styles in east Asian context." *TESOL Journal* 11, no. 2 (2002): 5–11.

Considers characteristics of traditional East Asian learning styles, then suggests appropriate actions for teachers dealing with these learners: diagnosing learning styles and developing students' self-awareness, adapting teaching styles to suit students' learning styles, fostering guided style-stretching and encouraging changes in student behaviors, providing activities with different groupings.

121. Rifkin, William, Susan Helmundt, Christine Fox, and Celia Romm. "Getting international students to speak up." *Overview (University of Wollongong, Australia)* 4, no. 2 (1997). http://www.uow.edu.au/cedir/CEDIR/overview/overviewv4n2/rifkin.html (September 30, 2008).

Discusses lesson plans and strategies designed to stimulate class discussion by international students. Results were tested using before-and-after surveys of almost five hundred students. Written for teaching faculty, but contains useful ideas for library instruction.

122. Robertson, Joan E. "User education for overseas students in higher education in Scotland." *Journal of Librarianship and Information Science* 24, no. 1 (1992): 33–51.

Reports on two surveys completed by ten students from each of the institutes of higher education in Scotland. The first survey aimed to identify the status of user education for all Scottish students using academic libraries, to find out if special user education programs were created for overseas students, and to determine if librarians were aware of problems of overseas students. The second survey examined how well overseas students understood and utilized academic libraries and how they perceived benefits from user education. Concludes that the importance of user education is recognized and most institutions make some attempt to provide library instruction. However, there is a need for better librarian/faculty liaison and for cooperation between librarians and other institutional bodies that deal with international students. Library staff were unenthusiastic about user education in general, and overseas students were not coping as well as library staff thought they were.

123. Rodrigues, Helena Frances. *Bibliographic instruction for international students: A comparison of delivery methods.* D.A. dissertation, Simmons College, 1992. xiii, 114 p.

Reports on a study examining differences between test scores of international students who receive peer tutoring and those who receive traditional bibliographic instruction (lecture/demonstration). Also compares international and American students who receive peer tutoring. Recommendations include the implementation of a peer-tutoring program and course-integrated instruction for students at the Roger Williams College Library in Bristol, Rhode Island.

124. Ryan, Janette. *A guide to teaching international students.* Oxford: Oxford Brookes University, 2000. 91 p.

Basic textbook covering such issues as understanding approaches to knowledge and learning in different cultures; operating effectively as a teacher of international students; assessment; course content and design; issues for personal tutors (forms of names, providing support); post-graduate supervision; experiences of international students and what universities can do to help; useful cultural information. Written for teaching faculty, but some material relevant to library instruction.

125. Sarkodie-Mensah, Kwasi. "The international student in the U.S. academic library: Building bridges to better bibliographic instruction." 105–20 in *Diversity and multiculturalism in libraries*, edited by Katherine Hoover Hill. Greenwich, CT: JAI Press, 1994.

Discusses international students' academic library use and perceptions of the library, then considers staff training, student instruction, creating appropriate alliances with other academic campus offices, and integrating bibliographic instruction into English-as-a-second-language classes. Also presents an outline of a library session for international students. Based on results from the survey created by the author for his 1988 dissertation (388 respondents); see no. 288.

126. Seton, J., and N. Ellis. "Information literacy for international postgraduate students." 61–68 in *Learning for life: Information literacy and the autonomous learner: Proceedings of the Second National Information Literacy Conference conducted by the University of South Australia Library, 30 November–1 December 1995*, edited by Di Booker. Adelaide: University of South Australia Library, 1996.

Notes that information literacy is crucial for the success of all post-graduate students. Post-graduates from international non-English-speaking backgrounds face additional linguistic and cultural difficulties. Article describes the Integrated Bridging Program at the University of Adelaide, Australia, and points to areas in which further development is required.

127. Shana'a, Joyce. "The foreign students: Better understanding for better teaching." *Improving College and University Teaching* 26, no. 4 (1978): 243–46.

Brief discussion of international students and issues that they face. Provides advice for instructors aimed at encouraging understanding of students' language problems, classroom behavior, and social customs.

128. Sigsbee, David L., Bruce W. Speck, and Bruce Maylath. *Approaches to teaching non-native English speakers across the curriculum.* San Francisco: Jossey-Bass, 1997. 104 p.

Textbook on teaching English-as-a-second-language students. Includes essays discussing international variations in standard English, differences between international students and language minority students, cultural norms that affect oral communication in the classroom, and what teachers can do to relieve problems identified by international students.

129. Smith, Andrew James McGregor. *International students at university in the United States: Faculty perceptions of instructional difficulties and effective instructional strategies.* Ph.D. dissertation, Georgia State University, 2001. UMI no. 3023304. xi, 234 p. Full text in *Dissertations and Theses* database.

Discusses opportunities and challenges international students present to teaching faculty. Study examined perspectives of twelve faculty members at a large urban university in the southeastern United States with respect to learning difficulties displayed by international students. Instructional solutions found to be effective in overcoming difficulties are also presented. Problems identified included language and communication issues, social interaction, cultural effects on learning styles, technology-based difficulties, lack of acculturation, gender roles, and teacher/student expectations. Appendices include interview questions, sample page from a reflective journal, data analysis coding book, researcher biases and expectations.

130. Spanfelner, Deborah L. "Teaching library skills to international students." *Community & Junior College Libraries* 7, no. 2 (1991): 69–76.

Describes the international student makeup (mostly Spanish-speaking) at Broome Community College in Binghamton, New York, then discusses lesson planning and preparation for a bibliographic instruction course taught in both English and Spanish. Includes sample exercises and student comments.

131. Spaven, Claire, and Anne Murphy. "Parlez-vous technologie? Teaching information skills in a second language." *INSPEL* 34, no. 3/4 (2000): 179–86.

Authors were responsible for teaching information skills to post-secondary students in a government-funded college system in the United Arab Emirates. In developing a curriculum they first had to review their own assumptions of their students' existing information literacy skills, for example, did students understand and appreciate library "culture" and know how to find information in their native language; what was the role of books in society; what type of learning style was prevalent (rote learning rather than learner-centered). Paper discusses obstacles faced and lessons learned, and offers advice to other librarians teaching information skills to students in a second language.

132. Tao, Dorothy. "Bibliographic instruction for a diverse population: Understanding, planning, and teaching in the twenty-first century." *Art Documentation* 24, no. 1 (2005): 29–37.

Describes planning for bibliographic instruction at the School of Architecture and Planning at the University of Buffalo in Buffalo, New York. Notes that the student population included many international students. Discusses cultural difficulties, staff training, learning styles, affectivity, and language difficulties. Outlines strategies for improving communication and describes an international student workshop conducted at the university. Also considers approaches for use with nontraditional or re-entry students and multicultural students.

133. Thompson, Susan N. *Teaching library skills to ESL students.* ERIC document no. ED408831, 1997. 18 p. http://www.eric.ed.gov/ERICDocs/data/eric docs2sql/content_storage_01/0000019b/80/16/ad/48.pdf (July 24, 2008).

Presents support materials for a program to teach library research skills to Japanese university students of English as a second language (ESL) studying in the United States. The program, instituted at Mukogawa Fort Wright Institute in Spokane, Washington, was designed to assist English majors from Mukogawa University in Japan in the use of the institute's specialized library collection. Introductory section describes the institution and its library collection, then outlines the rationale for library research instruction, student needs, and lesson contents, and lists examples of student research projects undertaken at the institute. Student materials include a library and research vocabulary list, worksheets for four lessons, a sample topic worksheet, and a brief list of additional resources. Lesson topics include finding one's way around the library, using general reference books, the Dewey Decimal System, and the card catalog. Material is dated.

134. Tsai, Benhong. *Special bibliographic instruction for international students: A survey of academic libraries in medium sized state universities.* M.S. in I.M. research report, St. Cloud State University, 1988. ii, 49 p.

Examines the amount and types of formalized bibliographic instruction for international students offered in medium-sized state universities. Based on results of a mail survey (sixty respondents). Results indicated most international students at the surveyed universities came from Asian regions; 58 percent of universities offered some form of bibliographic instruction exclusively for international students; most existing instruction programs consisted of brief introductory sessions and individual assistance at the reference desk; few instruction programs were mandatory and student participation rates tended to be 50 percent or lower; instruction sessions were most frequently conducted by reference librarians; lack of funding and staff were cited most often as reasons for not providing specialized instruction. Study was designed as a counterpart to the 1984 survey of large university libraries by Goudy and Moushey (no. 63). Copy of the questionnaire, list of participating libraries, and summary of results mailed to respondents are appended.

135. Valiente, Carolina. "Are students using the 'wrong' side of learning?: A multicultural scrutiny for helping teachers to appreciate differences." *Active Learning in Higher Education* 9, no. 1 (2008): 73–91.

Discusses learning styles and ways in which teachers can develop a richer multicultural learning and teaching approach in Western higher education institutions. Considers the importance of memorization as a tool for learning and how motivation, communication, and collaborative patterns work in different cultures. Compares Western learning theory and Confucian principles with the aim of increasing academics' awareness of international students' backgrounds and the challenges they face.

136. Wallin, Margie, Debbie Orr, and Jillian Litster. "Information literacy: Assessing the needs of international students at Central Queensland University." 1–9 in *Proceedings of the 3rd Pacific Rim Conference on the First Year in Higher Education, Auckland NZ, 5–8 July 1998, Volume II,* edited by Roger Stokell. Auckland, NZ: Auckland Institute of Technology, 1998.

Reports on a survey of international students in the introductory tourism unit at Central Queensland University in Australia (fifty-five respondents) aimed at determining the learning backgrounds and cultural issues that shaped expectations and information-gathering approaches of this student group. Results showed many students had limited prior access to libraries, limited understanding of the technology needed to access information sources, and limited experience and understanding of the need for information literacy skills. Concludes that appropriate teaching strategies need to be employed to maximize learning outcomes for this group. A program integrating information literacy skills into the unit content was subsequently developed.

137. Watkins, Nan. "A case in point: Individual library instruction for international students." *North Carolina Libraries* 54 (1996): 76–79.

Reviews the rationale for introducing a bibliographic instruction program for international students at Western Carolina University in Cullowhee, North Carolina. Discusses the development and refinement of the program and offers tips for teaching international students.

138. Wilson, Vicky. "Independent learning skills and the overseas student: The role of the library." 657–79 in *Conference proceedings: Papers presented at the Australian Library and Information Association 1st Biennial Conference, Perth, W.A., September 30–October 5, 1990, volume 2.* Applecross, WA: Promaco Conventions, 1990.

Examines current thought on the acquisition of independent learning skills by students and barriers created for overseas students studying in Australia. Considers the design of library programs, from initial orientation sessions through the teaching of specific research assignments. Concludes that overseas students will continue to require specially designed courses to help them cope with the Anglo-American style of education.

139. Wong, Joseph Kee-Kuok. "Are the learning styles of Asian international students culturally or contextually based?" *International Education Journal* 4, no. 4 (2004): 154–66.

Reports on a survey conducted with seventy-eight first-year Asian international undergraduates at a south Australian university. Further interviews were conducted with nine students. Major difficulties highlighted by students were different learning styles, cultural barriers, and language problems. However, Chinese learners were found to be highly adaptive for learning. Concludes that there is no apparent reason for Australian higher learning institutions to adapt to the Asian style of teaching and learning, but those teaching Asian students should try to understand the initial learning difficulties faced by these students and take measures to support them when necessary.

140. Yoshida, Norman J. "In pursuit of trivia—Game theory and research skills." Paper presented at the TRI-TESOL Conference, Bellevue, Washington, November 14–16, 1985. ERIC document ED267623, 1985. 5 p. http://www.eric.ed.gov/ERICDocs/data/ericdocs2sql/content_storage_01/0000019b/80/2f/2a/3e.pdf (July 22, 2008).

Discusses an intermediate course designed to help develop students' world knowledge through language. This was part of a group of modular courses created for a college-level English-as-a-second-language program at Lewis and Clark College in Portland, Oregon. The course, modeled on the Trivial Pursuit game, required students to learn library skills, research a variety of topics, discuss material researched and other relevant cultural information in classroom sessions, and prepare as a final project a student-designed version of the game. *See also* nos. 152, 182, 185, 186, 192, 194, 203, 210, 211, 236, 245, 274, 279, 282, 374, 384, 391, 392, 448, 578, 579.

BIBLIOGRAPHIES

141. Association of College and Research Libraries. Instruction for Diverse Populations Committee. *Library instruction for diverse populations bibliography.* Chicago: American Library Association, 2008. 21 p. http://www.ala.org/ala/acrlbucket/is/publicationsacrl/fullbib.pdf (July 21, 2008).

Annotated bibliography dealing with instruction to a variety of populations in academic libraries, including ethnic minorities; first-generation college students; gay, lesbian, bisexual, and transgender students; students with disabilities; transfer students; and international students (twenty entries).

142. Davis, Kaetrena D. *Global evolution: A chronological annotated bibliography of international students in U.S. academic libraries.* Chicago: Association of College and Research Libraries, 2007. 30 p.

Annotated bibliography containing 191 items. Entries are arranged by decade: 1970s (three entries), 1980s (forty-seven entries), 1990s (sixty-six entries), 2000s (thirty-five entries). Special sections list items relevant to specific ethnic/cultural groups, library administration, staffing, bibliographies, international library education, international research, and general works of note. Many citations are inaccurate or incomplete.

143. Greis, Naguib. *ESL bibliography.* ERIC document no. 126732, 1975. 19 p.

Bibliography of materials in English as a second language especially at college level (117 entries). Materials are classified under categories of oral skills; reading, patterns, and vocabulary; writing and grammar exercises; orientation, library and study skills; technical English; and tests.

144. Liestman, Daniel. *Library users whose second language is English: A bibliography of sources, 1964–1989.* ERIC document no. 311911, 1989. [iii], 37 p.

Bibliography (514 entries), with items arranged by broad subject areas in twenty-five categories: academic libraries, services to Asians, automated services, bibliographies and checklists, bilingualism in the library, children's services, collection management, community analysis, general, services to Hispanics, intercultural interaction, library education, mass media, media, services to migrants, services to native populations, professional concerns, public libraries, recruitment of librarians, reference, school libraries, special libraries, technical services, user education, and young adult services. Not annotated.

145. Loomis, Abigail A., and Karen Havill Bingham. "Reaching out: Library instruction for special user groups: A bibliography." *Illinois Libraries* 70 (1988): 670–76.

Briefly annotated bibliography listing sixty-one articles related to various nontraditional library users (the disabled, international students, high school students in academic libraries, older adults, gifted students).

146. Macomber, Nancy. "Academic library services to international students: A selected bibliography." *Urban Academic Librarian* 5 (1987): 49–51.

A selective, briefly annotated listing of twelve sources that address cultural differences and language problems that potentially lead to negative encounters between international students and library staff.

147. McSwiney, Carolyn. "Academic library needs of students from non-English speaking backgrounds in Australia: A position paper and select bibliography." *Australian Library Journal* 43 (1994): 197–217.

Considers needs of both international students and students from immigrant families who communicate at home in a mother tongue other than English. Focus is on students of Asian origin, who form the largest group of overseas students in Australia. Annotated bibliography lists fifty items.

148. Moeckel, Nancy, and Jenny Presnell. "A companion bibliography to: Recognizing, understanding, and responding: A program model of library instruction

for international students." 327–53 in *Library instruction revisited: Bibliographic instruction comes of age*, edited by Lynne M. Martin. New York: Haworth Press, 1995. Co-published as *The Reference Librarian* 51/52 (1995): 327–53.

Lists 193 entries with brief annotations. Divided into three sections: library programs/instruction; cultural attributes of international students; general education/interpersonal communication issues. Companion work to no. 101.

149. Penchansky, Mimi B., Evelyn Apterbach, and Adam Halicki-Conrad. *International students and the library: An annotated selective bibliography on the theme of the LACUNNY 1988 Institute*. New York: The Library Association of the City University of New York, 1988. ERIC document no. ED295679. 29 p.

A seventy-one-entry annotated bibliography including books, articles, and reports. Focuses on international students but also contains topics related to immigrant students from non-English-speaking countries and their adjustment to the educational system in the United States. Includes a list of organizations working with international students and a list of suggestions for helping students in the library.

150. Sapon-White, Richard. "International librarianship: Resources for further exploration." *OLA Quarterly (Oregon Library Association)* 6, no. 4 (2000): 8–10.

Brief annotated bibliography listing five books and articles, six journals, and five web resources on issues related to international librarianship.

151. Wu, Connie. *Library services and foreign users—A comprehensive bibliography*. ERIC document no. ED308867, 1988. 14 p.

Lists 135 journal articles, books, book chapters, conference papers, and documents on bibliographic instruction, minority librarianship, and cultural/ethnic-specific services for non-English-speaking users. *See also* nos. 379, 496.

COLLECTION DEVELOPMENT

152. Chabrán, Richard. "Latino reference arrives." *American Libraries* 18 (1987): 384, 386–88.

Provides a short history of the development of Latino-centered collections in American colleges and universities and offers a listing of relevant reference sources and successful bibliographic instruction programs.

153. Chabrán, Richard. "Mapping emergent discourses: Latino bibliographic services in academia." 116–19 in *Alternative library literature 1986/87*, edited by Sanford Berman. Phoenix, AZ: Oryx Press, 1988.

Brief discussion of issues related to the development of research collections for Latino students. Identifies a number of important indexes and reference sources.

154. Dickinson, Donald C. "The reviewing of foreign language reference books: woeful inadequacy." *RQ* 32, no. 3 (1993): 373–80.

Discussion of reviewing media used to evaluate reference books published in non-English languages. Based on a survey of eighty Association of Research Libraries institutions.

155. Evans, G. Edward. "Needs analysis and collection development policies for culturally diverse populations." *Collection Building* 11, no. 4 (1992): 16–27.

Provides an outline of a method of determining library user needs, then provides an example of needs analysis in California. Focuses primarily on minority ethnic groups within the general population, but guidelines would be applicable in an academic library setting.

156. Figueredo, Danilo H. "The many we are: Guidelines for multicultural collections based on the Bloomfield College project." 63–74 in *Diversity and multiculturalism in libraries*, edited by Katherine Hoover Hill. Greenwich, CT: JAI Press, 1994.

Discusses efforts at Bloomfield College in Bloomfield, New Jersey, to develop a multicultural library collection. Notes the project was successful because faculty supported the initiative. Emphasizes the importance of a written library policy statement that reflects a commitment to multicultural diversity in collection development.

157. Hodge, Stanley P., and Marilyn Ivins. "Current international newspapers: Some collection management implications." *College and Research Libraries* 48, no. 1 (1987): 50–60.

Discusses newspaper collection management practices among research libraries, based on two surveys, one of eighteen members of the Association of Research Libraries and one at Texas A&M University in College Station. Emphasizes the importance of incorporating use patterns into selection decisions and offers a methodology for surveying the library's international user group. Also provides a list of factors to consider when drafting a collection development policy for newspapers.

158. Mood, Terry Ann. *Library resources for the foreign born college student.* ERIC document no. ED233725, 1982. 34 p.

Begins with a brief essay on difficulties faced by college students who have recently immigrated to the United States. Notes that immigration to the United States has been increasing, particularly from the Asian and African countries, and that immigrant students must deal with language problems and also must adjust to new educational methods and different types of library service. The major component of the paper is an annotated list of 108 general reference books and works on Africa, Asia, and the Middle East that college libraries can provide for the use of immigrant students. This listing includes general encyclopedias, sources of international statistics, biographical dictionaries, sources of international business information, news directories, and periodical indexes covering international affairs.

Also includes encyclopedias, handbooks, yearbooks, dictionaries, atlases, sources of statistics, biographical sources, news summaries, bibliographies, and periodical indexes specific to Africa, Asia, and the Middle East. Material is dated.

159. Pettingill, Ann, and Pamela Morgan. "Building a retrospective multicultural collection: A practical approach." *Collection Building* 15, no. 3 (1996): 10–16.

Outlines an action plan designed to meet cultural diversity goals of the strategic plan of Old Dominion University in Norfolk, Virginia. The library action plan included purchasing videos, creating a printed library resource guide on multiculturalism, and evaluating library resources by checking against bibliographies on selected minority and ethnic groups.

160. Scarborough, Katherine. "Collections for the emerging majority." *Library Journal* 116, no. 11 (1991): 44–47.

Reports on an ethnic collection development conference held in San Francisco in September 1990 and sponsored by the Bay Area Library and Information System and the School of Library and Information Studies, University of California, Berkeley. Over 350 public, academic, and school librarians attended the conference, which was entitled "Developing Library Collections for California's Emerging Majority." Sessions covered such issues as the need for strong ethnic collections, sources of materials, making collections accessible, and technical processing issues.

161. Scarborough, Katherine T. A. (ed.). *Developing library collections for California's emerging majority: A manual of resources for ethnic collection development.* Oakland: Bay Area Library and Information System, 1990. ii, 296 p.

Collection development manual produced in conjunction with the conference described above, no. 160.

162. Schomberg, Jessica, and Michelle Grace. "Expanding a collection to reflect diverse user populations." *Collection Building* 24, no. 4 (2005): 124–26.

Reviews rationale, development, and outcome of a collection development project focusing on Somalia and Somalis at Minnesota State University in Mankato. Highlights difficulties in establishing the project and reviews all phases, from finding funding to assessing the impact of the collection on the university community.

163. Vocino, Michael. "International newspapers for U.S. academic libraries: A case study." *Collection Management* 9 (1987): 61–68.

Reports on an analysis of the international newspaper collection at the University of Rhode Island Library in Kingston. The project resulted in extensive changes in the library's holdings both in number and format.

164. Ziegler, Roy A. "International students and country of origin news." *Serials Review* 23, no. 1 (1997): 33–47.

Discusses challenges faced by students living in a foreign culture and notes that international news sources are generally neglected in collection development. Discusses three common library "solutions": it's not the library's job; the library will subscribe as long as it supports the curriculum; and the library will do everything it can. Reports on a survey of international news resources at ten midwestern U.S. university libraries, then outlines the specific response at Southeast Missouri State University in Cape Girardeau. Includes a table listing a selection of international news websites and a brief catalog of country-of-origin news sources in English. *See also* nos. 97, 202, 205, 218, 227, 228, 232, 245, 309, 327, 376.

COMPUTERS AND THE INTERNET

165. Abdullah, Aman Salem. *Factors affecting international students use of the online catalogue and other information sources.* Ph.D. dissertation, Florida State University, 2000. UMI no. 9973229. xvi, 220 p. Full text in *Dissertations and Theses* database.

Based on a survey of three hundred international graduate students at Florida State University in Tallahassee. Examines search behaviors, particularly preference among academically oriented information resources and how students used the online catalog. Findings showed subjects preferred to learn through exploration and that they searched using English even when native language interfaces were available. Copy of the questionnaire is appended.

166. Adeoye, Blessing, and Rose Mary Wentling. "The relationship between national culture and the usability of an e-learning system." *International Journal on E-Learning* 6, no. 1 (2007): 119–46.

Discusses globalization and the increasing need for business, educational, and training organizations to be involved in e-learning as a training tool. Reports on a study exploring possible relationships between the usability of e-learning systems and national culture. Participants were twenty-four international students from a large university in the midwestern United States. Concludes with discussion of factors to consider when conducting e-training with those from varying cultural backgrounds.

167. Al-Mashaqbeh, Ibtesam F. *Computer applications in higher education: A case study of students' experiences and perceptions.* Ed.D. dissertation, Ball State University, 2003. UMI no. 3091874. viii, 123 p. Full text in *Dissertations and Theses* database.

Qualitative study describing the educational experiences with computers of nine female international graduate students at Ball State University in Muncie, Indiana. Describes subjects' computer use before coming to the United States, current use of computers, challenges faced related to the use of computers during graduate study, and support received from the university to help them overcome these barriers. Reports on ways computers supplemented and enriched the experiences of these students in the completion of their graduate work. Each participant was interviewed for two hours, then asked to complete a brief questionnaire to identify age, country of origin, academic program, and length of time spent in the United States. Results indicated most participants did not use computer applications on a daily basis during their undergraduate study in their native countries, but all participants used computer applications on a daily basis during their study at BSU. Some participants faced two important academic adjustments at the same time: adjustment to the English language and adjustment to the use of computers. Most participants received support from friends regarding the use of computers and most faced problems regarding their typing skills. Using the library website was a challenge. All participants believed that the use of computers enriched their experiences during their study at BSU and all used the Self-Learning Theory to improve their computer skills. Demographic and interview questions are appended.

168. Anderson, Renee Nesbitt. "Utilization of computerized services in the academic library: The freshman and international student experience." Paper presented at the Third International Conference on New Information Technology, Guadalajara, Mexico, 26–28 November 1990. http://web.simmons.edu/~chen/nit/ NIT'90/001-and.html (July 23, 2008).

Discusses results of a study undertaken at the University Library and North Campus at California State University, Long Beach involving the use of computers by incoming students in a required introductory course. Usage of the online catalog, online search services, and compact disc products were observed and participants (twenty-five first-year and sixteen international students from thirteen countries) completed a questionnaire on library use (appended). Statistical tables differentiate between international and undergraduate student responses, but analysis does not deal specifically with differences between the two student groups.

169. Ariyapala, P. G., and N. N. Edzan. "Foreign postgraduate students and the online catalogue at the University of Malaya library." *Malaysian Journal of Library and Information Science* 7, no. 1 (2002): 57–67.

Describes a study investigating international students' ability to use an online library catalog. Data was collected through a questionnaire survey (forty-two respondents) on availability of OPACs in their country of origin, OPAC usage, frequency and type of OPAC use, ease and difficulties in using the OPAC, success in locating items, types of searches, most frequently conducted searches, and how students learned OPAC use. Most respondents indicated there were no OPAC facilities in their home countries and, if available, they were limited to university libraries. Students found the OPAC at the University of Malaya library relatively easy to use, but they were only moderately successful in locating items.

Recommends more effective bibliographic instruction sessions, preparing printed instructions on OPAC use, encouraging students to seek help from librarians, and making additional OPAC terminals available.

170. Barlow, Michael. *Working with computers: Computer orientation for foreign students.* ERIC document no. 286478, 1987. 304 p. http://www.eric. ed.gov/ERICDocs/data/ericdocs2sql/content_storage_01/0000019b/80/1b/eb/ e5.pdf (July 23, 2008).

Two-part guide written for international students. Includes instructions on how to use computers for general and efficient academic use. Part I reviews basic components and major areas of computing. Part II reviews specific academic tasks, including library research, online searching, taking notes, organizing information, and word processing. Appendices discuss fundamentals of common text editors, major operating systems, and list of common computer functions. A glossary of technical terms is also provided. Material is dated but provides some guidelines with respect to format and content for instruction.

171. Ben Omram, Abdulaziz Ibraheem. *Library anxiety and internet anxiety among graduate students of a major research university.* Ph.D. dissertation, University of Pittsburgh, 2001. UMI no. 3013234. x, 114 p. Full text available in *Dissertations and Theses* database.

Examines the relationship between library anxiety and Internet anxiety among graduate students of the University of Pittsburgh, Pennsylvania (164 subjects). Considers whether selected variables (year of study, major, grade point average, number of library instruction sessions attended, gender, age) are correlated with and can predict anxiety. Also explores the differences in anxiety levels between American and international students. Results indicated that library anxiety and Internet anxiety existed among the subjects of this study, but age was the only variable that predicted library anxiety. The frequency of Internet use and major were significant in predicting Internet anxiety. Finally, findings suggested that differences exist between the levels of library anxiety and Internet anxiety of American and international students among some groups. Appendices include anxiety scales, questionnaire, statistical tables.

172. Bentley, Joanne P. H., Mari Vawn Tinney, and Bing Howe Chia. "Intercultural Internet-based learning: Know your audience and what it values." *Educational Technology Research and Development* 53, no. 2 (2005): 117–27.

Target audience is designers of Internet-based learning courses taken by students from various cultures, but provides useful information on how international learners perceive quality in instruction. Considers such factors as language, educational culture, technical infrastructure, primary audience, learning styles, reasoning patterns, cultural context, and social context.

173. Blackhall, Gael. "Multilanguage features for public access computers." *Feliciter* 50, no. 1 (2004): 24.

Report of efforts at Calgary Public Library in Calgary, Alberta, to meet the needs of users who require public computers to display websites in non-English languages, send and receive e-mail from web-based e-mail accounts in non-English languages, and compose MSWord documents in non-English languages and scripts. Based on experience in a public library, but relevant to academic library settings.

174. Burns, Elizabeth Clerkin. *A comparison of the language specific problems encountered by native-English-speaking and English-as-a second-language undergraduate students searching the University of Washington library's online catalog.* M.Libr. Thesis, 1998, University of Washington. vii, 68 p.

Report of a field observation study comparing the online catalog searching techniques of thirteen ESL students with those of twelve native-English-speaking students at the University of Washington in Washington state. Notes that all of the ESL students had attended a fifty-minute bibliographic instruction class less than four days prior to being observed. Only six of the English-speaking students had taken a library class and only three reported having had a class within the past year. Results indicated that native English speakers employed significantly larger numbers of search terms and executed a significantly larger number of searches on a single topic than did ESL searchers. Both groups underutilized truncation, Boolean operators, and the limit features on the catalog. ESL searchers scanned retrieval sets more slowly and needed help finding physical documents in the library. Worksheets and statistical tables are appended.

175. Chiang, Ching-hsin. *Learning COMCAT (Computer Output Microform Catalog): Library training program for foreign students at New York Institute of Technology.* M.Sc. thesis, New York Institute of Technology, 1991. vi, 113 p.

Describes the development and implementation of COMCAT training for foreign students at New York Institute of Technology in New York. Concludes with recommendations for the possible use of skills presented. Material is dated.

176. DiMartino, Diane, William J. Ferns, and Sharon Swacker. "CD-ROM searching techniques of novice end-users: Is the English-as-a-second-language student at a disadvantage?" *College and Research Libraries* 56, no. 1 (1995): 49–59.

Report of a controlled experiment comparing CD-ROM search strategies of forty-two undergraduate native English speakers and thirty-four undergraduate English-as-a-second-language speakers. All were students at Baruch College, City University of New York in New York City. Findings showed native speakers experimented more with search terms (e.g., using plural word forms, synonyms, and alternative works), but both groups of students underutilized basic search techniques, such as Boolean operators and indexing, and searched inefficiently. Suggests future areas of study and offers recommendations on developing future CD-ROM databases and interfaces.

177. DiMartino, Diane, William J. Ferns, and Sharon Swacker. "A study of CD-ROM search techniques by English-as-a-second-language (ESL) students."

107–17 in *Proceedings of the Fourteenth National Online Meeting, New York, May 4–6, 1993*, edited by Martha E. Williams. Medford, NJ: Learned Information Inc., 1993.

Presents preliminary findings of a study comparing CD-ROM search techniques of native English speakers and English-as-a-second-language speakers. Subjects were nineteen English-speaking and eighteen ESL undergraduates at Baruch College, City University of New York in New York City, and had no formal training using CD-ROM databases. Results suggested there were a few significant differences between the groups, but generally, search strategies for both groups were inconsistent, inefficient, and relatively imprecise. Notes that effective retrieval may be influenced more by interface design than by users' language skills.

178. Howze, Philip C., and Dorothy M. Moore. "Measuring international students' understanding of concepts related to the use of library-based technology." *Research Strategies* 19, no. 1 (2003): 57–74.

Presents results of a survey of international students' knowledge of terms in the American College and Research Libraries Instruction Section's Committee on Instruction for Diverse Populations multilingual glossary. The 153 respondents were enrolled in the Intensive English laboratory course at Wichita State University in Wichita, Kansas. Highlights varying levels of student understanding. Includes copies of the glossary and survey tools.

179. Hughes, Hilary. "Actions and reactions: Exploring international students' use of online information resources." *Australian Academic & Research Libraries* 36, no. 4 (2005): 169–79.

Discusses interim findings of a research project investigating the use of online information resources by a group of twelve international students at the Brisbane International Campus of Central Queensland University in Australia. Describes students' online behavior (actions), their affective and cognitive responses (reactions), and associated difficulties. Data was collected through semi-structured interviews and observation. Considers the implications for information literacy education and online resources development related to cultural and linguistic diversity. *See also* no. 180.

180. Hughes, Hilary, and Christine Bruce. "Cultural diversity and educational inclusivity: International students' use of online information." Paper presented at the 12th International Conference on Learning, Granada, Spain, July 2005. *International Journal of Learning* 12, no. 9 (2006): 33–40.

Discusses the experiences of a group of twelve students from nine different countries enrolled at the Brisbane International Campus of Central Queensland University in Australia. Participants were interviewed and their responses analyzed to identify difficulties in online use attributable to cultural or linguistic diversity and to foster the development of information literacy strategies that would respond to the students' learning needs. Proposes a holistic approach to information literacy learning that would address the diverse needs of international students. *See also* no. 179.

181. Kamentz, Elisabeth, and Thomas Mandl. "Culture and e-learning: Automatic detection of a users' culture from survey data." Paper presented at the 5th Annual International Workshop on Internationalization of Products and Systems, Berlin, Germany, July 2003. http://eprints.rclis.org/archive/00007083 (August 20, 2007).

Notes that knowledge about the culture of a user is especially important for the design of e-learning applications. Reports on a study in which questionnaire data was used to build machine learning models to automatically predict the culture of a user. Participants were seventy-four students from fourteen countries. Suggests this work can be applied to automatic culture detection and subsequently to the adaptation of user interfaces in e-learning. Concludes by suggesting further avenues for research. Of interest to those designing computer systems for use by multinational populations.

182. Kamhi-Stein, Lia D. "Making online databases accessible to ESL students." *CATESOL Journal* 9 (1996): 73–83.

Describes a model of online database instruction that draws on the collaboration of content faculty, reference librarians, and English-as-a-second-language teachers. Model was implemented at California State University, Los Angeles through Project LEAP (Learning English for Academic Purposes). Online database instruction is hands-on and integrated into a multi-step writing assignment. Article describes the rationale for the model and the sequence of activities designed to promote independent online database use by ESL students. *See also* no. 86.

183. Main, Linda. *Building websites for a multinational audience.* Lanham, MD: Scarecrow Press, 2002. vi, 179 p.

Reference guide highlighting issues to be considered when building a website aimed at an international audience (e.g., writing systems, character sets, encoding, graphics, etc.). Also examines cultural issues to be considered.

184. Mehra, Bharat, and Dania Bilal. "International students' perceptions of their information seeking strategies." Paper presented at the Canadian Association of Information Science conference, Montreal, Quebec, May 2007. http://www.caisacsi.ca/proceedings/2007/mehra_2007.pdf (November 30, 2007).

Explores the information needs and information-seeking strategies of ten Asian graduate students at the University of Tennessee, Knoxville. Quantitative and qualitative methods were used to assess students' use of information and communication technologies (search engines, internet, library website, OPAC, online databases). Makes recommendations for improving information support services and participants' cross-cultural learning process.

185. Mestre, Lori. "Accommodating diverse learning styles in an online environment." *Reference & User Services Quarterly* 46, no. 2 (2006): 27–32.

Outlines four common theories and models used to explain how students' learning styles vary, including the single learning-style continuum and the multidimensional learning style. Also discusses implications of the theory of field dependence and field independence cognitive styles for cross-cultural learning and its impacts on users' information processing. Offers suggestions for tutorial design.

186. Mestre, Lori. "Designing internet instruction for Latinos." 185–99 in *The challenge of internet literacy: The instruction-web convergence*, edited by Lyn Elizabeth M. Martin. New York: Haworth Press, 1997. Co-published as *Internet Reference Services Quarterly* 2, no. 4 (1997): 185–99.

Discusses cultural issues, needs, and learning styles of Latino students and implications for librarians instructing them. Focus is on finding information in an online environment.

187. Park, Il-Jong. *Evaluation by Korean students of major online public access catalogs in selected academic libraries*. Ph.D. dissertation, University of North Texas, 1995. UMI no. 9517638. ix, 168 p.

Notes that library and information science professionals are hindered in making the best decisions when designing, acquiring, and managing library information systems by a lack of understanding of the characteristics, skills, and searching abilities of specific user groups. Questionnaires and skills tests were administered to Korean students enrolled at the University of North Texas in Denton (eighty-four responses). Students' perceptions and behaviors were measured in their use of DRA, Geac, INNOPAC, NOTIS, and VTLS OPAC systems. Results of analysis showed academic level of study and age of the students affect the preference for the type of OPAC system selected, but academic major of the students does not affect the preference; system designers should prepare more specific instructions regarding searching methods; system designers should focus on the design of the system menu, since menu instructions represented the most common method of learning about the OPAC; there was a negative relationship between the number of searching methods that the respondents knew in using OPACs and the frequency of manual card catalog use; and menu-driven systems should be the first selection of OPAC systems for Korean students. Makes recommendations for designing, adopting, or managing a new online system.

188. Purmensky, Kerry. "How educational media can benefit the international student population in the United States university setting." *Journal of Educational Media & Library Sciences* 42, no. 3 (2005): 363–68.

Report of web-based survey investigating international students' access to the Internet, their use of web-based educational media, and differences between those who utilized a website designed to decrease acculturative stress and those who did not (ninety-three participants). The website, the Global Survival Guide, was developed at Southern Illinois University to meet the needs of incoming students. It provided information on coming to the United States, housing and other student services, academic and social issues while at university, and personal issues, as well as serving as a bulletin board for student questions. Results indicated international students applying to American universities have excellent access to the Internet, though it is very expensive in some areas. Of students using the website designed for them, most found it helpful, and these students also reported they used web-based educational media to help them decide which university to attend. Concludes that universities need to focus their attention on using web-based educational media to attract and assist international students in adjusting to life in a new country. Not specifically library-related, but useful in understanding international students' prior Internet experience.

189. Song, Yoo-Seong. "International business students: A study on their use of electronic library services." *Reference Services Review* 32, no. 4 (2004): 367–73.

Examines perceptions and expectations of international students studying business at the University of Illinois at Urbana-Champaign, particularly in the area of electronic resources. Results of a survey of 143 subjects indicated a significant number had no prior experience with electronic library services in their home countries. About half preferred to use libraries other than the Business and Economics Library, making reference service more challenging. Most students did not see virtual reference as an important library service. Implications for information literacy and virtual reference service are discussed. Also includes suggestions for further research, including the idea of differing library-use patterns between international students in other disciplines.

190. Taylor, Carol, Joan Jamieson, and Daniel Eignor. "Trends in computer use among international students." *TESOL Quarterly* 34 (2000): 575–85.

Report on computer familiarity among English-as-a-second-language students learning English for higher education programs in North America. Participants (191,493) were Test of English as a Foreign Language (TOEFL) examinees, who were tested twice. Frequency of computer use, frequency of using English word-processing software, and Internet use were among factors used in developing profiles and determining if the profile was changing. Includes an outline of the report's purpose, methodology, and results by test region and by Asian language groups. Results indicated increased use of computers, English word processing, and, most notably, the Internet over the test period (one and a half years), with dramatic differences evident from what was reported in a similar study done in 1989.

191. Vöhringer-Kuhnt, Thomas. "The influence of culture on usability." Diploma paper, Freie Universität Berlin, 2002. http://userpage.fu-berlin.de/~kuhnt/thesis/results.pdf (October 1, 2008).

Report of two surveys testing the usability of websites. Participants in the main survey (145 students and professionals from 30 countries) tested a Cross-Cultural Usability Questionnaire developed by the author. Results indicated differences in attitude toward usability across members of different national groups and these differences are attributed to different cultural values.

192. Welch, Jeanie M., and William E. King. "Using the Internet to teach US business research to students of English as a second language." *The Reference Librarian* 58 (1997): 5–12.

Describes a course taught at the American Graduate School of International Management in Phoenix, Arizona, that included a semester-long project involving finding information about a U.S. company and its place in industry. Notes the challenges reference librarians faced in dealing with patrons for whom English is a second language and in integrating the possibilities of the Internet into their reference and library instruction functions. Suggests that working closely with classroom instructors and integrating a course-specific website into a research project can be beneficial in meeting both these challenges.

193. Ye, Jiali. "Acculturative stress and the use of the Internet among East Asian international students in the United States." *CyberPsychology & Behavior* 8, no. 2 (2005): 154–61.

Investigates relationships between stress and use of the Internet, taking into account Internet types (English-language and native-language) and Internet motives. Data was derived from a survey of 115 East Asian international students at a large urban university in the southeastern United States, all of whom had lived in the United States for an average of over three years. Results indicated that students generally used English-language Internet more than native-language, with a positive correlation found between using English-language Internet and English proficiency. Three Internet motives were identified: information seeking, social utility, and relaxation/entertainment. Acculturative stress was not related to information seeking. Older students tended to use the Internet as a source of information, while younger students used it more for social purposes.

194. Zhuo, Fu, Jenny Emanuel, and Shuqin Jiao. "International students and language preferences in library databases use." *Technical Services Quarterly* 24, no. 4 (2007): 1–13.

Notes that library database interfaces such as EBSCO, OCLC's FirstSearch, CSA, and JSTOR provide additional language features to assist international students. Reports on a survey conducted by librarians at Central Missouri State University and St. Louis University in Missouri aimed at determining preferences of international students (128 respondents). Data was collected on use of multilingual features, bibliographic instruction given in the students' home nations, and questions about the literal translation of search keywords and terms. Librarians were able to tailor their instruction to best meet these students' database searching needs based on results. Recommendations include activating database language interfaces, maintaining contact between the library and the international office, providing cultural sensitivity training to library staff, providing multilingual library instruction, conducting ongoing assessment of library services to international students, and making full use of international students who are familiar with the library as peer counselors. Copy of the survey is appended.

195. Zoe, Lucinda R., and Diane DiMartino. "Cultural diversity and end-user searching: An analysis by gender and language background." *Research Strategies* 17, no. 4 (2000): 291–305.

Study on end-user searching focusing on gender and language variables. Subjects (131, including 52 who were native English speakers) were graduate students at Baruch College at the City University of New York. Participants conducted searches using LEXIS/NEXIS, then completed a detailed survey. Searching success, techniques, and satisfaction with results were analyzed. A correlation was found between native language and searching ability. Students who did not speak English as a first language employed different search strategies from those who did, for example, students from East Asian backgrounds did not use Boolean operators as often as English speakers but they made more use of proximity operators. *See also* nos. 29, 50, 77, 80, 109, 203, 240.

DISTANCE EDUCATION

196. Chakraborty, Mou, and Johanna Tuñón. "Taking the distance out of library services offered to international graduate students: Considerations, challenges and concerns." 163–76 in *distance learning library services: The tenth off-campus library services conference*, edited by Patrick B. Mahoney. New York: Haworth Press, 2002. Co-published in *Journal of Library Administration* 37, no. 1/2 (2002): 163–76.

Discusses library services offered to international distance education students at Nova Southeastern University in Fort Lauderdale, Florida. Seven areas of service provision and delivery are considered, including document delivery, online resource access, setting up formal agreements with local libraries, and providing services in the language of instruction. *See also* nos. 103, 315.

GENERAL WORKS

197. Abadi, Jawad Mahmoud. *Satisfaction with Oklahoma State University among selected groups of international students*. Ed.D. dissertation, Oklahoma State University, 1999. UMI no. 9942416. x, 155 p. Full text in *Dissertations and Theses* database.

Examines extent to which international students from selected countries at Oklahoma State University in Stillwater, Oklahoma, were satisfied in their academic, social, personal, and financial experiences. Data was collected through face-to-face semi-structured interviews with thirty-five international students from ten different countries. Analysis of data showed: 64 percent of participants were satisfied with their academic experience; 55 percent were generally satisfied with their financial situation; 42 percent expressed overall satisfaction with their personal experience; only 36 percent were satisfied with their overall social life. Library-related recommendations included improving and updating of resources in libraries and computer labs to provide a more satisfactory educational experience for all students. Interview script and guide appended.

198. Abdoulaye, Kaba. "Information-seeking behaviour of African students in Malaysia: A research study." *Information Development* 18, no. 3 (2002): 191–96.
      Reports on a survey to investigate information-seeking behaviors of African students at the International Islamic University Malaysia's library in Kuala Lumpur (twenty subjects). Discusses channels used by students to get information (social networks, computers, library staff, etc.) and how often they used library services. Notes that using the library had a positive effect on changing students' information-seeking behaviors.

199. Abdullahi, Ismael. "Multicultural issues for readers advisory services." *Collection Building* 12, no. 3–4 (1993): 85–88.
      Brief general survey of issues related to multicultural library services and the role of multicultural advisory groups.

200. Adams, Elaine P. "Internationalizing the Learning Resources Center." *The College Board Review* 119 (1981): 19, 27–28.
      Discusses programs at the Learning Resources Center at Texas Southern University in Houston, designed to help international students cope with adjusting to American life skills. Also provides tips for collection development and workforce diversification to help students understand American academic libraries.

201. Ahmadi, Hassan. *Reactions of international students to academic library services and resources: Problems and difficulties encountered by international students in terms of using library services and resources at two sample American universities (USC and UCLA).* Ph.D. dissertation, University of Southern California, 1988. iii, 138 p.
      Examines impressions held by international students at the University of Southern California (USC) and the University of California, Los Angeles (UCLA) related to services provided by the university libraries. Evaluates international students' views regarding reference services, bibliographic assistance, and needs for additional public services. Also discusses characteristics of the user population and difficulties experienced in using libraries and resources, then suggests new programs and services to remedy problems. Based on questionnaires and interviews. Concludes that international students have difficulties in using various segments of the library. The language barrier presents many difficulties. Recommends that special library programs be developed for international students and that library staff be specially trained in assisting them. Self-guided audio tours supplementing a printed tour of the library were also suggested.

202. Alire, Camila, and Orlando Archibeque. *Serving Latino communities: A how-to-do-it manual for librarians.* 2nd ed. New York: Neal-Schuman, 2007. xii, 229 p.

Designed primarily for public libraries, but much information could be adapted to academic settings. Includes information on Latino culture and cultural traits, needs assessment, developing programs and services, preparing staff to work with Latinos, improving collection development, and performing effective outreach and public relations.

203. Allen, Mary Beth. "International students in academic libraries: A user survey." *College and Research Libraries* 54, no. 4 (1993): 323–33.

Analyzes results of a survey of international graduate students at the University of Illinois (395 respondents) to determine patterns of library use. Major aims were to identify which aspects of library service were new to students and which were different from libraries in countries of origin, and to examine students' prior use of computers and perceived challenges using libraries. Findings showed students with prior experience using computers for bibliographic research had greater confidence in their skills using the online catalog. However, a significant number of students did not have this prior experience. Concludes with discussion of the importance of offering distinct forms of bibliographic instruction for international graduate students.

204. American Library Association. "Guidelines for library services to Hispanics." *RQ* 27, no. 4 (1988): 491–93.

Lists guidelines related to collections, programs and community relations, personnel, and buildings.

205. American Library Association. "Guidelines for multilingual materials collection and development and library services." *RQ* 30, no. 2 (1990): 268–71.

Guidelines developed to promote the development and maintenance of multilingual library services and collections and to serve as models against which the provision of services and materials can be assessed. Aimed primarily at public libraries, but relevant to academic collections.

206. Arishee, Jebreel H. *Personal and cultural values as factors in user satisfaction: A comparative study of users of library services.* Ph.D. dissertation, University of Pittsburgh, 2000. UMI no. 9998539. xv, 176 p. Full text available in *Dissertations and Theses* database.

Investigates the extent to which the personal and cultural values of American and international students are factors in their satisfaction with library services. Considers conceptual linkages between cultural and personal values, as well as the effects of values on customer satisfaction. Survey population included 435 American and international graduate students enrolled in the Graduate School of Public and International Affairs at the University of Pittsburgh (Pennsylvania). Data was collected on demographics, cultural values, and user satisfaction. Analysis of results showed a significant positive correlation between personal values, service quality, and satisfaction and between power distance, service quality, and satisfaction. There was no significant relationship between geographic area and any of the eight personal values identified. Only Japanese students showed less satisfaction with American library services; this is probably due to two major factors: the Japanese students' high expectations and the fact that they had come from a more developed and technologically enhanced background than other international students included in the study. Includes recommendations and suggestions for further research. A copy of the questionnaire is appended.

207. Association of College and Research Libraries. *Cultural diversity programming in ARL libraries*. Association of Research Libraries, 1990. 189 p.

Association of Research Libraries (ARL) SPEC kit. Based on a survey of forty-five ARL libraries that aimed to identify practices in the areas of affirmative action, minority recruitment, and cultural diversity. A major focus is on issues related to the recruitment and retention of a diverse workforce. Also discusses library diversity programs designed to enhance staff multicultural awareness/sensitivity training and to meet the needs of diverse user groups, including international students, through such initiatives as the appointment of librarians with responsibility for diversity programs and the creation of peer-counseling groups.

208. Ayala, John, Luis Chaparro, Ana Maria Cobos, and Ron Rodríguez. "Serving the Hispanic student in the community college library." 111–20 in *Library services to Latinos: An anthology*, edited by Salvador Güereña. Jefferson, NC: MacFarland, 2000.

Four-part essay, with separate sections discussing the demographic profile of Spanish-speaking students in American colleges, challenges for community colleges, outreach to Latino community college students, and an administrator's perspective. Primarily concerned with domestic students, but some ideas relevant for international students.

209. Baker, Susan. "Providing library services to overseas students." *Library Association Record* 92, no. 7 (1990): 509–10.

Brief outline of results of a questionnaire administered to ninety-six international students at Liverpool School of Tropical Medicine in the United Kingdom. Section 1 of the survey asked about previous library use, access to online facilities, use of abstracts, loan period, previous library instruction, and how easy it was to use libraries. Section 2 covered questions about copyright and photocopying, while section 3 included more indirect questions about library use (e.g., finding specific materials). Once results were tabulated, students were streamed into seminar groups for instruction based on their particular needs.

210. Ball, Mary Alice, and Molly Mahony. "Foreign students, libraries and culture." *College and Research Libraries* 48, no. 2 (1987): 160–66.

Discusses two approaches to placing the international student and the academic library in cultural context: bibliographic instruction and staff development. Notes that the first step to building relationships is understanding that libraries reflect culture. Discusses teaching research methods, increasing staff sensitivity to international student issues, and designing a staff development workshop. Also highlights the impact of stereotypes and cultural traits in library interactions, citing the University of Michigan Libraries program as a reference point.

211. Ballard, Brigid. "Academic adjustment: The other side of the export dollar." *Higher Education Research and Development* 6, no. 2 (1987): 109–19.

Discusses the problems of Asian students in Australian universities and factors that affect their success. Considers support services (accommodation offices, counseling services, health services, language centers, learning/study skills services), then examines the need for institutional adjustment. This could include providing assistance with language and academic deficiencies, changing teaching styles, reorienting student study habits, and understanding reasons for plagiarism. Based on experiences of the Study Skills Unit of the Australian National University, Canberra.

212. Bent, Moira, Marie Scopes, and Karen Senior. "Discrete library services for international students: How can exclusivity lead to inclusivity?" 205–15 in *Libraries without walls 7: Exploring "anywhere, anytime" delivery of library services*, edited by Peter Brophy, Jenny Craven, and Margaret Markland. London: Facet, 2008.

Report on research being undertaken for the United Kingdom Society of College, National, and University Libraries (SCONUL) aimed at determining how UK university libraries can best support international students. This research examines issues surrounding the debate over exclusivity versus inclusivity, and includes a description of techniques libraries are currently employing, feedback from international students about their priorities for library support and how that matches library staff perceptions, and discussion of groups with which libraries need to collaborate to improve service provision. Based on a survey of SCONUL member institutions (fifty responses) that collected data on designated staff support for international students, staff development, library web pages, publications, services provided, and emerging themes. *See also* SCONUL, no. 298.

213. Bigdeli, Zahed. *Library services to overseas students in Australian universities*. Ph.D. dissertation, University of New South Wales, 1996. UMI no. 0597070 2 vols. (xv, 175; 329, [83] p.)

Examined effectiveness of library use by comparing international post-graduate students with their local counterparts. A mail questionnaire completed by post-graduate students (197 responses) collected data on how well subjects were able to use library resources as well as their attitudes toward the library and librarians at the University of New South Wales in Sydney, the cultural proximity of their own experience to the dominant culture in Australia, their previous library experience, English proficiency, and language of instruction at different levels of study. Results of analysis indicated local post-graduate students scored higher than international students on all investigated variables, with differences in culture the most significant variables. Concludes that libraries and librarians need to take into account cultural differences when dealing with international students. Notes that European students found their culture closer to the dominant culture in Australia than did non-European international students, and European students used the library more effectively than international students from non-European countries.

214. Bilal, Dania M. *Library knowledge of international students from developing countries: A comparison of their perceptions with those of reference librarians.* Ph.D. dissertation, Florida State University, 1988. UMI no. 8814400. xvii, 240 p. Full text in *Dissertations and Theses* database.

Outlines the rationale, methodology, and results of a study examining the relationship between international students' perceptions of the importance of library knowledge and their success in using the library, particularly with respect to certain variables (length of stay at an American university, participation in library instruction programs, sex, region of origin, English language proficiency, previous library experience). Reference librarians' perceptions of students' success in using the library and the importance of library knowledge to them were also examined, as well as differences between student and librarian perceptions. Study sample involved 53 librarians and 104 students at forty-two large Association of Research Libraries (ARL) member institutions. Includes thirty-eight tables and sixteen figures of data and sixteen appendices.

215. Bilal, Dania M. "Problems of foreign students in using United States libraries and the difficulties of translating an international education to Lebanon." 23–36 in *Translating an international education to a national environment: Papers presented at the International Doctoral Guild at the University of Pittsburgh, School of Library and Information Science, September 23–25, 1988,* edited by Julie I. Tallman and Joseph B. Ojiambo. Metuchen, NJ: Scarecrow Press, 1990.

Two-section report. Part I reviews purposes and results of a nationwide study conducted by the author on the assessment of international students' perceptions of the library and successful U.S. academic library use (see no. 214). Also outlines what U.S. academic librarians should know about students from developing countries, with an emphasis on those from Arab-speaking countries. Part II discusses library education in Lebanon and offers recommendations on how the library at Lebanese University can improve the use and status of libraries.

216. Bonta, Bruce. "American higher education and international programs: Background, issues, and a future agenda." 1–23 in *The role of the American academic library in international programs,* edited by Bruce Bonta and James G. Neal. Greenwich, CT: JAI Press, 1992.

Provides a brief history of American universities' and colleges' involvement in international programs. Considers study programs abroad, faculty and staff exchanges, and issues related to international students on American campuses. Also examines the role of academic institutions in promoting world cooperation, multiculturalism, and the development of education in the developing world.

217. Bonta, Bruce, and James G. Neal (eds.). *The role of the American academic library in international programs.* Greenwich, CT: JAI Press, 1992. xviii, 294 p.

Ten papers examine four major aspects of international involvement by American academic libraries and librarians: international resources sharing, work of American librarians abroad, international librarians and students who come to the United States for study, and area studies collections in academic libraries. *See also* Bonta, no. 216; Kalin, no. 245; Kaniki, no. 246; Segal, no. 331; Snyder and Griffin, no. 545; Welch and Okuizimi, no. 561.

218. Buckner, Terry, and Tiana French. "International students and the academic library: How one library is working to make its international students feel at home." *Kentucky Libraries* 71, no. 2 (2007): 8–11.

Discusses initiatives at the Learning and Resource Center at Bluegrass Community and Technical College in Kentucky, where diversity has been identified as a priority. Discusses exchange and visiting scholar programs; diversity programs in the library, such as art, literature, and thematic displays; provision of resources in various languages, including search interfaces, e-books, and print resources; development of a small language lab in the library; and marketing the library through brochures in various languages.

219. Burhans, Skip. *Serving the information needs of the international and minority students at a small college library: A librarian's view.* ERIC document no. ED335714, 1991. 6 p. http://www.eric.ed.gov/ERICDocs/data/ericdocs2sql/content_storage_01/0000019b/80/23/00/f7.pdf (July 31, 2008).

Notes that international and minority students often pose challenges for public service librarians due to cultural, linguistic, or socio-economic differences. Outlines likely areas where miscommunication may arise and suggests that listening carefully, speaking slowly and clearly, and being patient are a few ways to handle language problems. Awareness of the educational hierarchies and differences in library resources in other cultures is helpful. In addition, librarians can provide bibliographic instruction courses and expand book and journal collections to include works dealing with minority issues or written by minority authors.

220. Bush, Simon, Chris Tzourou, and William Archer. *How important is a multicultural learning environment for international students compared with domestic students?* Report prepared by the i-graduate Research Service and published by the International Graduate Insight Group (IGI), 2007. http://www.cihe-uk.com/docs/0711igradexp.pdf (September 24, 2008).

Report commissioned by the Council for Industry and Higher Education in the United Kingdom. Based on results from a survey at thirty-eight British universities (29,968 respondents). Online questionnaires included questions on demographics of respondents, how important they rated university services, and how satisfied they were with these services. Results indicated a multicultural learning environment was significantly more important to international than domestic students.

221. Chadley, Otis A. "Addressing cultural diversity in academic and research libraries." *College & Research Libraries* 53 (1992): 206–14.

Discusses the current state of cultural diversity in American academic research libraries. Reports on results of a survey of Association of Research Libraries member libraries (thirty-five responses) that collected data on recruitment of librarians, services to students, and collection development. Results suggested research libraries were making increased efforts to create a more culturally diverse environment, but more sustained effort was needed, especially with respect to attracting underrepresented minorities to the library workforce.

222. Chau, May Ying, and Michael Culbertson. "Library services for international students: A study at Colorado State University." *Colorado Libraries* 20 (1994): 40–41.

Reports on the methodology, results, and conclusions of a study examining the success of international students at Colorado State University in Fort Collins in locating library materials (seventy survey respondents). Results indicated 80 percent used the library regularly and 64 percent thought they could use the library successfully. In response a workshop was designed for international students on library use and efforts were under way to publicize the service through the International Student Services Office and other channels.

223. Curry, Deborah A., Susan Griswold Blandy, and Lynne M. Martin. *Racial and ethnic diversity in academic libraries: Multicultural issues.* New York: Haworth Press, 1994. 374 p.

Collection of essays dealing with various aspects of work with culturally diverse populations. *See also* Blenkinsopp, no. 372; Huston, no. 79; Irving, no. 342 ; Rosen, no. 283.

224. DuMont, Rosemary Ruhig, Lois Buttlar, and William Caynon. *Multiculturalism in libraries.* Westport, CT: Greenwood Press, 1994. 240 p.

Four-part study covering various aspects of cultural diversity and libraries: the context of multiculturalism; administrative services (dealing largely with staff diversity); case histories of practices at three American libraries (California State, University of Michigan, Lorain Public in Ohio); and a bibliographic essay on cultural pluralism. Section dealing with multiculturalism in academic libraries considers both ethnic minority groups and international students. Discusses problems of adjustment, differences in educational systems, differences in libraries, and staff recruitment and training, then provides brief outlines of programs and services offered for minority and international students at a number of American academic libraries.

225. Farid, Mona. *A study of information seeking behavior of Ph.D. students in selected disciplines: Final report.* ERIC document no. ED252213, 1984. 128 p.

Investigated information-seeking behavior of Syracuse University (Syracuse, New York) doctoral students in six disciplines: economics, English, geology, history, philosophy, and physics. Questionnaire responses from sixty-nine subjects provided data on their educational environment, search strategies, selection of information channels, and demographic information. Special attention was given to the students' use of tools and services offered by Syracuse University Libraries. Differences in information patterns among students in the six disciplines and between international and U.S. students are described, and suggestions made concerning methods of library instruction. Statistical tables and a copy of the survey instrument included.

226. Gale, Caroline. "Serving them right? How libraries can enhance the learning experience of international students: A case study from the University of Exeter." *SCONUL Focus* 39 (2006): 36–39.

Outlines steps taken by the author, a subject librarian and International Officer at the University of Exeter in England, to better support international students. These included development of web pages, creating a jargon list of library terms, compilation of an introductory leaflet, providing extra teaching sessions on library use, offering drop-in sessions for extra library help, and obtaining books for students that used basic English.

227. Güereña, Salvador (ed.). *Latino librarianship: A handbook for professionals.* Jefferson, NC: MacFarland, 1990. xiii, 192 p.

Anthology designed to provide guidance to librarians serving Latino communities in both academic and public libraries. Does not consider international students specifically, but provides useful articles on such topics as Latino reference sources, Latino databases, and collection development for Latinos. For an updated collection of articles see no. 228.

228. Güereña, Salvador (ed.). *Library services to Latinos: An anthology.* Jefferson, NC: MacFarland, 2000. xi, 249 p.

Anthology that includes several chapters relevant to college and university librarians, in particular those on language issues, community college libraries, and electronic resources. *See also* Berlanga-Cortéz, no. 343; Ayala, no. 208; and Vega García, no. 587.

229. Hagey, A. R., and Joan Hagey. "The international students and the junior college: Academic and social needs." *Journal of College Student Personnel* 13, no. 2 (1972): 140–44.

Presents results of a study in which 272 Middle Eastern students from 17 two- and four-year institutions in Oregon were surveyed with respect to social adjustment, academic adjustment, services used, and services wanted. Results showed the majority of students in junior colleges did have either formal courses in library use or special tours of the library, while almost half of those in four-year colleges used more informal means to learn about the library. Reasons for this difference are suggested.

230. Hagey, A. R., and Joan Hagey. "Meeting the needs of students from other cultures." *Improving College and University Teaching* 22 (1974): 42–44.
Reports on a questionnaire survey conducted at Portland State University in Oregon involving Middle Eastern students (265 respondents). Data was collected on student adjustment to the American academic environment, particularly with respect to general orientation programs, library orientation programs, support from classroom instructors, advising services, and involvement in international student organizations. Results suggested many students felt inadequate in library use despite a library tour. Recommends that institutions of higher education provide more direction in teaching library skills.

231. Hao, Junhong. *Chinese students' use of a medium-sized American academic library.* M.S. thesis, Central Missouri State University, 1992. 47 p.
Study of difficulties faced by Chinese students as users of libraries and library services at Central Missouri State University in Warrensburg. Subjects identified items perceived to be new and difficult in the academic library and commented on available bibliographic instruction. Analysis suggested unfamiliarity with an American library, lack of concepts of using the library, and insufficient language skills were major problems. Recommendations included redesigning library tours and providing both general library instruction and instruction specially designed for this group of library users.

232. Haro, Roberto. *Developing library and information services for Americans of Hispanic origin.* Metuchen, NJ: Scarecrow Press, 1981. xvi, 286 p.
Discusses services at public, school, and academic libraries. Relevant chapters include those on geographical distribution and concentrations, attitudes, and pertinent sociocultural factors of Mexican Americans, Puerto Ricans, Cubans, and Latinos; assessment of an Hispanic community and the development of appropriate library and information services; library programs developed for Hispanic groups; Mexican American and Chicano attitudes toward libraries; library acquisitions, technical processing, and training; bilingual/bicultural education and library services; library staff and service programs; building and site considerations; library education; library collections and informational services for Hispanic students in community and four-year colleges and universities; evaluation of library staff, holdings, and services; and domestic and international implications regarding library and information services for Spanish-speaking people. Appendices list domestic distributors and publishers of Hispanic materials,

sample questions for a library survey, and a discussion of the structured interview methodology. Aimed primarily at Hispanic Americans, but presents many ideas adaptable for use with international students from Spanish-speaking countries.

233. Heery, Mike. "Academic library services to non-traditional students." *Library Management* 17, no. 5 (1996): 3–13.

"Non-traditional students" are identified as students with disabilities, overseas students, part-time students, and distance learners. Specific needs of each group are outlined and ways to improve services to them suggested. With respect to international students, the importance of staff awareness regarding such issues as communication difficulties, culture shock, library jargon, subject headings, and alphabetical order are highlighted. Specialized library instruction, providing a basic guide on how the library operates (which could include such information as guidance about surnames), and regular library liaison with other campus units working with international students are recommended.

234. Heggins, Wille J., III, and Jerlando F. L. Jackson. "Understanding the collegiate experience for Asian international students at a midwestern research university." *College Student Journal* 37, no. 3 (2003): 379–91.

Examines levels of student adjustment by international students at an unidentified American midwestern research university. Participants (twenty-eight Asian students) were interviewed individually and divided into two focus groups. Results showed students had difficulties with adjusting to the campus environment. A lack of proficiency in English was one of the greatest problems. Social interaction was also identified as a problem, as were external pressures from family and differing cultural values. Students tended to seek information and support from friends and family rather than formal university support services such as the library.

235. Hill, Katherine Hoover. *Diversity and multiculturalism in libraries.* Greenwich, CT: JAI Press, 1994. xii, 264 p.

Collection of essays dealing with various aspects of work with culturally diverse populations. *See also* Figueredo, no. 156; Gomez, no. 390; Mandernack, no. 97; Miller, no. 271; Sarkodie-Mensah, no. 125; Su, no. 302; Welburn, no. 358; Yates, no. 312.

236. Hughes, Hilary. "The international-friendly library: Customising library services for students from overseas." Paper presented at ALIA 2001 TAFE Libraries Conference, Brisbane, Australia, 21–23 October 2001. http://conferences .alia.org.au/tafe2001/papers/hilary.hughes.html (September 11, 2007).

Identifies eight obstacles that international students face when studying in Australian universities (emotional roller coaster, language barriers, nonverbal communication, physical problems, culture shock, racism and stereotyping, study shock, library shock) and offers recommendations for creating an "international-friendly library." Suggests services can be improved through staff development and campus-wide collaboration and offers pointers on teaching information literacy courses to international students.

237. Hughes, Hilary. "Researching the experiences of international students." 168–74 in *Lifelong learning: Whose responsibility and what is your contribution? Refereed papers from the 3rd International Lifelong Learning Conference, Yeppoon, Australia, 13–16 June 2004*, edited by Patrick Alan Danaher, Colin Macpherson, Fons Nowens, and Debbie Orr. Rockhampton, QLD: Central Queensland University Press, 2004.

Discusses the experiences of Australian international students based on published literature and the author's extensive experience working with and researching this population. Outlines the challenges of conducting research on international students, including cultural and linguistic/communication considerations, and suggests strategies for addressing these challenges. Also considers the benefits of researching international students to both researchers and participants.

238. Iivonen, Mirja, Diane Y. Sonnenwald, Maria Parma, and Evelyn Poole-Kober. *Analyzing and understanding cultural differences: Experiences from education in library and information studies.* Paper presented at the 64th IFLA General Conference, Amsterdam, Holland, 16–21 August 1998. http://www.ifla.org/IV/ifla64/077-155e.htm (August 23, 2007).

Discusses the need to understand cultural differences when providing library services to multicultural populations. Provides an analytic framework for examining cultural differences that takes into consideration such factors as cultural views on: the nature of people, personal relationships to the external environment, personal relationships to other people, primary mode of activity, physical space, temporal orientation, beliefs and orientation, and differences in language and communication styles. Also describes how cultural information was exchanged and analyzed during a library and information studies course taught via the Internet simultaneously in Finland and North Carolina.

239. Insaidoo, Albert, and A. A. Alemna. "Information needs and the provision of information for overseas students in England." *Education Libraries Journal* 38, no. 1 (1995): 45–55.

Examines information needs of international students at universities in Northeast England. Discusses how these needs are met and if the information provided supports subjects' social, economic, and academic issues and concerns. Participants were sixty-one overseas students from twenty-seven countries studying at Newcastle and Northumbria Universities in Newcastle upon Tyne and the Universities of Sunderland in Sunderland and Teeside in Middlesbrough.

240. Jackson, Pamela A. "Incoming international students and the library: A survey." *Reference Services Review* 33, no. 2 (2005): 197–209.

Reports on a survey designed to assess incoming international students' library- and computer-use proficiencies and to determine their library needs. Study took place over a three-week period at San Jose State University in San Jose, California. Results indicated the majority of incoming students were computer literate and had used computers previously to conduct library research. However, services such as interlibrary loan, live online reference, and one-on-one reference appointments were new. Study's rationale, methodology, and findings are summarized and recommendations for partnership, collaboration, liaison, and technology services are suggested.

241. Jiao, Qun G., and Anthony J. Onwuegbuzie. *Library anxiety among international students.* ERIC document no. ED437973, 1999. 10 p. http://www.eric .ed.gov/ERICDocs/data/ericdocs2sql/content_storage_01/0000019b/80/16/ 0a/6d.pdf (August 7, 2008).

Investigates the prevalence of library anxiety among non-native English-speaking students at an unidentified northeastern American university. Participants (125) were administered the Library Anxiety Scale (LAS), which has five subscales: barriers with staff, affective barriers, comfort with the library, knowledge of the library, and mechanical barriers. Of the five dimensions studied, mechanical barriers (feelings that emerge as a result of students' reliance on mechanical library equipment, e.g., computer printers, copy machines, and change machines) were the greatest source of library anxiety. Affective barriers (feelings of inadequacy about using the library) were the second-most prevalent dimension. This dimension was followed by barriers with staff and comfort with the library respectively. Knowledge of the library was the source of least anxiety. Based on these finding, librarians and library educators should be cognizant of the role that technology plays in inducing library anxiety among international students. *See also* no. 242.

242. Jiao, Qun G., and Anthony J. Onwuegbuzie. "Sources of library anxiety among international students." *Urban Library Journal* 11, no. 1 (2001): 16–27.

Reports on a study conducted at an urban university in the northeastern United States. Participants were 125 undergraduate international students. Notes that many international students come to the United States with insufficient library skills, incorrect assumptions about academic libraries, and lack of familiarity with American classification schemes. These problems are compounded by language, cultural, and technological difficulties, and combine to make library use overwhelming. Results of study indicated that mechanical barriers (use of library technology) and affective barriers (feelings of inadequacy regarding library research skills) were the two greatest sources of library anxiety, while knowledge about the library, often cited as a major barrier in the literature, caused the least anxiety. *See also* no. 241.

243. Kahne, Merton J. "Cultural differences: Whose troubles are we talking about?" *International educational and cultural exchange* 11 (1976): 36–40.

Does not deal with libraries and library staff specifically, but offers advice for all who deal with international students. Notes they should be viewed more as students than as foreigners. Warns against stereotyping and highlights the importance of becoming familiar with diverse cultural issues.

244. Kaikai, Septimus M., and Regina E. Kaikai (eds.). *Understanding the international student*. New York: McGraw Hill, 1992. xii, 331 p.

Textbook discussing various facets of dealing with international students in universities and colleges. Part I, focusing on the background of international students, includes chapters on understanding students from diverse cultures, intercultural communication, international student admissions, hosting international education visitors, and food consumption patterns of international students. Part II focuses on promoting literacy skills of international students and includes chapters on international students and the research process (see Peck, no. 117), international students in the library (see Preston, no. 282), international students' difficulties with writing, English language study in the United States, and scaling the language barrier. Part III considers the impact of African and Asian cultures on students' education, and includes chapters on promoting cross-cultural friendships, understanding Japanese university students, the experiences of an African student in the United States, Vietnamese students and culture conflict, and Kenyan students. Part IV discusses host country gains from the support of international students.

245. Kalin, Sally Wayman. "The international student in the American academic library." 147–74 in *The role of the American academic library in international programs*, edited by Bruce D. Bonta and James G. Neal. London: JAI Press, 1992.

Identifies major obstacles international students face in academic libraries and suggests ways librarians can eliminate these barriers to the mutual benefit of both students and librarians. Considers such issues as communication, cultural differences, learning styles, and international students' prior experience with libraries, then discusses staff training programs, outreach, collection development efforts, tours, special materials, and bibliographic instruction.

246. Kaniki, Andrew M. "Reentry of international students to home library environments." 175–95 in *The role of the American academic library in international programs*, edited by Bruce Bonta and James G. Neal. Greenwich, CT: JAI Press, 1992.

Discusses problems that may be faced by international students, especially those from developing countries, when they complete their courses of study and return home. These include cultural and social readjustments; linguistic difficulties; and political, professional, and educational problems. Makes suggestions for American academic libraries to help prepare students for reentry to their home library environments.

247. Keller, Shelley G. *Harmony in diversity: Recommendations for effective library service to Asian language speakers*. Sacramento: California State Library, 1998. 31, [1] p.

Not specifically about international students, but provides helpful general information on library services to Asians, including commonalities and differences between and within Asian cultures, tips on communicating, and suggestions for conducting needs analyses.

248. Kirkendall, Carolyn. "Accommodating international students: How much is too much?" *Research Strategies* 2 (1984): 85–87.

Presents responses given by librarians from three academic libraries (Boston University; the University of California, Los Angeles; and the University of Michigan) to the question of what should be considered appropriate levels of assistance for international library users.

249. Knapp, Amy E., and Marilyn Whitmore. *Bridging cultural gaps: A workshop for international students.* ERIC document no. ED34538, 1992. 20 p.

Reports on a workshop for international students held at the University of Pittsburgh in Pennsylvania. Goals were to help international students transition to American academic life and to alert the library's public service staff to these students' needs. Provides an agenda of the workshop, which included a get-acquainted session, keynote speaker who addressed the pervasive effect of culture, a role-play video featuring interactions of international students and reference librarians, and a summary of discussions. Participants' evaluations were positive.

250. Kuang, Jian Qun. *A study to determine how international students utilize the library resources and services of the Bowling Green State University.* M.Ed. thesis, Bowling Green State University, 1989. vi, 61 p.

Identifies problems encountered by international students at Bowling Green State University in Bowling Green, Ohio, in using library services and resources. A questionnaire survey gathered data from 238 graduate and international graduate students from 52 countries. Results discuss student use of the library and specific library services that were unfamiliar.

251. Lafon, Felicia Sulia Kimo. *A comparative study and analysis of the library skills of American and foreign students at the University of Michigan.* Ph.D. dissertation, University of Michigan, 1992. UMI no. 9303767. x, 209 p. Full text in *Dissertations and Theses* database.

Identifies and analyzes similarities and differences between American and international students in their perceptions, experiences, expectations, knowledge, and use of U.S. academic libraries, then considers whether differences merit the creation of separate bibliographic instruction programs. Data was gathered through questionnaires mailed to students at the University of Michigan in Ann Arbor (312 American and 527 international respondents). Results indicated library education needs of international students differed significantly from those of American students, and various recommendations are made. Appendices include statistical tables and a copy of the questionnaire used.

252. Lai, Ting Ming. *A comparative study of the use of academic libraries by undergraduates in the United States and Taiwan.* Ph.D. dissertation, University of Wisconsin–Madison, 1990. UMI no. 9033783. xv, 281 p. Full text in *Dissertations and Theses* database.

Examines purposes and frequency of library use. Subjects were 379 students at the University of Wisconsin–Madison and 211 students at the National Taiwan University in Taiwan. Results indicated situational variables such as the requirement of term papers, assigned reading beyond textbooks, instructors' encouragement, and the need for quiet study space were the most important variables in the American sample, interacting with psychological traits, library-relationship variables, and demographic variables. In the Taiwanese sample, demographic variables such as the mother's educational level and psychological variables such as dogmatism and anti-intellectualism were more important than situational variables in their relationship to undergraduate library use. Questionnaires and statistical tables are appended.

253. Lai, Ting Ming. "A comparative study of the use of academic libraries by undergraduates in the United States and Taiwan." *Journal of Library and Information Science (Taipei)* 17 (1991): 52–63.

Summary article based on the author's 1990 dissertation, completed at the University of Wisconsin–Madison (see no. 252).

254. Lanz, Josefina Garcia. *Factors relating to academic social adjustment of international graduate students in the School of Education at the University of Pittsburgh.* Ph.D. dissertation, University of Pittsburgh, 1985. UMI no. 8601418. vi, 130 p. Full text in *Dissertations and Theses* database.

Based on results of a questionnaire survey of seventy-two students from seven countries and follow-up interviews with twenty-one students. Most important findings included the perception that library use and understanding lectures and textbooks were the most important factors influencing academic adjustment. Copy of Michigan International Student Problem Inventory is appended.

255. Li, Suzanne D. "Library services to students with diverse language and cultural backgrounds." *The Journal of Academic Librarianship* 24, no. 2 (1998): 139–43.

Report of study on library service needs of undergraduate students born and mostly educated outside the United States. Conducted at Queens College, City University of New York. Focus group comments centered on needs relating to hours, physical surroundings, materials, research tools, personnel, and copy services. Issues surrounding language and culture differences were not an expressed concern as had been anticipated. Follow-up included the development of library workshops, adding new computer terminals, display racks with materials on how to use the library catalog and databases, extra photocopiers, and extending library hours. Notes that most improvements benefited all patrons, not just international students. List of focus group questions appended.

256. Liao, Yan, Mary Finn, and Jun Lu. "Information-seeking behavior of international graduate students vs. American graduate students: A user study at Virginia Tech 2005." *College and Research Libraries* 68, no. 1 (2007): 5–25.

Reports on a web-based survey conducted at Virginia Tech University in Blacksburg aimed at determining how students initiated research, their searching process, and how they located items. Respondents included 224 American students and 91 international students. Also compares the information-seeking behaviors (ISB) of international and American graduate students and investigates the relationship between international students' ISBs and their English-language proficiency and length of time in the United States. Results showed technological resources (the Internet, the library's electronic resources) were the most popular method with both groups. However, the international students utilized the Internet more often while the American students preferred the library's e-resources. Also concludes that although barriers due to language/cultural differences and differing technology in home countries still exist, these are becoming increasingly less pronounced.

257. Lin, Shao-Chen. *Perceptions of United States academic library services of first-year graduate students from Taiwan: A photo-elicitation study.* Ph.D. dissertation, University of Wisconsin, 2006. UMI no. 3234607. v, 266 p. Full text in *Dissertation and Theses* database.

Uses a qualitative method, photo-elicitation, to study how previous library experiences influence international students' current perceptions of American academic libraries. Focuses on four dimensions of library service: access to information, affect of service, library as place, and personal control. These four dimensions are adapted from the LibQUAL+(TM) survey tool. Five first-year graduate students from Taiwan were interviewed about how they perceived the library services of the Center for Instructional Materials and Computing (CIMC), an academic library serving students and faculty of the School of Education at the University of Wisconsin, Madison. Findings confirmed those of previous studies.

258. Liu, Mengxiong. "Ethnicity and information seeking." 123–34 in *Library users and reference services*, edited by Jo Bell Whitlatch. New York: Haworth Press, 1995. Co-published as *The Reference Librarian* 49/50 (1995): 123–34.

Summarizes approaches to information-seeking by students of various ethnic backgrounds in American academic libraries and identifies barriers to effective communication. Discusses concepts of informal social networks and gatekeepers and their role in information seeking. Outlines guidelines for effective communication with English-as-a-second-language students and makes recommendations for reference service, instruction, and outreach.

259. Liu, Mengxiong. "Library services for ethnolinguistic students." *Journal of Educational Media & Library Sciences* 32, no. 3 (1995): 239–46.

Notes that international students, who form a large proportion of the student body on university campuses in the United States, face difficulties in the use of academic libraries due to language barriers, communication skills, and the lack of a concept of self-service. Librarians need a better understanding of information-seeking behaviors of these students in order to serve them better. Suggests that librarians need to develop new approaches to engage in effective intercultural conversation and need to learn to identify gatekeepers among student groups.

260. Liu, Mengxiong, and Bernice Redfern. "Information-seeking behavior of multi-cultural students: A case study at San Jose State University." *College and Research Libraries* 58 (1997): 348–54.

Reports on a 1995 survey at San Jose State University in San Jose, California, which showed minorities made up 50.7 percent of the total student population, with Asians being the largest ethnic group. Discusses factors that hindered interaction at the reference desk or during library instruction sessions. Analysis showed students who used/spoke English as a primary language were more successful in library-use skills. Length of time in the United States, behaviors when asking questions, and self-perceptions of their mastery of the English language also impacted on success rates.

261. Liu, Ziming. "Difficulties and characteristics of students from developing countries in using American libraries." *College and Research Libraries* 54 (1993): 25–31.

Reports on a study involving fifty-four mostly Asian students enrolled at the University of California–Berkeley. Data was collected on previous library environments and strategies for coping in an American academic library through one-on-one interviews. Problems identified included lack of proficiency in English, unfamiliarity with classification systems and subject headings, confusion when online catalogs and database searches retrieved too many results, the concept of open stacks, and American concepts of plagiarism. The relationship between study disciplines and library acclimatization is also discussed. Notes that students from countries with cultures more similar to America often do not face the same issues or use the library in the same way as students from less developed countries. Makes recommendations for improving library services for international students.

262. Lu, Cathy Anne. "Services for new American users: Indochinese students' behavior in using academic libraries." 328–32 in *Crossing the divide: Proceedings of the Tenth National Conference of the Association of College and Research Libraries, March 15-18, 2001, Denver, Colorado*, edited by Hugh A. Thompson. Chicago: Association of College and Research Libraries, 2001.

Study of how Indochinese students enrolled at San Jose State University and the University of California at Berkeley used academic libraries. Findings showed 89 percent of students sampled did not attend instruction workshops, preferring to learn library skills through handouts. While they came to the library frequently, they did not often use resources/services such as reference, circulation, and interlibrary loan. Suggests that the format and pace of instruction workshops may overwhelm students and recommends less information-packed sessions, more one-on-one consultation, and clear, concise handouts. Also advocates student involvement in the development of training plans.

263. MacDonald, Gina, and Elizabeth Sarkodie-Mensah. "ESL students and American libraries." *College and Research Libraries* 49 (1988): 425–31.

Discusses cultural differences in library use by international students and the often ineffective response of American library staff. Suggests that analogy, universal humor, hands-on experience, and an English-as-a-second-language program that emphasizes collaboration and integration of ESL and library personnel create a foundation for better library services and interactions.

264. Marama, Ishaya D. "Use of the technological university library by international students." *International Information & Library Review* 30, no. 2 (1998): 87–96.

Report of questionnaire and interview-based study exploring problems faced by international students at Abubakar Tafawa Balewa University, an English-speaking university in Bauchi, Nigeria. International students in the experimental group spoke French natively and came from various African countries. Data was collected on problems faced by students, services that were new or different from their home countries, and services from which they had benefited. Includes recommendations to address problems identified, which were similar to those encountered by international students at North American universities: unfamiliar services, confusing library terminology, and language barriers.

265. Martin, Rebecca R. *Libraries and the changing face of academia: Responses to growing multicultural populations.* Metuchen, NJ: Scarecrow Press, 1994. x, 263 p.

Three-part monographic study. Part I provides an overview of the changing face of academia in light of the evolution of multiculturalism in the United States, with discussion of both minority and international students. Part II describes research undertaken at three academic libraries: University of California, Santa Cruz; University of New Mexico in Albuquerque; and State University of New York, Albany. Part III discusses these libraries' responses to change in the face of multiculturalism.

266. McCullagh, Lyn, and Steve O'Connor. "Overseas students, full-fee paying students, and the utilization of library resources in Australian tertiary institutions." *Australian Academic and Research Libraries* 20, no. 2 (1989): 100–112.

Discusses problems faced by international students in Australia: language, cultural differences in library perception, confronting library personnel who are unaware of special information needs. Also reports on a survey sent to registrars and libraries of selected higher education institutions to determine kinds of orientation programs offered to international students. Makes suggestions for establishing effective programs and notes issues for library management.

267. McKenzie, Darlene E. *A survey of library and information needs of the international students at Kent State University.* Master's research paper, Kent State University, 1995. ERIC document no. ED390410. iv, 32 p. http://www.eric.ed.gov/ERICDocs/data/ericdocs2sql/content_storage_01/0000019b/80/14/4f/e3.pdf (August 5, 2008).

Reports on a questionnaire survey administered to international students at Kent State University in Kent, Ohio, designed to collect demographic and other information regarding students' use of the library and their information needs (fifty-six respondents). Results showed that the greatest number of Kent State international students were twenty-six to thirty years old, male, and in a graduate program and attended school full-time. Many respondents (78.8 percent) expressed a desire for multicultural materials in the library, such as more current native language books, journals, magazines, and newspapers. Many respondents also indicated a general lack of familiarity with online catalogs and other library automation. A literature review explored ways in which other colleges dealt with the problem of bibliographic instruction and library orientation for international students.

268. McSwiney, Carolyn. *Essential understandings: International students, learning, libraries.* Adelaide: Auslib Press, 1995. i, 201 p.

Monograph based on the author's 1994 Master of Librarianship thesis (Monash University, Australia). Interviews with sixty-five students from South or Southeast Asia at Swinburne University in Melbourne, Australia, collected data on their linguistic and academic backgrounds, use of the library, library orientation and user education, library facilities, library anxiety, attitudes toward the library, and expectations of the academic library prior to coming to Australia. Includes case studies of four students, two from Vietnam and one each from Indonesia and Thailand. Results showed students were surprised at the differences between libraries in their home countries and in Australia, at the emphasis on self-directed learning in Australia, and at the ease of access to library materials through online catalogs and open shelves. The majority of students reported they only sometimes found what they wanted in the library, although 90 percent rated user education classes positively and 85 percent reported they used the library more than twice a week. Study also considers the attitudes and perceptions of library staff, based on group discussions with twenty-six user services staff.

269. McSwiney, Carolyn. "Students, libraries and the international student adviser: We are in this together!" 183–90 in *International education—In it together: Proceedings of the eighth ISANA Conference, Melbourne, Australia, December 1997,* edited by Heather Bigelow et al. Melbourne: ISANA, 1997.

Paper given at a conference of professionals working in the field of international education. Aims to promote understanding and cooperation between international student advisers and academic librarians by identifying shared concerns and exploring the academic library world of international students in Australia. Emphasizes the need for academic library staff to identify and understand the information needs of this group.

270. Meredith, Meri. "Confronting the styles and needs of an international clientele (library services)." *Information Outlook* 3, no. 6 (1999): 18–23.

Discusses ways to address information needs of international patrons in academic libraries, including creating a comfort zone, respecting each student's learning process, stressing demonstrative actions rather than verbal directions, and being proactive and patient.

271. Miller, Rush G. "Leading the way to diversity: The academic library's role in promoting multiculturalism." 1–18 in *Diversity and multiculturalism in libraries*, edited by Katherine Hoover Hill. Greenwich, CT: JAI Press, 1994.

Discusses the situation at Bowling Green State University in Bowling Green, Ohio, and its efforts to deal with increasing cultural diversity on campus. Focus is on minority rather than international students, but the description of how the library worked to create a more positive multicultural environment for students and staff through recruitment of minority staff and student assistants, staff training programs, and multicultural collection building is useful.

272. Mood, Terry Ann. "Foreign students and the academic library." *RQ* 22 (1982): 175–80.

Discusses results of a questionnaire survey of U.S. academic libraries (sixty-five responses) that suggested international students continued to be a marginalized user group, despite their increasing numbers on university campuses. Discusses problems faced by these students and concludes that even small efforts in staff development, particularly in reference service, can have a highly positive impact on their American academic experience. Library instruction, especially orientation sessions and classes in research methods that emphasize hands-on experience, is a key component in helping students become acclimated. Recommends providing specialized handouts, purchasing and promoting materials about the students' home countries, and appointing a library staff liaison for international students.

273. Mood, Terry Ann. "Library services to foreign students in Colorado." *Colorado Libraries* 8 (1982): 8–11.

Based on a questionnaire survey of selected academic libraries in Colorado and other states aimed at determining what libraries were doing to serve foreign students (sixty-five returns). Outlines responses and compares Colorado data with that from other institutions. Many findings are comparable, though Colorado libraries kept better and more up-to-date information lists for foreign students.

274. Morrissey, Renee. *Understanding ESL/international students' experiences using Canadian academic libraries: A proposal.* Research proposal, School of Library and Information Studies, University of Alberta, 2006. http://capping.slis .ualberta.ca/cap06/renee/abstract.html (August 10, 2007).

Proposed research project developed as part of a Research Methods seminar at the School of Library and Information Studies, University of Alberta, Edmonton. Includes a literature review and proposed implementation plan, including project budget. Although the project was not implemented, the report provides a useful outline for future research.

275. Natowitz, Allen. "International students in US academic libraries: Recent concerns and trends." *Research Strategies* 13, no. 1 (1995): 4–16.

Content analysis of eighteen journal articles written between 1985 and 1993 on international students and their use of American academic libraries. Highlights common issues, problems, and concerns. Considers cultural diversity, language, cultural, and technological barriers and solutions to each. Makes recommendations for further research and discusses implications for staff development and bibliographic instruction programs.

276. Onwuegbuzie, Anthony J., and Qun G. Jiao. "Academic library usage: A comparison of native and non-native English-speaking students." *Australian Library Journal* 46, no. 3 (1997): 258–69.

Compares frequency of usage and reasons for library use between native and non-native English-speaking university students at two unidentified American academic libraries (522 subjects in various fields of study). Also explores levels of library anxiety between the two groups. Results showed that non-native students visited the library more often and for a greater variety of reasons than their counterparts. International students often experienced significantly greater problems adapting to and using the library and exhibited higher levels of overall library anxiety. *See also* no. 277.

277. Onwuegbuzie, Anthony J., Qun G. Jiao, and Christine E. Daley. *The experience of non-native English-speaking students in academic libraries in the United States.* ERIC document ED438815, 1997. 16 p. http://www.eric.ed.gov/ERIC Docs/data/ericdocs2sql/content_storage_01/0000019b/80/16/15/9d.pdf (July 24, 2008).

Compares native and non-native English-speaking university students with respect to frequency of library usage and reasons for using the library, as well as differences between these groups with respect to levels of library anxiety. Findings were intended to be used in the planning and implementation of library services for international students. Subjects were 522 undergraduate and graduate students from two unidentified universities. Students came from fifteen non-English-speaking countries representing the continents of Europe, Asia, Africa, and South America. Findings suggested non-native English-speaking students visited the library more frequently than native English speakers. For both non-native and native English-speaking students, obtaining a book or article for a course paper was the most common reason for using the library, followed by studying for a test. Non-native English speakers had higher levels of library anxiety associated with barriers with staff, affective barriers, and mechanical barriers, and lower levels of library anxiety associated with knowledge of the library than native English speakers. *See also* no. 276.

278. Parker, Orin D. "Cultural clues to the Middle Eastern student." 77–84 in *Culture bound: Bridging the culture gap in language teaching*, edited by J. M. Valdes. Cambridge: Cambridge University Press, 1986.

Outlines distinctive characteristics of Middle Eastern students. Designed to assist those working with them on North American university campuses.

279. Patton, Beth Ann. *International students and the American university library*. M.A. thesis, Biola University, 2002. ERIC document ED469810. vi, 122 p. http://www.eric.ed.gov/ERICDocs/data/ericdocs2sql/content_storage _01/0000019b/80/1a/7e/fb.pdf (July 25, 2008).

Notes that the transition to independent research is one of the major adjustments faced by international students when studying at colleges in the United States. Studies indicate that non-native speakers of English are also likely to suffer from library anxiety and are most at risk for lowered academic achievement. In addition to overcoming differences from national education systems and library cultures, international students also face language barriers that escalate difficulties in help-seeking behaviors and formulation of search strategies. Recent literature showcases the development of critical thinking as one of the most important facets of information literacy instruction programs. Study analyzes the way this emphasis interfaces with the particular needs of international students and suggests effective strategies for working with international students. Primarily a literature review, with some additional data collected through faculty and international student focus groups.

280. Paul, Jeff. "Changing library services in response to Chicano student needs: The Chicano Library Resource Center at San Jose University." *CMLEA Journal* 6 (1983): 22.

Describes briefly the needs of and library's response to Chicano students.

281. Pfau, Richard H. *Foreign student orientation needs at the University of Connecticut: Results of a survey*. ERIC document no. ED230154, 1983. 27 p.

Reports on a survey of forty-eight foreign students concerning orientation needs at the University of Connecticut. Orientation activities identified as most important, in the approximate order of importance were: American government regulations (visas, immigration, social security, taxes); needs of spouses (including English-language training, educational opportunities, work opportunities, health care, and social activities); the International Student Office and foreign student advisor; health care; services available to students at the university (including library, counseling, writing clinics, and career placement); on- and off-campus student employment; information on student housing accommodations (mailboxes, laundry, cooking); bus service; housing; the registration procedure; the international center services, programs, and staff; a tour of the campus; the American system of higher education; and the role of the American advisor. It is recommended that orientation activities for foreign students be publicized more widely. Suggestions provided by students are included, along with students' ranking of orientation activities and a sample questionnaire. Not library-focused, but provides a useful overview of issues faced by international students.

282. Preston, Bonita. "Foreign students: Lost in the library?" 106–18 in *Understanding the international student*, edited by Septimus M. Kaikai and Regina E. Kaikai. New York: McGraw-Hill, 1992.

Reviews cultural, philosophical, and educational obstacles faced by international students studying in the United States, particularly when using the academic library: communication problems, learning styles and behaviors, previous experience in libraries. Recommendations to alleviate these obstacles include course-integrated library instruction, library orientation tours and programs created specifically for international students, and staff training programs focusing on cultural cross-training and the acquisition of appropriate communication techniques.

283. Rosen, C. Martin, Mary G. Wrighten, Beverly Stearns, and R. Susan Goldstein. "Student employees and the academic library's multicultural mission." 45–55 in *Racial and ethnic diversity in academic libraries: Multicultural issues*, edited by Deborah A. Curry, Susan Griswold Blandy, and Lynne M. Martin. New York: Haworth Press, 1994.

Recruitment of minority student workers is a way in which libraries can contribute to university efforts to foster diversity. Strategies employed by the Libraries and Learning Resources Multicultural Affairs Committee at Bowling Green University in Bowling Green, Ohio, to increase the hiring of minority student workers are described.

284. Russell, Ralph E., Joseph S. Sturgeon, James E. Prather, and James E. Greene, Jr. *The relationship of documented library use to academic achievement, program of study, and progress toward a degree*. ERIC document no. ED220045, 1982. ii, 21 p.

Report of a study based at a large urban non-residential American university with a full-time equivalent of 15,000 students. Among results of survey findings were: students attending under student visas had high levels of measured library use, and minority students, especially females, had substantially higher book checkout activity. Suggests that higher levels of library use by foreign and minority students may result from fewer resources to purchase books, fewer community book resources, and/or a tendency to live closer to the university.

285. Ryland, Elisabeth K. "International students at CSU San Bernardino—Obstacles and opportunities." 105–9 in *Internationalizing the California State University: Case studies*, edited by Richard L. Sutter. Long Beach: California State University System, 1992.

Discusses the challenges and benefits of working with international students at California State University, San Bernardino. Most foreign students are from Asian countries. Considers questions related to culture, language, and working with students in the classroom.

286. Safahieh, Hajar, and Diljit Singh. "Information needs of international students at a Malaysian university." 479–85 in *Proceedings of the Asia-Pacific Conference on Library & Information Education & Practice 2006*, edited by C. Khoo, D. Singh, and A. S. Chaudhry. Singapore: School of Communication & Information, Nanyang Technological University, 2006.

Reports on a study investigating the information needs of international students at the University of Malaya in Kuala Lumpur. A questionnaire survey (fifty-four respondents) found that the main information needs were related to the university, the faculty, and programs of study. Students used the library to attempt to meet their needs, though frequency of library usage was generally low. Major barriers in seeking information were language proficiency and unfamiliarity with the library organization and mission. The majority of students considered themselves computer and Internet literate.

287. Saladyanant, Tasana. "Meeting the needs of foreign student users in Chiang Mai University and Payap University libraries, Chiang Mai, Thailand." Paper presented at the 65th IFLA Council and General Conference, Bangkok, Thailand, 20–28 August 1999. http://www.ifla.org/IV/ifla65/papers/096-106e.htm (August 20, 2007).

Discusses issues surrounding meeting the information needs of foreign students at two universities in Thailand. Notes concerns related to provision of books and journals in English, availability of up-to-date material, loan periods, and language issues.

288. Sarkodie-Mensah, Kwasi. *Foreign students and U.S. academic libraries: A case-study of foreign students and libraries in two universities in New Orleans.* Ph.D. dissertation, University of Illinois at Urbana–Champaign, 1988. xxvii, 328 p.

Examines difficulties encountered by foreign students in their use of American academic libraries, their patterns of library use, and the nature of libraries in their home countries. Based on a survey of 388 students from Tulane University and the University of New Orleans in Louisiana. Results indicated students would readily ask for assistance in times of need; large library collections were not new to the majority; and the concept of open library stacks was not as foreign to as many students as might have been expected. Statistical analysis showed language of instruction had the strongest relationship with variables used to measure patterns and difficulties in library use, followed by years spent on American library campuses and years spent in the United States as a whole. Previous exposure to libraries and country of origin were the least statistically relevant variables in measuring patterns and difficulties in library use. *See also* no. 125.

289. Sarkodie-Mensah, Kwasi. "In the words of a foreigner." *Research Strategies* 4 (1986): 30–31.

Discusses the experiences and challenges the author faced as a foreign student at an American library school. Highlights differences in his native home use of the library (as a quiet place to study) and how language, especially idiomatic phrases, caused anxiety even with basic requests. Highlights confusing behaviors of American librarians.

290. Sarkodie-Mensah, Kwasi. "The international student on campus: History, trends, visa classification, and adjustment issues." 3–16 in *Teaching the new library to today's users: Reaching international, minority, senior citizens, gay/lesbian, first generation, at-risk, graduate and returning students, and distance learners*, edited by Trudi E. Jacobson and Helene C. Williams. New York: Neal Schuman, 2000.

Documents the increasing numbers of international students in the United States between 1784 and the present, then provides additional background on numbers of international students from various regions of the world. Outlines popular areas of study for international students, gender of international students, and common sources of funding for international study. Also discusses visas, language issues, acculturation to American classrooms, serving as graduate or teaching assistants, culture shock, and stress.

291. Sarkodie-Mensah, Kwasi. "International students in the U.S.: Trends, cultural adjustments, and solutions for a better experience." *Journal of Education for Library & Information Science* 39, no. 3 (1998): 214–22.

Provides a brief overview of international education in the United States and recent international student enrollment trends. Discusses differences in classroom structure and perceptions of the role of the instructor, along with factors that affect the daily lives of international students (social isolation, culture shock). Highlights programs that can help international students adjust, including library orientation, training graduate students to teach, accent reduction training, and counseling services.

292. Selvadurai, Ranjani. "Problems faced by international students in American colleges and universities." *Community Review* 12 (1992): 27–32.

Does not deal specifically with library issues, but provides a useful overview of common problems faced by international students studying in the United States, including language and cultural difficulties both inside and outside of the classroom.

293. Sharkey, Jennifer. *Academic library services: A study of perceptions of librarians and international students.* Master's Alternate Plan paper, Minnesota State University, 1998. v, 52 p.

Highlights unique challenges faced by international students when using American academic libraries and how librarians may be missing opportunities to help those students adjust to a new learning environment. Six international students and four academic librarians at Minnesota State University in Mankato were interviewed to help understand libraries in the students' home countries, students' perception of the library at MSU, and librarians' perceptions of international students' library use. Makes recommendations for improved library service. Copies of the survey questions and a table profiling the international student population at MSU are appended.

294. Sharma, Madhav P., Charles B. Klasek, and Jared H. Dorn. "How United States students perceive academic and nonacademic needs of international students." *The Journal of Studies in Technical Careers* 9 (1987): 297–315.

Reports on a survey of subjects at six selected midwestern U.S. universities regarding the effect the presence of international students on campus had on the attitudes of American students.

295. Sibgatullina, Diana Rais. "International students and the UNL libraries." *Nebraska Library Association Quarterly* 29, no. 1 (1998): 26–28.

Briefly outlines the library orientation process for international students at the University of Nebraska in Lincoln libraries and provides a short description of international students' participation in Library 110, a credit-bearing information literacy course. Also highlights international students' perception of reference services and the availability of resources from their home countries.

296. Singer, Helen. "Learning and information services support for international students at the University of Hertfordshire." *SCONUL Focus* 35 (2005): 63–67.

Describes the activities undertaken by the author when she assumed a new role offering learning and information services support to international students at the University of Hertfordshire in Hatfield, England. Efforts included fact finding about what colleagues were doing, conducting desk research to see what had been written, identifying and producing relevant materials, promoting library materials and services, and training staff in dealing with international students.

297. So, Soo Young. *International students and American academic libraries: An empowering relation.* ERIC document no. ED369403, 1994. 26 p. http://www.eric.ed.gov/ERICDocs/data/ericdocs2sql/content_storage_01/0000019b/80/15/82/c0.pdf (July 24, 2008).

Considers international clientele, usually foreign-born students, in American society as a whole, then discusses specific ways to improve library services to meet these students' needs. Notes international students are frequently hampered in their library use by language and cultural barriers, and also by a limited understanding of the potential resources and services a library may offer. The proper relationship between the library and the student is one of mutual empowerment. International students benefit from their time in the United States and take information and library knowledge with them when they return to their native countries. Cultural sensitivity on the part of library staff can be fostered by increased training.

298. Society of College, National, and University Libraries (SCONUL). *Library services for international students.* London: SCONUL Access, 2008. v, 52 p.

Guidelines prepared as a result of research undertaken in 2007 on behalf of the SCONUL Access Group aimed at determining ways in which libraries in institutions of higher education were supporting international students. Research involved a literature survey; a survey of SCONUL member institutions; a web survey of most UK library and institutional websites; a web survey of a sample of international institutional and library websites in Australia, New Zealand, and North America; focus groups with international students; surveys and interviews with international students; and institutional visits overseas. Guidelines are designed to provide a practical tool for library practitioners by providing them with a comprehensive overview of issues as seen by both their peers and students, along with suggested solutions and best practices case studies. Appendices include summary of survey and results, strategy document examples, sample library websites reflecting good practice, samples of glossaries of library terms, samples of websites on academic writing skills, list of companies offering staff training on international issues, "good ideas and special touches," key concepts checklist. *See also* Bent, Scopes, and Senior, no. 212.

299. Song, Yoo-Seong. "A comparative study on information-seeking behaviors of domestic and international business students." *Research Strategies* 20, no. 1–2 (2004): 23–34.

Reports on a study of information-seeking behaviors and impressions of library services of business students at the University of Illinois at Urbana–Champaign. Data was collected through a web-based survey (thirty domestic and fifty-four international respondents). Focuses on three areas: how domestic and international business students assess the effectiveness of library instruction sessions, how each group uses library services, and how each group uses the Internet for research. Results offered insights into understanding differences between the two groups with respect to library-use patterns and research strategies. It was decided to begin offering specialized training sessions for international students and for reference staff who worked with them.

300. Stafford, Thomas H., Jr., Paul B. Marion, and M. Lee Salter. *Relationships between adjustment of international students and their expressed need for special programs and services at a U.S. university: Research and implications.* ERIC document no. ED155579, 1978. 25 p.

Reports on results of a survey of international students (278 respondents) enrolled at North Carolina State University in Raleigh. Aims were to correlate student classification and geographic area of origin with a number of other variables: use of selected university services and programs, including the library; university services and programs that were needed but not used; and student satisfaction with the use of university services and programs. Also considered the relationship between adjustment in selected areas and use of university services and programs. Includes an outline of methods and results. With respect to the library, 90 percent of students had used the library and 96 percent were satisfied with their experiences. No details are provided on specific areas of library use.

301. Stoffle, Carla. "A new library for the new undergraduate." *Library Journal* 115, no. 16 (1990): 47–50.
    Examines the potential role of the undergraduate library as a model for the multicultural, pluralistic environment in society and on university campuses. Discusses activities and programs, staff diversity, appropriate staff behavior, collections, access to electronic resources, and teaching critical judgment.

302. Su, Julie Tao. "Library services in an Asian American context." 121–43 in *Diversity and multiculturalism in libraries*, edited by Katherine Hoover Hill. Greenwich, CT: JAI Press, 1994.
    Discusses the Asian population in the United States and diversity within this population. Separate sections deal with public libraries and the Asian population and academic libraries and the Asian population. Considers demographics of Asian students on college campuses, Asian studies programs, and the general issues relating to Asian Americans and Asian international students and faculty in academic libraries (orientation and instruction, collections, library outreach, visiting scholars). Offers suggestions for meeting their particular needs, for example, through personalized library consultation services.

303. Varga-Atkins, Tünde, and Linda Ashcroft. "Information skills of undergraduate business students: A comparison of UK and international students." *Library Management* 25 (2004): 39–55.
    Reports on objectives, methodology, data analysis, and results of a study created to measure and compare information skills of UK and international students studying business at two British universities: Liverpool John Moores University and Manchester Metropolitan University (141 subjects). No significant differences were found. The majority of students felt negative or neutral toward library and information skills, with international students having a more positive attitude than home students. One of the main sources of negativity cited was the inability to find information without help.

304. Wales, Barbara, and Harry Harmon. "A comparison of two user groups: International and US students in an academic library." *Public and Access Services Quarterly* 2, no. 4 (1998): 17–37.
    Report of a survey created to determine library-use patterns and library perceptions of international students. Administered to students at Central Missouri

State University in Warrensburg (150 international student and 194 "traditional student" respondents). Data was collected on rate of use for various library services, frequency of asking for help, library orientation experiences, importance of holdings and services, familiarity with library services, ease of use of resources (online catalog, LC classification system, indexes, web). Results indicated international students were frequent library users, with the library serving as not only a place to fill information needs but a place to study and meet friends. Both groups displayed similar assistance-seeking behavior, but the language barrier sometimes prevented international students from seeking help needed. Both groups found orientation events of similar importance, with international students seeing more potential benefit for all activities; approaches that were more "hands-on" and group-oriented were most valued. Findings were used to improve orientation and collection development needs of international students. Copy of the survey is appended.

305. Wang, Belle Xinfeng. *Academic library services to Chinese international students in New Zealand.* Master of Library Science paper, Victoria University of Wellington, 2006. ix, 115 p. http://www.nzcer.org.nz/pdfs/T01025.pdf (August 8, 2008).

Discusses a research project investigating the provision of academic library services to Chinese international students in New Zealand. Analyzes students' perceptions, experiences, and expectations of library services. Subjects were six undergraduates and two graduates at Victoria University of Wellington. Concludes that despite generally positive evaluations, four issues needed to be addressed: book retrieval, library as study place, library collections, and underused library services such as library instruction, reference services, journal resources, subject librarians, and interlibrary loan service.

306. Wang, Jian, and Donald G. Frank. "Cross-cultural communication: Implications for effective information services in academic libraries." *Portal: Libraries & the Academy* 2, no. 2 (2002): 207–17.

Explores the need for libraries to be proactive in providing effective services for international students in American university and college libraries. Uses data from focus groups at Harvard University in Cambridge, Massachusetts; the Georgia Institute of Technology in Atlanta; Portland State University in Portland, Oregon; and the 2001 American Library Association annual conference. Notes that underutilization of library services by international students is often due to their unfamiliarity with the mission of the American academic library and low skill levels with technologies. Unique concerns of international students and scholars and cultural differences in communication and learning styles are also discussed. Makes recommendations to assist academic librarians in efforts to help international students improve their research skills and become more comfortable in an American research and education environment.

307. Wayman, Sally G. "The international student in the academic library." *The Journal of Academic Librarianship* 9, no. 6 (1984): 336–41.

Examines potential sources of conflict in interactions between international students and librarians, including communication problems (verbal, nonverbal, and written); different learning styles, attitudes, and behaviors; group and individual success; expectations; and previous library experience. Makes suggestions to promote better librarian/international students interactions. Article was one of the first to address the needs of international students and challenges they face. *See also* no. 308.

308. Wayman, Sally G. "The international student in your library: Coping with cultural and language barriers." 93–109 in *Bibliographic instruction and the learning process: Theory, style, and motivation: Papers presented at the Twelfth Annual Library Instruction Conference, held at Eastern Michigan University, May 6–7, 1984*, edited by Carolyn A. Kirkendall. Ann Arbor, MI: Pierian Press, 1984.

Outlines language and cultural differences of international students and discusses how understanding these differences is crucial to creating effective library instruction and meaningful reference interactions. Discusses communication issues; learning styles, attitudes, and behaviors; and knowledge of libraries. Makes recommendations for improving the adjustment of international students to American academic library systems. *See also* no. 307.

309. Wilson, Vicky. "Library services for overseas students." 228–31 in *Western perspectives: Library and information services in Western Australia*, edited by Robert C. Sharman and Laurel A. Clyde. Perth: ALIA, Western Australian Branch, 1990.

Presents a brief summary of results of a survey of libraries in Western Australia (twenty-eight responses). Findings are discussed with respect to collection development (English-as-a-second-language collections, fiction collections, nonfiction collections), the library environment, cultural problems, and reader services.

310. Wyman, Andrea. "Working with nontraditional students in the academic library." *The Journal of Academic Librarianship* 14, no. 1 (1988): 32–33.

Defines nontraditional students, a group which includes international students, and suggests ways to help them: network involvement, staff specialization, advertising programs, responsiveness, a concrete approach, fostering independence (through guidelines and signage), in-depth answers, quiet study areas, and reaffirmation.

311. Yang, Eveline L. "Library services to ethnic populations: An Asian-American's perspective." *Colorado Libraries* 21 (1995): 27–29.

Does not deal with international students or academic libraries specifically, but offers useful information on differences between Asian cultures from the perspective of a member of an ethnic minority group. Discusses the growth of Asian populations, in the United States generally and in Colorado more specifically, then highlights the diversity among Asian Americans. Offers a number of suggestions for serving multicultural populations in libraries.

312. Yates, Carol J., Rafaela Castro, and Lillian Castillo-Speed. "Voices of diversity in University of California libraries: Impact, initiatives and impediments for cultural and racial equity." 19–28 in *Diversity and multiculturalism in libraries*, edited by Katherine Hoover Hill. Greenwich, CT: JAI Press, 1994.

Discusses the nine campuses of the University of California as a microcosm of cultural diversity and the formation of the Ad Hoc Committee on LAUC (Librarians' Association of the University of California) Regional Workshops on Cultural Diversity in Libraries and its work.

313. Yi, Zhixian. "International student perceptions of information needs and use." *The Journal of Academic Librarianship* 33, no. 6 (2007): 666–73.

Examines international student information needs and whether education level, age, and gender affect their information use. Data was gathered through an e-mail survey undertaken at Texas Woman's University (sixty-one respondents). Information was collected on demographics, how often the students used library resources and services to find needed information, and format preferences. Concludes that TWU international students frequently need information for augmenting their academic course work, improving library skills, and enhancing their use of software applications. They make full use of library printed materials as well as online resources. The higher the education level they had attained, the more likely they were to use databases, remote access to library offerings, and e-journals.

314. Zhang, Wei-Ping. "Foreign students and U.S. academic libraries." *College Student Journal* 28, no. 4 (1994): 446–51.

Considers barriers to library service for international students and describes common concepts and services offered at American academic libraries that may be unfamiliar, such as open stacks, reference service, and interlibrary loan. Makes recommendations for assisting international students to achieve academic success in a different educational setting.

GLOBALIZATION/INTERNATIONALIZATION AND ACADEMIC LIBRARIES

315. Becker, Linda K. W. "Globalisation and changing practices for academic librarians in Australia: A literature review." *Australian Academic & Research Libraries* 37, no. 2 (2006): 82–99.

Provides an overview of historical research related to changes brought on by globalization in Australian academic libraries. Examines the role of academic librarians in internationalizing their own experiences and perspectives in order to improve library, instructional, and service activities. Part 1 of a three-part study. *See also* nos. 316, 318.

316. Becker, Linda K. W. "Globalisation and internationalisation: Models and patterns for change for Australian academic librarians." *Australian Academic & Research Libraries* 37, no. 4 (2006): 282–98.
   Describes case studies of Australian academic libraries in which a successful pattern for internationalization emerged. Discusses conclusions of the research and makes recommendations for practice and further research. Part 3 of a three-part study. *See also* nos. 315, 318.

317. Becker, Linda K. W. *Globalization and structural change: Internationalization and the role of librarians in Australian universities.* Ed.D. dissertation, University of Massachusetts, 2005. UMI no. 3172772. xii, 245 p. Full text available in *Dissertations and Theses* database.
   Discusses increasing globalization in higher education, with emphasis on the Australian context. Study examines strategies employed by Australian librarians in internationalizing their practice and perspective in the library and the university and within higher education. Data was gathered in part from a questionnaire survey of twenty-three Australian university library directors and extensive case studies of libraries at two public universities whose practice indicated a commitment to the goal of internationalization: a regional mid-sized university located in a coastal city and a major university located in its state capital. Interviews were conducted with library directors and administrators at these two institutions. Results indicated models of internationalization at universities varied widely. Internationalization was stimulated when librarians were proactive in international activities, when a stable budget was established for internationalization, when librarians engaged in strategic planning, when library leadership was consistent, and when sufficient time was allotted to achieve the goal of internationalization. Copies of the survey and a list of interview questions are appended.

318. Becker, Linda K. W. "Internationalisation: Australian librarians and expanding roles in higher education." *Australian Academic & Research Libraries* 37, no. 3 (2006): 200–220.
   Presents an overview of a research project designed as a way to understand the role of Australian academic librarians in internationalizing the library, university, and higher education practice. Discusses findings of a survey of university library directors (twenty-three respondents) aimed at finding out how they develop international experience and perspective and what they describe as effective institutional practice. Part 2 of a three-part study. *See also* nos. 315, 316.

319. Brogan, Martha L. "Trends in international education: New imperatives in academic librarianship." *College & Research Libraries* 51, no. 3 (1990): 196–206.

Provides an overview of new directions in international education over the previous decade and links them to changing imperatives for academic librarians. Five major areas of development are considered: foreign language instruction, study abroad, internationalizing the curriculum, foreign students and scholars, and technical assistance and international development. Recommends ways in which the Association of College and Research Libraries might strengthen its role as an advocate of international education.

320. Connolly, Pauline. "Is there a need for a library twinning focal point? The IFLA twinning project and beyond." Paper presented at the 66th IFLA Council and General Conference, Jerusalem, Israel, 13–18 August 2000. http://www.ifla .org/IV/ifla66/papers/163-168e.htm (September 4, 2008).

Provides background on the International Federation of Library Association's twinning database and its contents. Database was set up in October 1996 and discontinued in 2000 due to lack of funding. The twinning project aimed to match libraries in first and developing countries and set up partnerships between them.

321. Doyle, Robert P., and Patricia Scarry. *Guidelines on library twinning.* Paris: UNESCO, 1994. http://unesdoc.unesco.org/images/0009/000973/097322eo.pdf (August 29, 2008).

UNESCO document describing ways to set up twinning relationships between libraries, especially those in two different countries. Describes benefits, ways to set up a twinning arrangement, and examples of twinning programs.

322. Kim, Mijin. "Introducing multicultural resources and services at Library and Archives Canada." *Feliciter* 50, no. 1 (2004): 19–20.

Brief report of efforts to expand the multicultural and multilingual component of the collection at the Canadian national library and archives. These efforts include collections building, hosting exhibits, promoting multilingual collections and services, consulting with libraries and the multicultural community, developing online resources, and participating in international cooperation initiatives. Also discusses the Multicultural Resources and Services Program, announced in the fall of 2001, which has been involved in consultations and in the development of a Multicultural Resources and Services web portal and the multicultural-resources-l listserv.

323. Kuzilwa, Matilda S., and Else-Margrethe Bredland. "Co-operation between the libraries at Mzumbe University (Tanzania) and Agder University College (Norway): An overview for the present and the future." Paper presented at the World Library and Information Congress: 71st IFLA General Conference and Council, Oslo, Norway, 14–18 August 2005. http://www.ifla.org/IV/ifla71/ papers/118e-Kuzilwa_Bredland.pdf (September 5, 2008).

Describes a successful twinning program between a library in Tanzania and one in Norway. Discusses the model of collaboration; the main activities undertaken, which included joint research projects, staff exchanges, sharing of library materials and bibliographic resources, informational workshops and seminars, and joint publications; and the impact of the collaboration, especially on the African university.

324. Lipu, Suzanne. "Beyond books: The library's role in internationalisation on a university campus." 10–15 in *Proceedings of the ISANA 13th National Conference, Inveresk Tramsheds, Launceston, Tasmania, 3–6 December 2002.* Launceston: ISANA, 2002.

Discusses increasing diversity on university campuses in Australia, with focus on the University of Wollongong in New South Wales. Outlines the university library's vital role in helping the university to achieve its internationalization goals of integrating international perspectives, in particular through its cultural diversity workshop, which is part of core training for all staff.

325. McSwiney, Carolyn. "Cultural implications of a global context: The need for the reference librarian to ask again 'Who is my client?'" Paper presented at the 68th IFLA Council and General Conference, Glasgow, Scotland, 18–24 August 2002. http://ifla.org/IV/ifla68/papers/001-128e.pdf (August 20, 2007).

Defines globalization and related concepts as a contextual framework, with special reference to librarianship and information management, then discusses culture-related issues and their implications for library professionals. Finally, reflects on approaches taken at two Australian academic libraries (University of Melbourne and University of South Australia) to develop attitudes and skill sets of information professionals to work in increasingly diverse library environments.

326. McSwiney, Carolyn. "Global influences: Implications for the reference librarian." 103–8 in *Symposium proceedings: Revelling in reference 2001: ALIA/ RAISS–reference and information services section, Melbourne, 12–14 October 2001,* edited by Margaret Smith. Kingston, ACT: Australian Library and Information Association, 2001.

Describes the impact of globalization on the library profession generally, then considers its implications for reference services. Discusses implications of globalization for the information workplace, draws attention to issues related to cultural diversity in the area of reference services, identifies skills that assist in responding to cultural diversity, and offers practical suggestions for dealing with cultural complexity.

327. McSwiney, Carolyn. *Internationalisation of the university: Implications for the academic library.* Ph.D. dissertation, Monash University, 2001. xii, 244 p. Full text available at http://arrow4.lib.monash.edu.au:8080/vital/access/services/ Download/monash:6347/SOURCE2?view=true.

Explores social and cultural changes associated with the internationalization of the university and the academic library, noting that these changes have an impact on the library user group and on the use and provision of information resources made accessible through the library. Study consists of two main parts. A conceptual study develops a schematic framework and examines the context and influence of global trends and internationalization on the university and its library, with emphasis on the situation in Australia. Part 2 provides a multi-site case study; the central case is Monash University in Melbourne, Australia, and its offshore campus in Malaysia. Findings are discussed with respect to policy and planning issues, the library user group, and the library collection.

328. McSwiney, Carolyn. "Think globally! Libraries, cultural diversity and the 21st century." Paper presented at the Australian Library and Information Association 2000 Conference, Canberra, Australia, 24–26 October 2000. http://conferences.alia.org.au/alia2000/proceedings/carolyn.mcswiney.html (August 6, 2008).

Discusses globalization and cultural diversity, with focus on three aspects: creating an awareness of the implications globalization might have on the information workplace; outlining cultural issues, influences, and circumstances that might further understanding of cultural diversity; and offering practical suggestions on ways in which librarians can build these and other issues into continuing professional development.

329. McSwiney, Carolyn, and Stephen Parnell. "Transnational expansion and the role of the university library: A study of academics and librarians in an Australian university." *A Routledge Journal: New Review of Libraries and Lifelong Learning* 4, no. 1 (2004): 63–75.

Explores the role of the academic library in providing information services in a transnational context. Based on discussions with the authors' colleagues, academics and librarians at the University of South Australia in Adelaide, initiated as part of a review of the library's response to transnational expansion. Highlights the value of strong partnerships between academics and the library and strategies adopted to deal with increasing internationalization.

330. Rader, Hannelore. "The international role of U.S. librarians." *The Bowker Annual of Library & Book Trade Information* 39 (1994): 91–94.

Notes that American librarians have been involved in international cooperation since 1867 and have taken active roles in cultural and library activities and in exchange programs worldwide. Discusses the globalization of telecommunications and electronic information networks on international communication and its impact on sharing of business information, on the role of libraries in institutions of higher education, and in the development of new technologies to meet the needs of a wide range of users. Global communication also enables U.S. and foreign librarians to learn from one another.

331. Segal, JoAnn. "American academic librarians and international library organizations." 85–103 in *The role of the American academic library in international programs*, edited by Bruce Bonta and James G. Neal. Greenwich, CT: JAI Press, 1992.

Provides an overview of the role played by American academic librarians in the work of ten major international library organizations and the impact of their efforts in the advancement of librarianship. Discusses activities in a variety of areas: leadership, publications, meetings, and continuing professional education; resource provision; exchanges and visits; development of standards; philosophy of librarianship; political activity; and collection development. Notes problems Americans have in working with international colleagues and offers suggestions for becoming involved in international library organizations.

332. Woods, L. B., Tamie Willis, Dan Chandler, Beth Manoir, and Paula Wolfe. "International relations and the spread of information worldwide." *International Library Review* 23, no. 2 (1991): 91–101.

Discusses the role librarians can take in the international transfer of information. Topics include the International Federation of Library Associations and its activities, preservation of materials, international networks and information services, international telecommunications, international library exchanges, and international material exchanges. *See also* nos. 77, 105, 216, 217.

GUIDES FOR INTERNATIONAL STUDENTS

333. Badke, William B. *Beyond the answer sheet: Academic success for international students.* Lincoln, NE: Writer's Club Press/iUniverse.com, 2003. v, 152 p.

Guide for international students covering various aspects of Western education. Includes chapters on differences in the approach to education, skills needed to succeed, the North American classroom, professors, writing research papers (with a special focus on plagiarism), other types of assignments, and quizzes and examinations. Includes a chapter on the use of the library and final chapter lists the reference librarian as one of the Important People to Know in your Academic World. Concludes with an appendix on graduate study and thesis work.

334. Byrd, Patricia, Carol A. Drum, and Barbara Jean Wittkopf. *Guide to academic libraries in the United States: For students of English as a second language.* New Jersey: Prentice-Hall, 1981. vii, 184 p.

Monograph written in English and designed for students who speak languages other than English. Individual chapters describe roles and services of the academic library in the United States; arrangements of materials in the U.S. academic library; types of research materials available in academic libraries; research for questions posed in chapter 3; advanced research in scientific and technical fields; applications (taking notes, exercises, the relationship between the library and laboratory research). Explains common library services such as reference, interlibrary loan, private study areas, and copying. Appendices provide list of common abstracting and indexing sources and an answer key to sample exercises outlined in text. Material is very dated but general outline is useful.

335. Flanders, E. Lorene. *Georgia College Libraries handbook for international students.* Milledgeville: Georgia College, 1989. ERIC document no. 320583. 45 p. http://www.eric.ed.gov/ERICDocs/data/ericdocs2sql/content_storage_01/0000019b/80/20/7d/8c.pdf (July 31, 2008).

Guidebook created for international students at Georgia College in Milledgeville, Georgia. Provides an introduction to academic and public library service in Milledgeville; a general introduction to operating procedures and facilities of the Ina Dillard Russell Library; a description of the library's collections (books and other cataloged materials, the periodical collection, U.S. government documents, ERIC documents, college catalogs, telephone directories, and special collections); a directory of information services (including sections on the circulation and information desks, interlibrary loan, "Books in Print," DIALOG online computer searching, and using other University System libraries); guidelines for finding information (with sections on using the library's microfiche catalog, the Library of Congress classification system, and using periodical indexes) and for conducting library research (including information on using bibliographies and indexes). Also includes a directory of Georgia College Media Services, a glossary of terms used, and directories of library and media services faculty and staff. Material is dated.

336. Larson, Darlene. *Library explorations: Activities for international students.* Ann Arbor, MI: University of Michigan Press, 2000. xii, 129 p.

Manual for international students covering such areas as getting acquainted with the library, exploring different types of library material such as almanacs and atlases, the Library of Congress classification system, using the card catalog, searching for biographical material, using the Readers' Guide to Periodical Literature, working on a library project, using the current periodicals reading area, using the New York Times index, using specialized subject indexes, learning about call numbers, and checking out books. Much material is dated.

337. Muroi, Linda, and Philip White. *Library research guide for international students.* ERIC document no. ED286524, 1987. 76 p. http://www.eric.ed.gov/ERICDocs/data/ericdocs2sql/content_storage_01/0000019b/80/1b/ed/06.pdf (July 30, 2008).

Guidebook created for international students entering San Diego State University in California. Introduces basic library materials and search techniques. Uses examples, illustrations, and maps, to cover the following topics: introductions to San Diego State University and its library, choosing and focusing on a topic, locating background information, using the Library of Congress classification system, finding books and articles, defining government publications, evaluating the information found, and using style manuals. Two appendices provide samples of four types of information available on education in Japan and a glossary of basic library terminology in Chinese, Japanese, Arabic, Spanish, and English. Much material is dated, but provides a useful format and outline.

338. Muroi, Linda, and Philip White. *Library research guide for international students*. ERIC document no. ED328280, 1990. 64 p. http://www.eric.ed.gov/ERICDocs/data/ericdocs2sql/content_storage_01/0000019b/80/22/c2/08.pdf (July 30, 2008).

Revised version of the above guidebook, created for international students entering San Diego State University. Covers the following topics: introductions to San Diego State University and its library; locating reference librarians and research materials; library terminology; locating the major service points and areas in the library; locating library materials using the Library of Congress classification system and call numbers; library search strategy; overview sources (encyclopedias and other reference books); locating books using the online public access catalog; identifying periodical articles in indexes and locating them in the library using the online catalog; locating and using government publications; additional library services, including computer search services, reserve books, library instruction, group study rooms, interlibrary loan, the map collection, the media center, and the university archives and special collections. Exercises are included for many sections. Appendices provide a glossary of basic library terminology in English and lists of representative subject encyclopedias and periodical indexes. Much material is dated, but provides a useful format and outline.

339. Rutgers University Library. *Library guide for international students*. ERIC document no. ED431405, 1998. 13 p. http://www.eric.ed.gov/ERICDocs/data/ericdocs2sql/content_storage_01/0000019b/80/17/9c/33.pdf (July 24, 2008). See also online version: http://www.libraries.rutgers.edu/rul/lib_servs/intl_students.shtml.

Library guide prepared for students at Rutgers University in New Jersey includes welcoming remarks; brief discussion of American academic library systems; list of the locations and abbreviations of the twenty-five libraries, collections, and reading rooms on the Rutgers campuses; library policies on loan period, library hours, checking out books, and eating and smoking; brief descriptions of reference services and the Integrated Rutgers Information System (IRIS), the library online catalog; brief descriptions of online databases (indexes and abstracts); electronic journals (e-journals); the Internet; CD-ROMs; an introduction to library orientations, classes and workshops; and notes on the Rutgers Request Service, Interlibrary Loan Service, and library reserves. Guidelines for finding books and journal articles are also provided, as are tips for library research. Provides a useful format and outline of content for similar projects.

340. Rutgers University Library. *Library terminology: A guide for international students*. ERIC document no. ED433806, 1999. 9 p. http://www.eric.ed.gov/ERICDocs/data/ericdocs2sql/content_storage_01/0000019b/80/15/dc/7a.pdf (July 24, 2008). See also online version: http://www.libraries.rutgers.edu/rul/lib_servs/intl_students_terms.shtml.

Provides definitions of commonly used library terms. Created for use by students at the Rutgers University Libraries (New Jersey).

341. Wu, Connie. *American library terminology—A guide for international students*. ERIC document no. ED308863, 1988. 8 p.

Lists twenty-seven common library-related terms in English, Chinese, Spanish, Korean, and Arabic, with definitions in English.

INTERLIBRARY LOAN

342. Irving, Suzanne. "Addressing the special needs of international students in interlibrary loan: Some considerations." 111–17 in *Racial and ethnic diversity in academic libraries: Multicultural issues*, edited by Deborah A. Curry, Susan Griswold Blandy, and Lynne M. Martin. New York: Haworth Press, 1994. Co-published as *The Reference Librarian* 45/46 (1994): 111–17.

Considers challenges international students may face when dealing with the concept and use of interlibrary loan (ILL) services. Describes a typical ILL encounter and highlights the importance of the ILL interview. Also outlines how ILL staff can access foreign materials for international students.

LANGUAGE/COMMUNICATION

343. Berlanga-Cortéz, Graciela. "Cross-cultural communication: Identifying barriers to information retrieval with culturally and linguistically different library patrons." 51–60 in *Library services to Latinos: An anthology*, edited by Salvador Güereña. Jefferson, NC: MacFarland, 2000.

Considers four main issues perceived as barriers to effectively serving the information needs of culturally and linguistically diverse library users: cultural differences in verbal and nonverbal communication styles, cultural awareness of ethnic minority groups on the part of library staff, cultural sensitivity training for library staff, and training on the use of information technology for diverse users. Makes recommendations to help reduce the impact of these barriers.

344. Bordonaro, Karen. "Language learning in the library: An exploratory study of ESL students." *The Journal of Academic Librarianship* 32, no. 5 (2006): 518–26.

Report of a study examining how higher-level English-as-a-second-language students used the academic library in a self-directed way to improve their English skills. A series of open-ended, qualitative oral and written questions were administered to a group of twenty students at a medium-sized academic institution in the northeastern United States over the course of the academic year. Results indicated students used the library to improve their reading, writing, speaking, and listening skills in both formal and informal ways.

345. Briguglio, Carmela. "Generic skills: Attending to the communication skills of international students." 285–90 in *Proceedings of the Lifelong Learning Conference, Yeppoon, Queensland, Australia, 17–19 July 2000*, edited by Ken Appleton, Colin MacPherson, and Debbie Orr. Rockhampton: Central Queensland University, 2000.

Discusses issues surrounding educational support required by international students from non-English-speaking backgrounds to enable them to become more proficient in English language communication. Suggestions offered are based on findings of several research projects undertaken at Curtin University of Technology in Perth/Sydney, Australia. *See also* no. 346.

346. Briguglio, Carmela. "Language and cultural issues for English-as-a-second/ foreign language students in transnational educational settings." *Higher Education in Europe* 25, no. 3 (2000): 425–34.

Discusses linguistic and cultural differences faced by international students and issues of educational support for them. Suggestions are based on findings of several research projects undertaken at Curtin University of Technology in Perth/Sydney, Australia. *See also* no. 345.

347. DuPraw, Marcelle E., and Marya Axner. *Toward a more perfect union in an age of diversity: Working on common cross-cultural communication challenges.* 1997. http://www.pbs.org/ampu/crosscult.html (August 21, 2008).

Outline of fundamental patterns of cultural difference, including differences in communication styles, attitudes toward conflict, approaches to completing tasks, decision-making styles, attitudes toward disclosure, and approaches to knowing. Includes guidelines for respecting differences and working together. Put together by the Public Broadcasting Service (U.S.).

348. Gudykunst, William B. *Bridging differences: Effective intergroup communication.* 4th ed. Newbury Park, CA: Sage, 2004. xi, 171 p.

Popular textbook on interpersonal and intercultural communication. Includes chapters on understanding cultural differences, attributing meaning to strangers' behaviors, exchanging messages with strangers, managing intergroup conflict, and building community with strangers.

349. Hall, Patrick Andrew. "Peanuts: A note on intercultural communication." *Journal of Academic Librarianship* 18, no. 4 (1992): 211–13.

Challenges librarians to be aware of communication styles that occur even when both parties speak American English. Notes that the multicultural nature of the United States has led to numerous language codes that often go unnoticed or are ignored due to lack of knowledge of linguistic styles lying outside the American "mainstream." Also discusses concepts of linguistic bigotry, variables of culture and power in communication, cultural bias, and how dialects and accents impact perception of the speaker. Draws on the author's personal experience as a teacher at a Yupik Eskimo boarding school in western Alaska.

350. Karnes, David K., Francis Lajba, and Stephen R. Shorb. "Technology for providing materials in 94 world languages: A partnership for user-driven learning, and improved awareness of the people and events that shape our world." Paper presented at the World Library and Information Congress: 73rd IFLA General Conference and Council, Durban, South Africa, 19–23 August 2007. http://www .ifla.org/IV/ifla73/papers/146-Karnes-en.pdf (August 20, 2008).

Describes a partnership between the library at the University of Nebraska at Omaha and SCOLA, a nonprofit global television broadcaster, which has resulted in low-cost access to library and instructional materials in more than ninety languages. Discusses the importance of language learning and past difficulties for libraries in supporting language learners, the development of the library-based language center, and the nature of the university/SCOLA partnership. Notes that language students are the primary beneficiaries of the arrangement, but the language center is also widely used by international students.

351. Li, Hong, Roy F. Fox, and Dario J. Almarza. "Strangers in stranger lands: Language, learning, culture." *International Journal of Progressive Education* 3, no. 1 (2007): 6–28.

Investigates international students' perceptions of issues they face using English as a second language while attending American higher education institutions. The principal author is an international student from China who had lived in America for almost a year. Interviews were conducted with eight international graduate students from six different countries and regions and two professors at the University of Missouri–Columbia. Findings showed subjects were deeply concerned about their lack of proficiency in English. They expressed difficulties using English in America despite extensive English training in their home countries and noted the difference between formal and conversational English as a major obstacle to appropriate language use. Differences between their native cultures and American cultures also made it difficult for them to function in an American environment. Lack of vocabulary, individual personality traits, and study habits also impacted on language use. Recommendations are made to better assist international students' language development.

352. Lopez, Annette. "Did I see you do what I think you did? The pitfalls of nonverbal communication across cultures." *New Jersey Libraries* 27 (1993/1994): 18–22.

Discusses cross-cultural nonverbal communication issues, including para-kinesics (pitch, tone, intonation), kinesis (gestures), oculisics (eye contact), haptics (touch), proxemics (space), and monochronic and polychronic culture patterns.

353. Lustig, Myron W., and Jolene Koester. *Intercultural competence: Interpersonal communication across cultures.* 5th ed. Boston: Pearson, 2006. xiv, 386 p.

Recent textbook on interpersonal and intercultural communication. Includes chapters on why cultures differ, cultural differences in communication, cultural identity and cultural biases, nonverbal intercultural communication, the effects of code usage in intercultural communication.

354. Phipps, Alison M., and Manuela Guilherme (eds.). *Critical pedagogy: Political approaches to language and intercultural communication.* Buffalo, NY: Multilingual Matters, 2004. 61 p.

Recent textbook on interpersonal communications discussing cultural differences in communication and intercultural interaction.

355. Zhang, Li. "Communication in academic libraries: An East Asian perspective." *Reference Services Review* 34, no. 1 (2006): 164–76.

Discussion of how communication can be a barrier to international students in American academic libraries. Applies communication literature and theory to highlight how cultural-specific communication styles can cause unintentional obstacles in reference service. Makes recommendations to improve communication and understanding, in particular with respect to East Asian user groups. Includes an extensive literature review (1984–2001) of library literature on international students. *See also* nos. 9, 18, 32, 62, 84, 121, 258, 259, 306, 378, 383, 387, 395.

LIBRARY ADMINISTRATION

356. Buttlar, Lois. "Facilitating cultural diversity in college and university libraries." *Journal of Academic Librarianship* 20, no. 1 (1994): 10–14.

Reports on a survey of two hundred American academic library directors which showed 92 percent had appropriated financial resources to facilitate cultural diversity. Developing multicultural collections was the most common activity reported, with recruitment of minority librarians and provision of bibliographic instruction for international students also listed as high priorities.

357. Trujillo, Roberto J., and David C. Weber. "Academic library response to cultural diversity: A position paper for the 1990s." *The Journal of Academic Librarianship* 17, no. 3 (1991): 157–61.

Suggests ten actions U.S. academic libraries can take to advocate a larger role in the promotion of cultural diversity on their campuses. These include diversifying library staff so they reflect the multicultural community they serve, changing the composition of library management, developing internship and mentoring programs, adapting communication, and making contact with high schools.

358. Welburn, William C. "Rethinking theoretical assumptions about diversity: Challenges for college and university library planning." 75–84 in *Diversity and multiculturalism in libraries*, edited by Katherine Hoover Hill. Greenwich, CT: JAI Press, 1994.

Discusses the importance of library administrative leadership in promoting strategic change in academic institutions, with focus on the role of the academic library in supporting and promoting diversity. Examples considered include recruiting minority staff and students and initiating diversity training for student assistants. Focus is on minority students, but ideas are relevant to work with international students.

359. Welch, Janet E., and Errol R. Lam. "The library and the pluralistic campus in the year 2000: Implications for administrators." *Library Administration & Management* 5, no. 4 (1991): 212–16.

Discusses racial and cultural shifts in librarianship and in student bodies in American institutions of higher education. Considers responses to racism and ways to alleviate intolerance toward international students. Concludes with a listing of program ideas to raise sensitivity awareness of library staff and facilitate discussion. *See also* nos. 271, 390.

MARKETING/OUTREACH

360. Bordonaro, Karen. "We all have an accent: Welcoming international students to the library." *Feliciter* 52, no. 6 (2006): 240–41.

Notes that librarians need to develop the right attitude to overcome communication problems involving international students in libraries. Libraries should become welcoming places for students whose first language is not English and should help to promote and foster internationalization on campus. Suggests that the establishment of a library outreach program for international students also helps educate Canadians about foreign classmates.

361. Bryson, Montez. "Libraries lend friendship." *International Educational and Cultural Exchange* 10 (1974): 29–30.

Describes the Foreign Student Outreach Program at the University of Denver in Colorado, which was designed to help international students develop library skills. Librarians participated in relationship-building activities such as offering in-library luncheons and tours, holding regular afternoon coffee hours at the Center for Foreign Students, visiting ESL classes, and donating materials to the foreign student lounge. Notes that communication barriers were lessened as a result of the program.

362. Cuesta, Yolanda J., and Gail McGovern. "Getting ready to market the library to culturally diverse communities." *ALKI: The Washington Library Association Journal* 18, no. 1 (2002): 6–9.

Does not deal with academic libraries specifically, but provides useful suggestions for marketing any library that serves a multicultural population. Discusses needs assessment, setting priorities, examining assumptions, and analyzing the library's strengths and weaknesses. Includes a checklist for analyzing and reviewing your library.

363. Downing, Karen E., Barbara McAdam, and Darlene P. Nichols. *Reaching a multicultural student community: A handbook for academic librarians.* Westport, CT: Greenwood Press, 1993. xi, 223 p.

Monographic study with chapters on community analysis, the politics of program development, establishing a program budget, developing staff, program and service development, building a campus network, marketing and public relations, and program evaluation. Emphasizes the use of peer information counseling. Appendices provide training plans and exercises used at the University of Michigan in Ann Arbor, an undergraduate library minority student user survey, and sample advertisements. Focuses on domestic minority students, but ideas are adaptable for international students.

364. Dyson, Allan J. "Reaching out for outreach: A university library develops a new position to serve the school's multicultural students." *American Libraries* 20 (1989): 952–54.

Highlights the steps taken at the University of California, Santa Cruz to recruit a multicultural services librarian.

365. Espiñal, Isabel. "Multicultural outreach in academic libraries." Paper presented at the Office of Literacy and Outreach Services Pre-conference *Different Voice, Common Quest*, American Library Association Annual Conference, June 2002. http://www.ala.org/ala/pio/campaign/academicresearch/academic_multicultural.pdf (September 22, 2008).

Outline of paper presented. Suggests various avenues for multicultural outreach, including peer advisory programs, special programs and events, collections and special libraries, networking, minority residence programs, media, off-campus outreach, and library instruction. Refers to successful multicultural outreach instruction programs at the University of California at Berkeley and the University of Massachusetts at Amherst.

366. McClure, Jennifer, and Mangala Krishnamurthy. "Translating the libraries: A multilingual information page for international students." *The Southeastern Librarian* 55, no. 1 (2007): 26–31.

Discusses challenges faced by international students from non-English-speaking countries, and describes efforts made at the University of Alabama in Tuscaloosa to create a more welcoming environment for them. An online information page was first mounted on the UA libraries' website in 2004, but the value of providing library information in students' native languages became fully apparent only when this page was translated into Spanish and Chinese, two of the most prominent languages on campus, in 2006. This project was funded through a university Innovation Grant. Other efforts undertaken by the library include sponsorships of a weekly coffee hour for international students each term; maintaining two televisions with programming in Mandarin, Japanese, and South Asian languages, as well as international soccer programming; having the library's liaison for international students participate in the university's orientation session for international students at the beginning of each year and offering special library tours for international students; providing bibliographic instruction to English-as-a-second-language classes and to the international student sections of English composition classes; featuring international scholars and artists in the libraries' lecture series; and mounting periodic exhibits featuring international collections and programs.

367. Mu, Cuiying. "Marketing academic library resources and information services to international students from Asia." *Reference Services Review* 35, no. 4 (2007): 571–83.

Describes information literacy programs and activities suitable to accommodate the information needs of Asian international students and what teaching methodology should be used. Draws upon the author's personal experiences and observations as an international students information librarian at the University of Canterbury in Christchurch, New Zealand. Data was collected through surveys of Asian students on their experiences of using academic libraries and whether they were aware of services and resources available for them in a Western academic setting. Concludes that academic libraries need to market their services and resources proactively, and reference librarians need to consider students' characteristics, language proficiency, learning styles, and subjects of interest so that teaching methodology and examples used are effective.

368. Pan, Junlin. "Promoting the accessibility of Chinese resources to overseas Chinese communities." Paper presented at the Chinese American Librarians Association, Midwest Chapter Annual Program, Chicago, 1 June 2002. http://www.white-clouds.com/iclc/clieg/cl14pan.htm (July 25, 2008).

Study of library resource accessibility for ethnic Chinese users undertaken at the Northern Illinois University Founders Library in DeKalb. Discusses Chinese users' characteristics, needs, and frustrations when using the library, then considers ways to promote library resources to Chinese students, including library resources awareness, library instruction, and Romanization system standardization.

369. Walter, Scott. "Moving beyond collections: Academic library outreach to multicultural student centers." *Reference Services Review* 33, no. 4 (2005): 438–58.

Discusses collaboration between academic libraries and student services offices as a means of outreach. Case study involved targeted library programming for students at the cultural center for students of color at Washington State University, Pullman, but the process could be adapted to an international students center. A survey (sixty-three respondents) gathered data on frequency of library use, reasons for library use, problems encountered when using library resource or services, starting points for the research process, and desired library services. A number of opportunities for effective collaboration were identified. Copy of the questionnaire is appended.

370. Wei, Wei. "Outreach to international students and scholars using the World Wide Web." *Sci-tech News* 52, no. 2 (1998): 11–14.

Discusses a website created to support international students in the engineering program at the University of California, Santa Cruz. Reviews the site's design and content, which includes information on international news, travel, and weather, as well as "survival tips" at UCSC. Also summarizes how the website was promoted. *See also* nos. 71, 111, 200, 202, 208, 218.

REFERENCE SERVICES

371. Ajileye-Laogun, J. O. "Reference librarian/user relationship at the Obafemi Awolowo University Library." *Information for Social Change* 19 (2004). http://www.libr.org/isc/articles/19-Laogun-1.html (September 26, 2008).

Report of a study on the link between students' perceptions of librarians and the rate at which they approach them for services. A questionnaire survey administered at Obafemi Awolowo University in Ife-Ife, Nigeria (169 respondents), collected data on awareness of services at the reference desk, willingness to approach the desk for help, attitudes toward reference librarians, and perceptions of reference librarians and their duties. Findings showed that lack of awareness, poor expectations, and negative assumptions of services were major barriers to library use. Librarians' attitudes have a considerable impact on the rate of utilization of the library by users. Concludes that marketing and promotional activities applied effectively would increase the value status and awareness of librarians and what they can offer users. Study highlights the low professional image and low status of librarians in some cultures.

372. Blenkinsopp, Heather. "Communicating across cultures for reference librarians who supervise." 39–43 in *Racial and ethnic diversity in academic libraries: Multicultural issues*, edited by Deborah A. Curry, Susan Griswold Blandy, and Lynne M. Martin. New York: Haworth Press, 1994. Co-published as *The Reference Librarian* 45/46 (1994): 39–43.

Notes that as both student and employee populations become more culturally diverse, librarians need to increase their supervisory communication skills to effectively manage their departments.

373. Brown, Christopher C. "Reference services to the international adult learner: Understanding the barriers." 337–47 in *Reference services for the adult learner: Challenging issues for the traditional and technological era*, edited by Kwasi Sarkodie-Mensah. New York: Haworth Press, 2000. Co-published as *The Reference Librarian* 69/70 (2000): 337–47.

Discusses linguistic, technological, and cultural barriers faced by immigrant and foreign-born residents in the United States when seeking reference service. Suggests solutions to these barriers, including international travel for service providers, cultivating friendships, building multilingual library collections, developing a library vocabulary list, having reference staff become familiar with bibliographic searching in another language, and providing specialized instruction programs for international students.

374. Chattoo, Calmer D. "Reference services: Meeting the needs of international adult learners." 349–62 in *Reference services for the adult learner: Challenging issues for the traditional and technological era*, edited by Kwasi Sarkodie-Mensah. New York: Haworth Press, 2000. Co-published as *The Reference Librarian* 69/70 (2000): 349–62.

Notes that international adult learners constitute a large percentage of the international student and scholar population in the United States. International students not only face language, cultural, and educational barriers, but they are also hampered by librarians' limited understanding of differences in learning styles. Different learning styles and best practices for adjusting to these styles are discussed, along with recommendations for training librarians to deal with this user group.

375. Curry, Ann, and Deborah Copeman. "Reference service to international students: A field stimulation research study." *The Journal of Academic Librarianship* 31, no. 5 (2005): 409–20.

Evaluates the quality of reference service provided to non-native English-speaking international students at eleven college and university libraries in the lower mainland of British Columbia. Used field stimulation methodology, in which an individual posed as a library user and initiated a reference encounter in heavily accented English with library staff at each institution. In each case the same question was asked. After the interaction, observed behaviors were recorded. Each library was visited by the same individual twice. Results indicated that in 75 percent of cases service was satisfactory or very satisfactory. Reference librarians demonstrated approachability, but while most recognized the language barrier, they failed to ask enough questions and rushed the interaction to closure prematurely. A relationship was found between some library staff behaviors and the user's level of satisfaction and likelihood to return to the staff member in the near future. *See also* Kloda, no. 381.

376. Curry, Deborah A. "Assessing and evaluating diversity in the reference department." 115–20 in *Assessment and accountability in reference work*, edited by Susan Griswold Blandy, Lynne M. Martin, and Mary L. Strife. New York: Haworth Press, 1992. Co-published as *The Reference Librarian* 38 (1992): 115–20.

Discusses the concepts of diversity and multiculturalism and their relationship to assessment and evaluation of library reference staff and collections.

377. D'Aniello, Charles A. "Cultural literacy and reference services." *RQ* 28, no. 3 (1989): 370–80.

Does not refer to international or minority students specifically, but suggests that the extent and depth of cultural literacy possessed by reference librarians are major determinants of the quality of patron-librarian interactions in general. Also notes that reference sources can play an important role in the acquisition and enhancement of the cultural literacy of both librarians and patrons.

378. de Souza, Yvonne. "Reference work with international students: Making the most of the neutral question." *Reference Services Review* 24, no. 4 (1996): 41–48.

Discusses use of the neutral question technique with international students. Considers how reference service to international students differs from traditional reference, noting barriers to effective communication and ways of overcoming these barriers.

379. Foley, May. "Reference and information services in a multi-cultural environment." *Journal of Library and Information Science* 10 (1984): 143–62.

Bibliographic essay. Does not deal specifically with international students, but includes useful references.

380. Janes, Phoebe, and Ellen Meltzer. "Origins and attitudes: Training reference librarians for a pluralistic world." *The Reference Librarian* 30 (1990): 145–55.

Emphasizes the importance of reassessing existing training in light of demographic changes. Outlines barriers to reference service for multicultural library users and discusses desirable skills for librarians in multicultural settings. Notes that training should be ongoing and should include all reference staff.

381. Kloda, Lorie Andrea. "Academic librarians should be sensitive to language and cultural barriers when providing reference service to international students." *Evidence Based Library and Information Practice* 1, no. 4 (2006): 46–48.

Summary report of the study conducted by Ann Curry and Deborah Copeman (no. 375), which was designed to assess the quality of reference service received by international students in academic libraries in Lower Mainland British Columbia.

382. Kumar, Suhasini L., and Raghini S. Suresh. "Strategies for providing effective reference services for international adult learners." 327–36 in *Reference*

services for the adult learner: Challenging issues for the traditional and techno-logical era, edited by Kwasi Sarkodie-Mensah. New York: Haworth Press, 2000. Co-published as *The Reference Librarian* 69/70 (2000): 327–36.

Considers obstacles faced by international students in studying abroad, with emphasis on international students as adult learners. Reviews key literature on international students and discusses the librarians' role in dealing with them. Emphasizes the importance of university libraries making a commitment to multiculturalism and cultural diversity in their mission statements, and recommends the assignment of an international students' liaison librarian.

383. Lam, R. Errol. "The reference interview: Some inter-cultural considerations." *RQ* 27, no. 3 (1988): 390–95.

Focus is on issues surrounding interpersonal communication between white librarians and Afro-American students, but suggestions are useful when dealing with international students, in particular discussion of developing cultural sensitivity and of nonverbal behaviors.

384. Liestman, Daniel. "Reference services and the international adult learner." 363–78 in *Reference services for the adult learner: Challenging issues for the traditional and technological era*, edited by Kwasi Sarkodie-Mensah. New York: Haworth Press, 2000. Co-published as *The Reference Librarian* 69/70 (2000): 363–78.

Discusses characteristics of international adult learners and how they interact with reference staff. Considers general differences between North American and international libraries and language and communication barriers. Suggestions are made for meeting these learners' needs, including creating special programming and BI opportunities and developing partnerships with other organizations. Also considers staff training issues. Notes that international students generally prefer to receive instruction at point of need and point of use rather than committing time to an extra class on library use. Librarian instructors need to provide brief, relevant instruction, being careful not to overload students, and they should address affective issues such as stress and anxiety.

385. Marcus, Sandra. "Multilingualism at the reference desk." *College and Research Libraries News* 64, no. 5 (2003): 322–23, 336.

Discusses a reference desk policy that allows librarians, if they choose, to speak foreign languages along with English to international or culturally diverse students. Argues that doing so decreases students' feelings of isolation and falls in line with other language services many academic libraries offer. Benefits for librarians include a larger sense of accomplishment and an added service component.

386. Mykytiuk, Lawrence J. "From missionary and graduate student to reference librarian." 177–88 in *Philosophies of reference service*, edited by Celia Hales

Mabry. New York: Haworth Press, 1997. Co-published as *The Reference Librarian* 59 (1997): 177–88.

Discusses the author's background as a lay missionary in the Philippines and how this shaped his approach to library reference service. Notes that his own overseas experience helped him develop sensitivity to the needs of international students.

387. Osa, Justina O., Sylvia A. Nyuana, and Clara A. Obgaa. "Effective cross-cultural communication to enhance reference transactions: Training guidelines and tips." *Knowledge Quest* 35, no. 2 (2006): 22–24.

Notes challenges to non-American patrons in the United States including language and communication problems, adjusting to a new library system, and general cultural adjustments. Presents tips designed to enhance effective reference transactions and reports on a professional development workshop developed and conducted in the Penn State Libraries, University Park, Pennsylvania, and Texas State University Library in San Marcos, Texas.

388. Pyati, Ajit. "Limited English proficient users and the need for improved reference services." *Reference Services Review* 31, no. 3 (2003): 264–71.

Written from a public library perspective, but addresses issues of relevance in academic libraries: reference interviewing, information-seeking behavior, foreign language reference materials, and multi-lingual online catalogs.

389. Shachaf, Pnina, and Sarah Horowitz. "Are virtual reference services color blind?" *Library & Information Science Research* 28, no. 4 (2006): 501–20.

Reports on an experiment examining whether librarians provide equitable virtual reference services to diverse user groups. Each participating library (twenty-three Association of Research Libraries member libraries) received one request per week for six consecutive weeks. The targeted reference services received a version of the same request but with a different user name, suggestive of a different ethnic group or religious affiliation. Findings indicated the quality of service librarians provided to African Americans and Arabs was lower than the quality of service provided to Caucasian, Hispanic, Asian, and Jewish students. *See also* nos. 325, 326, 355.

STAFF DEVELOPMENT AND TRAINING

390. Gomez, Cheryl. "Cultural diversity staff training: The challenge." 29–42 in *Diversity and multiculturalism in libraries*, edited by Katherine Hoover Hill. Greenwich, CT: JAI Press, 1994.

Reports on a two-year staff training project based at the University of California, Santa Cruz Libraries. Describes the libraries' organizational culture before training, then outlines the elements of the program developed. Notes that commitment from library administration is the most important factor for success. Concludes with an evaluation of the training program.

391. Greenfield, Louise W. "Training library staff to reach and teach international students." 45–62 in *Reaching and teaching diverse library user groups: Papers presented at the Sixteenth National LOEX Library Instruction Conference held at Bowling Green State University, 5 & 6 May 1988*, edited by Teresa B. Mensching. Ann Arbor, MI: Pierian Press, 1989.

Seminar paper based on the author's experience working with international students at the University of Arizona Libraries in Tucson. Aims of staff training include making participants experience some of the kinds of pressures and emotions felt by international students, making staff aware of their own cultural assumptions and interpretations, demonstrating typical cultural differences, giving suggestions for improving intercultural communication, and showing how to be effective when teaching large groups of students from other cultures. Includes copies of a quiz on interlibrary loan policies and procedures, a handout on effective presentation for international students, a glossary of library terms, and a list of presentation suggestions for communicating with international users. *See also* no. 392.

392. Greenfield, Louise, Susan Johnston, and Karen Williams. "Educating the world: Training library staff to communicate effectively with international students." *The Journal of Academic Librarianship* 12, no. 4 (1986): 227–31.

Discusses a workshop at the University of Arizona library in Tucson designed to train library staff in cross-cultural communication. Presents goals, development, and organization of the workshop and highlights concerns. These included language challenges, cultural adjustment, and library instruction. Discusses results in the context of international students' experiences. *See also* no. 391.

393. Hannigan, Terence P. "Traits, attitudes, and skills that are related to intercultural effectiveness and their implications for cross-cultural training: Review of the literature." *International Journal of Intercultural Relations* 14, no. 1 (1990): 89–111.

Discussion of difficulties of adjusting to life in a foreign culture, with a focus on two populations: Peace Corps volunteers and international students. Examines recent definitions of such terms as adjustment, acculturation, assimilation, and effectiveness, then summarizes recent literature on traits related to intercultural effectiveness (e.g., ability to communicate, ability to establish and maintain relationships, interactions management, orientation to knowledge, world view, cultural empathy, linguistic ability, flexibility, a realistic view of target culture, organizational skills) and those which have inverse relationships to cross-cultural effectiveness (dependent anxiety, task-related behavior, authoritarianism, perfectionism, rigidity, ethnocentrism, narrow-mindedness, self-centered role behaviors). Final section deals with training implications.

394. Kathman, Jane McGurn, and Michael D. Kathman. "What difference does diversity make in managing student employees?" *College & Research Libraries* 59, no. 4 (1998): 378–89.

Discusses opportunities and challenges that arise for library staff as they supervise an increasingly diverse group of student employees. Suggests ways to rethink selecting, training, supervision, and evaluation of a diverse workforce.

395. Lukenbill, W. Bernard (ed). *Intercultural communication processes in libraries: Proceedings of the HEA Title II-B Institute, Austin, Texas, June 6–19, 1976.* Austin: University of Texas Graduate School of Library Science, 1976. ERIC document no. 126878. 68 p.

Proceedings from a two-week institute designed to help librarians and library educators expand their knowledge of the theory and practice of intercultural communication processes and environments. Program included sessions on verbal and nonverbal behavior, value and perceptual differences among minority cultures, life assumptions, and personal and group identification. Participants were given opportunities to evaluate their personal behavior through experience-based laboratory activities illustrating intercultural communication patterns. In-service and formal methods for teaching basic concepts of intercultural communication processes were designed and discussed. Report includes list of goals and objectives, program outline and plans, bibliographies, lists of staff and participants, information on facilities and resources used, and an evaluation instrument.

396. McSwiney, Carolyn, Diane Gabb, and Marie Piu. "An [un]likely partnership! Transcultural psychiatry and information professionals." *Australian Library Journal* 48, no. 3 (1999): 253–62.

Discusses an action-research program designed by psychologist/educators at the Victorian Transcultural Psychiatry Unit and an academic librarian at the University of Melbourne, Australia. The program was developed in response to the library's attempt to translate the university's cultural diversity awareness policy into practice in the library workplace. Goals were to enable library staff to interact effectively with international students, raise the level of awareness of the complex nature of culture, assist staff to identify and build on skill sets most needed to work in an internationalized climate, and to develop skills in transcultural communication in order to enhance the quality of information services offered.

397. Owens, Alison R. *Intercultural awareness and sensitivity in an Australian university: A study of professional practice of university staff.* Ph.D. dissertation, University of Technology, Sydney, 2005. xi, 299 p.

Report of a study conducted at Central Queensland University in Sydney, Australia, which aimed to identify pedagogical approaches to enhance the teaching and learning processes and learning outcomes for international students at Australian universities. Recommends the design and delivery of a professional development program in intercultural awareness and sensitivity for academic and learning support staff.

398. Pastor, Harriett M., and Lia S. Hemphill. "Acculturation of the international student employee in urban university libraries." 215–19 in *Academic libraries in urban and metropolitan areas: A management handbook*, edited by Gerard B. McCabe. New York: Greenwood Press, 1992.

Presents results of two surveys (locations and number of participants not specified). The first was a written survey of international students who worked or had worked in academic libraries and designed to determine if working in an academic library resulted in a more positive acculturation process. The second was a telephone poll of librarians who actively supervised international students and examined how librarians hired and placed international student workers in the library. Discussion highlights how finding a place to learn and observe American learning styles, humor, and language is an acculturation benefit for international student library workers.

399. Riedinger, Edward. "Ideas to meet the library needs of foreign students." *NAFSA Newsletter* 17 (1989): 17.

Reviews the articles by Ball and Mahony (no. 210) and Greenfield, Johnston, and Williams (no. 392) and recommends them for helping staff learn how to serve international students in American academic libraries.

400. Sapon-White, Richard. "Pamoja: Learning about international library issues through a simulation game." *OLA Quarterly (Oregon Library Association)* 6, no. 4 (2000): 16.

Reports on a cross-cultural game developed by two librarians with many years of international experience and designed to train librarians and others about the factors influencing international library and information resources development. The name, Pamoja, is the Swahili word for "together."

401. Sarkodie-Mensah, Kwasi. "Dealing with international students in a multicultural era." *The Journal of Academic Librarianship* 18, no. 2 (1992): 214–16.

The author, a foreign student and librarian, puts forward a number of suggestions for interacting with international students in library settings: dealing with pronunciation differences, listening to words not intonation, expressing interest in foreign cultures, having a basic knowledge of taboo subjects, navigating the subjects of politics and religion, resisting the urge to "noble-ize" international students, and self-education.

402. Sharpe, Dave. "Cross-sectoral staff development." *Library & Information Update* 2, no. 8 (2003): 51.

Discusses cooperation between various libraries (public, college, and university) in the Sunderland district in Northern England, with focus on staff development initiatives. Describes a joint staff development day aimed at training staff to work with users from different backgrounds and cultures, including international students, refugees, and immigrants.

403. Shirts, Gary R. *BaFà BaFà: A cross culture simulation.* Del Mar, CA: Simile II, 1977.
Kit used for a popular and widely used cross-cultural simulation exercise designed to teach sensitivity to difference. Provides participants with the opportunity to examine the effect that values, norms, and behaviors have on cross-cultural interactions. Helps build awareness of how cultural differences impact on interpersonal interaction. For further information see the BaFà BaFà website: http://www.simulationtrainingsystems.com/business/bafa.html. *See also* nos. 73, 83, 97, 199, 202, 207, 210, 245, 270, 282, 324, 343, 359, 371, 372, 373, 374, 376, 377, 380, 384, 387.

STAFF EXCHANGES AND INTERNATIONAL VISITS

404. Aamot, Gordon J. "Business library development in Vladivostok." *Business and Finance Division Bulletin (Special Libraries Association)* 103 (1996): 15–21.
Reports on a project between the University of Washington Business Administration Library in Seattle and the Vladivostok State University library in Russia set up during the development of a new undergraduate business school curriculum in Vladivostok. The project included exchanges between the librarians at the two institutions and the acquisition of materials to support the business curriculum and faculty research. Discusses the benefits of partnership exchanges.

405. ALA joint committee promotes international exchanges. *Library Personnel News* 7, no. 4 (1993): 3–4.
Report on efforts of the American Librarian Association International Relations Committee, working in conjunction with the International Relations Round Table Joint Committee on International Exchange, to set up a database of American and international libraries and librarians interested in international study visits or exchanges.

406. Atkins, David, Anthony D. Smith, and Barbara I. Dewey. "From the Great Smokies to the Mountains of the Moon: U.S. and Ugandan librarians collaborate in a digital world." *Information Technology and Libraries* 24, no. 4 (2005): 192–96.
Describes a partnership relationship between the University of Tennessee Libraries and Makerere University Libraries in Kampala, Uganda. Cooperative projects have included staff exchanges in which librarians taught seminars on various library-related issues, development of interlibrary loan services, and the identification of digitization projects.

407. Bao, Xue-Ming. "The National Science and Technology Library: A Chinese model of collaboration." *Issues in Science and Technology Librarianship*

2005 [online journal]. http://www.istl.org/05-summer/article4.html (October 20, 2008).

Account of a two-week visit by the author and a colleague at Seton Hall University Libraries in South Orange, New Jersey, to the Library of the Chinese Academy of Sciences in Beijing, China. During this time they made presentations on academic library websites and information literacy and met with librarians at major libraries in Beijing. Discussion focuses on developments at the National Science and Technology Library.

408. Barr, Sean P. "Discovering Columbus." *Legal Information Management* 2, no. 1 (2002): 40–45.

Report by a law librarian at the University of Wales Swansea who participated in an exchange with a librarian from the Ohio State University Moritz Law Library in Columbus.

409. Barton, Pamela. "The American Libraries Project." *The Bowker Annual of Library and Book Trade Information* 39 (1994): 94–101.

Describes the American Libraries Project (ALP), sponsored by the United States Information Agency (USIA). ALP brought professional librarians from abroad to the United States for a four-week program. Participants were exposed to a wide variety of libraries and library activities. Aims were to provide a better understanding of the role of American libraries and to foster institutional linkages between libraries. The USIA was disbanded in 1999.

410. Bedinger, Margery. "An exchange year abroad." *Wilson Library Bulletin* 28 (1953): 285–87.

Early article providing general discussion of the benefits and adjustments required for American librarians who participate in an exchange program.

411. Bell, Barbara. "When the rains came to Namibia." *International Leads* 9, no. 2 (1995): 5–7.

Describes experiences of the author, a documents/reference librarian at the College of Wooster, Ohio, as an American Library Association Library Fellow in Africa, where she spent nine months at the University of Namibia in Windhoek. Her project was to establish procedures and guidelines for a national bibliography, based on a legal deposit collection, and to train staff to continue the bibliography. She also visited local publishers and local libraries to encourage them to deposit materials.

412. Bolt, Nancy. "The ABLE Project: American/Bulgarian Library Exchange." *International Leads* 18, no. 4 (2004): 6, 8.

Describes a partnership project sponsored by the Colorado Association of Libraries and the Iowa Resources for International Service. Activities included an exchange program, in which Bulgarian librarians came to the United States for five weeks of training and American librarians went to Bulgaria for two weeks to provide further instruction. Further information about the project is available on the project website: http://cal-webs.org/interestg2.html.

413. Bonta, Bruce. "An American in Peru." *Library Journal* 113, no. 8 (1988): 45–50.
   Provides insights into what American librarians can learn from the practices of librarianship in developing countries such as Peru. Discusses merits of librarian exchange programs; background information on the exchange program between the Escuela de Administración de Negocios para Graduados in Lima, Peru, and Pennsylvania State University; and the commitment of Peruvian libraries to public service.

414. Brisson, Roger. "Spezialbibliotheken in der USA." *Information Outlook* 2, no. 9 (1998): 9–10.
   Report of a lecture on special libraries in the United States given by the author at the Hochschule für Technik, Wirtschaft und Kultur during a six-month assignment as an ALA library fellow in Leipzig, Germany. Notes that the Internet and other technological innovations have changed the face of research and learning in Germany.

415. Brownbridge, Heather. "To Peru on exchange." *Assistant Librarian* 70 (1977): 58–61.
   Discussion of the advantages and challenges of an exchange between developed and developing countries, based on the author's experience as a librarian at the Institute of Development Studies Library at the University of Sussex in Brighton, England, who participated in an exchange with a librarian at the Junta de Acuerdo Library in Lima, Peru.

416. Buckle, Eve. "A fair exchange was no robbery." *FOCUS on International and Comparative Librarianship* 15, no. 2 (1984): 19–20.
   Brief report offering advice to British librarians considering a job exchange. The author, the assistant social sciences librarian at Hatfield Polytechnic (now the University of Hertfordshire) in Hatfield, England, participated in a one-year exchange with a librarian at St. Lawrence College in Kingston, Ontario, Canada.

417. Burnett, Anne, and Laura Martino. "The adventures of two librarians in Buenos Aires, Argentina, and Athens, Georgia, U.S.A." 3–13 in *Law librarians abroad*, edited by Janet Sinder. New York: Haworth Press, 2000. Co-published in *Legal Reference Services Quarterly* 18, no. 3 (2000): 3–13.
   The authors, two law librarians, each spent one month at the other's library, then worked together on projects related to curriculum development in the area of alternative dispute resolution. Discusses the grant that made the projects possible, the authors' comments on their visit to the other country, and outcomes. Also considers ways to become involved in such exchanges, through securing grants and partnering with colleagues. Includes tips for working in a foreign country and comments on costs and benefits for participating libraries.

418. Chalfoun, Eileen. "Beyond the border: Research in Maasailand." *College & Research Libraries News* 68, no. 8 (2007): 522–23.

Report by a librarian from Prescott College in Prescott, Arizona, who accompanied students and three college faculty members engaged in a research project in Kenya over a three-week period.

419. Chepesiuk, Ron. "Field trip to Palestinian libraries yields audience with Arafat." *American Libraries* 29, no. 1 (1998): 40–42.

Report of a field trip to the Gaza Strip and West Bank, Palestine, made by the author and a colleague from the American Library Association International Relations Committee. Describes a discussion of library needs in the area with Palestinian President Yasir Arafat. *See also* Sharma, no. 537.

420. Chepesiuk, Ron. "In times of troubles: Library progress in Northern Ireland." *American Libraries* 28, no. 9 (1997): 56-58.

Report of a 10-day study tour of Northern Ireland undertaken by 14 American librarians and sponsored by the British Council. *See also* Snoeyenbos and Sharma, no. 544.

421. Clarke, Christine. *International exchange for educators and librarians in higher education resource guide.* Syracuse, NY: International Clearinghouse for Information Education and Training, School of Information Studies, Syracuse University, 1989. ERIC document no. ED329269. 42 p.

Provides an overview of international exchange and lists sources of government and intergovernmental information on exchange opportunities for American librarians and educators. Includes information on specific exchange programs and on foreign countries, including those in both the developed and the developing worlds. Much material is dated.

422. Coe, D. Whitney. "Global perspectives: Evaluating collections at Seoul National University Library." *Technicalities: Information Forum for the Library Services Practitioner* 15, no. 4 (1995): 1, 13–14.

Brief report of a visit by the author to Seoul, Korea, where he served as an American Library Association Library Fellow at Seoul National University Library and undertook the task of evaluating the library's collections.

423. Conklin, Curt. "Living and working in Australia." *Law Library Journal* 79, no. 4 (1987): 731–37.

The author, a catalog librarian at Brigham Young University in Provo, Utah, describes his experiences working in Australia for six months while on a sabbatical leave. He spent considerable time at the libraries of Monash University and Melbourne University in Melbourne, the University of New South Wales and Macquarie University in Sydney, and the National Library of Australia in Canberra. His aim was to study the procedures and policies for automated shared cataloging in Australia and to learn how to use Australian legal research materials. Article includes a brief description of his work activities, but focus is on the challenges of moving his family to Australia for the leave period.

424. Cooper, Catherine. "SLA member develops business library collections in Romania." *Interface: The newsletter of the Pacific Northwest Chapter of the Special Libraries Association* 26, no. 3 (1992): 3.

Reports on a visit by a business librarian from the University of Washington in Seattle to Bucharest, as part of a U.S. Agency for International Development project to promote Romania's transition to a market economy.

425. Copeland, Sally. "Library connections abroad." *CSLA Journal* 19, no. 1 (1995): 8–11.

Discusses exchange opportunities for librarians at overseas library schools. Covers settings, how to apply, and steps for getting involved internationally.

426. Cran, Liz. "Exchanging places: Organizing an overseas job swap." *Australian Academic and Research Libraries* 25, no. 3 (1994): 172–75.

The author, a librarian at Charles Sturt University–Mitchell in Bathurst, New South Wales, Australia, participated in a job exchange with a librarian at Durham University in England. Article focuses on the mechanics of setting up an exchange, formal arrangements, and the organization of personal matters such as housing, finances, and transportation.

427. Daniels, Wes. "Living and working in Switzerland." *Law Library Journal* 79, no. 4 (1987): 737–40.

The author, a reference librarian at Harvard Law Library in Cambridge, Massachusetts, describes his experiences on a three-month exchange with the deputy director of the Institut Suisse de Droit Comparé in Lausanne, Switzerland. Discusses his work activities and differences between life in Switzerland and the United States.

428. Davis, Thomas M. "Kent State University, Kent, Ohio, and Aristotle University, Thessaloniki, Greece: An exchange program." 197–204 in *Academic libraries in Greece: The present situation and future prospects*, edited by Dean H. Keller. New York: Haworth Press, 1993.

Provides background on the exchange program between the Ohio and Greek libraries and the types of exchanges undertaken since its inception in 1984. *See also* Salaba, no. 528 and Tolliver, no. 554.

429. Doksansky, Florence K. "Bamberg to Brown: A library exchange." *College and Research Libraries News* 48, no. 6 (1987): 338–43.

Discusses the merits and drawbacks of an overseas exchange. Based on the experiences of Regina Krepulat, a librarian at the Universität Bamberg in Bamberg, Germany, who spent three months at Brown University in Providence, Rhode Island. *See also* Yealy, no. 571.

430. Donley, Mary A. "Mexico journal: An exchange librarian reports." *Texas Library Journal* 4, no. 1 (1998): 48.

Brief review of the two-week visit by a librarian from the Fort Bend County Library system in Texas to a number of public and academic libraries in the Mexico City area.

431. Dorman, David. "A globetrotter librarian discusses her role in a changing world." *American Libraries* 31, no. 9 (2000): 48–50.

Reports on an interview with Marianna Tax Choldin, director of the Mortenson Center for International Library Programs at the University of Illinois, Urbana–Champaign. Discusses work of the center, which has brought 450 librarians from 74 countries to the United States, and offers insights about how libraries and collections differ around the world and about her experiences with librarians from other countries and cultures. Also outlines her involvement with the Soros Foundations' Network Library Program and with the International Federation of Library Associations. Helpful in providing cross-cultural understanding.

432. Dowling, Margaret. "The exchange experience: A British perspective." *College and Research Libraries News* 43, no. 10 (1982): 350–51.

Brief review of the author's experiences as an Edinburgh University librarian who participated in a one-year job exchange with a librarian from Indiana University in Bloomington. *See also* Griffin, no. 450.

433. Downs, Florence. "Exchange positions." *Wilson Library Bulletin* 15, no. 8 (1941): 648.

Early article promoting the benefits for librarians to undertake positions in other countries.

434. Duffy, Paula. "An American librarian visits overseas: A Czech experience." *International Leads* 12, no. 2 (1998): 7–8

Discusses a visit by the author, the documents and maps librarian at the Montana State University Library in Billings, to the Czech Republic, where she visited a number of different types of libraries. Describes briefly the Czech Management Center Library in Celekovice, one of the premier business libraries in the country; the National Library in Klementinum, Prague; and several monastery libraries.

435. Dyer, E. R., and D. Layzell Ward. "The international role of library consultants." *International Library Review* 14, no. 4 (1982): 379–90.

General overview of library consultants and their work and their role in the development of information services in the developing world. Discusses the definition of a consultant, recruitment and employment, and the consulting process. Criteria of the American Library Association International Relations Committee for the selection of consultants to serve abroad are appended.

436. Elliott, Carol. "A Library Fellow in equatorial West Africa." *Information Outlook* 2, no. 7 (1998): 8.

The author, a reference librarian at the University of Arizona College of Law Library in Tucson, reflects on her ten-month stay in Ghana, where she provided law librarianship training as a United States Information Service/American Library Association Library Fellow.

437. Erickson, Carol. "Library and archival programs with Central and Eastern Europe and the former Soviet Union." *International Leads* 7, no. 4 (1993): 4–5.

Brief report by the senior program officer for Library and Archival Programs at the International Research & Exchanges Board (IREX) in Washington, D.C. Discusses IREX initiatives, including administering research exchange programs with the countries of Central and Eastern Europe and the former Soviet Union.

438. Fardon, Chris. "Negotiating new horizons: The job exchange alternative." *Library Association Record* 92, no. 12 (1990): 921–22.

Brief discussion of the mechanics of job exchanges, including motivation, approaching your employer, finding a partner, setting the scene, and money matters.

439. Flake, Donna. "Planning a transatlantic job exchange." *North Carolina Libraries* 44, no. 2 (1986): 84–86.

Describes the experiences of the author, an American librarian in a health sciences library, in setting up a six-month exchange with a medical librarian from England. Provides sources of information to make such exchanges easier for others to arrange.

440. Flake, Donna. "A transcontinental job exchange." *Health Libraries Review* 2, no. 3 (1985): 112–20.

Discusses a six-month staff exchange between an English and a U.S. medical librarian. Participants exchanged jobs, houses, and cars, but not salaries. Considers the expectations and benefits of the exchange from the points of view of the exchange partners and library directors.

441. Foster, Connie. "Looking back and across the pond: 1980." *Kentucky Libraries* 63, no. 1 (1999): 7–9.

Reprint of an article from the fall 1980 issue of Kentucky libraries. See: Warth, no. 558.

442. Frail, Kim, and Chantal St. Louis. "Des montagnes rocheuses au Saint-Laurent: L'expérience d'une bibliothécaire albertaine au Québec." *Argus* 34, no. 1 (2005): 23–26.

Report of the experiences of a librarian from the University of Alberta Libraries in Edmonton who spent a month at Laval University in Ste-Foy, Quebec. During her stay she observed operations and participated in a number of library-related activities.

443. Frantz, Paul. "A library fellow in Greece." *Information Technology and Libraries* 15, no. 2 (1996): 122–26.

Describes the differences in the management and cultural styles between the author's employer, the University of Oregon in Eugene, and the Library of the Greek Parliament in Athens, where he worked for six months as an American Library Association Library Fellow. Also discusses projects undertaken, which included the development of a reference collection and catalog.

444. Fudan-Appalachian library exchange program. *College & Research Libraries News* 69, no. 7 (2008): 380–81.

Brief report of an agreement for future exchange of librarians between the Appalachian State University in Boone, North Carolina, and Fudan University Library in Shanghai, China. Aim of the program is to facilitate information sharing on culture and on library issues. The arrangement, begun in August 2009 and scheduled to continue for a minimum of four years, will allow a librarian from each university to be in residence at the partner university for one to six months per year.

445. Fulton, Gloria. "Networking not working in Yugoslavia." *International Leads* 6, no. 1 (1992): 4–5, 10.

The author served as an American Library Association Library Fellow at the City Library of Belgrade, Yugoslavia, during a time of political turmoil in the country. Her position description was to help set up the networking foundations for the new National Library of Serbia, teach database searching in the new library school at the University of Belgrade, and set up an American Studies collection. However, due to the political climate, this work proved difficult.

446. Fulton, Gloria. "Women librarians in Yugoslavia." *WLW Journal* 16, no. 1 (1993): 2–4.

Describes the situation of female librarians in Yugoslavia during a period of civil war. Based on the author's experiences as an American Library Association Library Fellow in Belgrade. *See also* no. 445.

447. Gordon, Ross. "Vladivostok libraries." *Feliciter* 6 (2000): 310–12.

Brief report of a short visit to Vladivostok, Russia, by a librarian from the Library of Parliament in Ottawa, Ontario. During his time there, the author attended a conference on library automation, gave several lectures to library staff, and served as a volunteer consultant to the two main universities in the region, Vladivostok State University of Economics and the Far Eastern State University.

448. Graubart, Marilyn. "Orientation sessions in Israeli academic libraries." *Research Strategies* 13, no. 3 (1995): 165–75.

Describes orientation programs offered at seven Israeli university libraries. Discusses implications for library orientations at the University of Missouri–Kansas City, including utilizing student tour guides and improving the learning environment for international students. A checklist of questions for interviews with Israeli librarians is appended. Library visits were undertaken while the author was on a three-month development leave.

449. Greey, Kathy, and Rosalind Wang. "The Oregon Fujian library connection." *OLA Quarterly (Oregon Library Association)* 6, no. 4 (2000): 14–15, 20.

Provides background on the history of relations between Oregon State Library in Salem and Fujian Province, People's Republic of China, noting that these can be traced back to 1984. Reports on a 1987 visit by Wang, education librarian at Portland State University, to the Fujian Provincial Library in Fuzhou. While in China she conducted a week-long workshop for librarians, library workers, and information retrieval officers of the Fujian Province. Subsequently Wang assisted in the establishment of the sister library relationship between Oregon State Library and Fujian Provincial Library. This led to further exchanges of both books and staff between the two institutions. *See also* Siegel, no. 535; Shaoning and Zhiminmg, no. 536.

450. Griffin, Larry W. "The exchange experience: An American perspective." *College and Research Libraries News* 43, no. 9 (1982): 310–12.

Brief review of the author's experiences as a librarian at Indiana University in Bloomington who participated in a one-year job exchange with a librarian from Edinburgh University in Scotland. *See also* Dowling, no. 432.

451. Grimes, David. "Turning corners: American librarians in post-Soviet Russia." *American Libraries* 34, no. 9 (2003): 56–58.

Describes the author's participation in an eighty-day Information Professionals-in-Residence (I-PIR) exchange program. He was the first public librarian (Queens Borough Public Library in New York) to participate in the I-PIR program, designed to provide training staff for the American Corners in Russia Program, an initiative begun in 2000 to expand the American Centers project throughout Russia. The project aims to help increase mutual understanding between Russia and the United States by making information about America available in a variety of formats. Librarians involved travel to five cities and spend two weeks in each location. Activities include in-service training sessions, visits and talks for library professionals and students, facilitation of English conversation groups, purchasing of equipment, extensive contact with library users, and project promotion in local news media. *See also* Johnson, no. 472.

452. Griner, Lily, Patricia Herron, and Heleni Pedersoli. "Sister libraries partners: Tecnologico de Monterrey, Mexico and University of Maryland–College Park." *College & Research Libraries News* 68, no. 9 (2007): 566–68, 589.

Discusses collaboration between academic libraries in Mexico and Maryland. Activities included a symposium dealing with library user education issues held in Monterrey in April 2005, in which four American librarians participated. Later that year a formalized partnership agreement was signed, and in both 2006 and 2007 two Mexican librarians visited the University of Maryland. Benefits to both institutions are outlined.

453. Hall, Bonlyn. "A Virginia librarian in Turkey." *Virginia Libraries* 42, no. 4 (1996): 16–17.

Describes the experiences of the author, music librarian at the University of Richmond, while working for three months as a visiting librarian at Bilkent University in Ankara, Turkey. Her job was to serve as a consultant, reviewing the university's music collection and recommending improvements. She also had the opportunity to visit a number of other libraries.

454. Hampel, Elisabeth. "The Riverside exchange." *College & Research Libraries News* 51, no. 2 (1990): 120–22.

Describes a six-month job exchange undertaken by the author, a cataloger at Regensburg University library in West Germany, and a librarian from the University of California, Riverside. Discusses how the exchange was set up and projects undertaken in California. *See also* Hutchinson, no. 465.

455. Hannon, Michael. "Report on Canadian exchange attachment." *FOCUS on International and Comparative Librarianship* 14, no. 3 (1983): 30–31.

Brief report of the experiences of the author, the deputy librarian of the University of Liverpool in England, as he participated in a one-month exchange with a librarian from the University of Calgary in Alberta. Focuses in particular on differences in library budgets, management structures, professional staff (Canadian librarians placed a strong emphasis on collegiality), and progress in automation.

456. Hannon, Michael. "Staff exchanges—new directions for academic libraries?" *Librarian Career Development* 5, no. 4 (1997): 124–27.

Discusses international academic library staff exchanges from three perspectives: the author's personal experience as an exchange participant, as director of a research library which hosted six exchanges, and as chairman of the Consortium of University Research Libraries (CURL) Staff Development Group in England, which was setting up a new intra-CURL staff exchange program beginning in 1997–1998. Describes a model of short, project-based reciprocal exchanges.

457. Hanson, Terry. "The mechanics of international job exchanges." *Library Association Record* 91, no. 4 (1989): 216–20.

Describes the experience of the author, a subject librarian at Portsmouth Polytechnic in England, who participated in a job exchange with a reference librarian at the University of Connecticut in Storrs. Discusses reasons for doing an exchange, finding the right exchange partner, making contact through LIBEX, and financial matters. Also highlights observations made during the exchange and differences between the exchange and home institutions.

458. Hary, Nicoletta M. "The University of Dayton Library hosting of an International Fellow." *Catholic Library World* 65, no. 2 (1994): 40–41.

Outlines the American Library Association's Library Fellows Program and describes the experiences of a Romanian librarian at the University of Dayton in Ohio.

459. Hary, Nicoletta Mattioli, and Francesca L. Hary. "Hosting an international librarian." *College & Research Libraries News* 56, no. 3 (1995): 162–64

Discusses the American Library Association's Library Fellows Program, begun in 1993, and offers suggestions for hosting an exchange visitor to the United States from another country. Considers training, publicity, scheduling, housing and accommodations, acculturation concerns, responsibility of the mentor, and debriefing.

460. Hensley, Randall, and Steve Pritchard. "California to Cardiff: Cardiff to California—A success story." *Library Association Medical Health and Welfare Libraries Group Newsletter* 15 (1982): 32–37.

Transcript of interviews with two librarians who participated in a six-month job exchange: a reference librarian at California State University, Chico and the Reader Services Librarian at the Welsh National School of Medicine in Cardiff, Wales. Discusses reasons for wanting an exchange, arrangements, domestic details, advice to others planning an exchange, and the value of the exchange.

461. Hindal, Sidsel. "Experiences of job exchange." Paper presented at the World Library and Information Congress: 71st IFLA General Conference and Council, Oslo, Norway, 14–18 August 2005. http://www.ifla.org/IV/ifla71/papers/200eHindal .pdf (September 1, 2008).

The author, an advisor for the Norwegian Archive, Library and Museum Authority, presents his views on the advantages of participation in international projects. Based on personal experiences as a result of various international activities undertaken over the previous five years, including training in Luxembourg and Denmark, a study tour to libraries in Singapore and Australia, and involvement in several European Union–funded library projects. Major benefits outlined are inspiration, network building, knowledge sharing, capacity building, and personal development.

462. Holmes, Jean. *Job exchanges in librarianship.* Leeds: Leeds Polytechnic School of Librarianship, 1986. 43, [20] p.

Reports on a British-based study of the concept of job exchange within librarianship. Also considers the potential of job exchange schemes as a solution to professional stagnation at a time when there was little opportunity within the profession for job mobility or advancement. Based on data collected through semi-structured interviews with librarians who had participated in job exchanges and management representatives from several local libraries (university library, polytechnic library, public library). Discusses both benefits and problems of exchanges and practicalities of organizing exchanges. Concludes that exchanges provide job stimulation and new learning experiences for participants; they forge links between libraries and improve mutual cooperation; and they improve morale, both on the part of the exchange partners and the staff working with them.

463. Hooker, Meg. "Luton to Washington, D.C.—Another success story." *Library Association and Medical Health and Welfare Libraries Group Newsletter* 16 (1982): 13–15.

Describes the experiences of a medical librarian from Bedfordshire, England, who participated in an two-month job exchange with a medical librarian in Washington, D.C. Discusses the arrangements for the exchange and presents impressions of the operation of American medical libraries. *See also* Knobloch, no. 484.

464. Hubbard, Marlis. "Exploring the sabbatical or other leave as a means of energizing a career." *Library Trends* 50, no. 4 (2002): 603–13.

Challenges librarians to create midlife leaves to inspire professional growth and renewal and help define future career directions. Presents a framework for a successful leave program, based on experiences of librarians at Concordia University in Montreal. Offers examples of various options, including internships, exchanges, conferences, community service, travel, and research.

465. Hutchinson, Heidi. "The Regensburg exchange." *College & Research Libraries News* 51, no. 2 (1990): 116–18, 120.

Describes a six-month job exchange undertaken by the author, a cataloger from the University of California, Riverside, and a librarian at the University Library in Regensburg, West Germany. Discusses how the exchange was set up, the library in Regensburg, and projects undertaken. *See also* Hampel, no. 454.

466. Hutton, Cate. "High-altitude librarianship: The adventures of an ALA Fellow in Tibet." *Information Technology and Libraries* 16, no. 1 (1997): 30–33.

Description of the experiences of a librarian from the University of California in Oakland who taught fundamental library science to the staff of the Tibet Autonomous Region Library in Lhasa as part of a nine-month American Library Association Library Fellow program. Part of the program involved developing a Tibetan language vocabulary for library professionals. Outlines the challenges of providing library and information resources in regions with rural and largely illiterate populations. *See also* no. 467.

467. Hutton, Cate. "How I came to be in Tibet." *International Leads* 9, no. 1 (1995): 1–4.

Similar to no. 466 above. Describes the author's experiences as an American Library Association Library Fellow at the Tibet Autonomous Region Library in Lhasa.

468. Hytnen, Phyllis. "Toward sustainable library development: The Inform the World Librarian Volunteer Program." *International Leads* 14, no. 4 (2000): 1–2.

Describes a program that placed volunteer librarians in rural African libraries. Volunteers lived in the communities and worked with local librarians to provide assistance and training. The ITW was sponsored by the World Library Partnership (WLP), a nonprofit organization that promoted literacy, learning, and access to information in developing countries. Article briefly describes experiences of volunteers in Zimbabwe and South Africa. WLP was suspended in 2004 due to a lack of funding. *See also* Mizzy, no. 499.

469. Intner, Sheila S. "Visiting libraries in the republic of Georgia." *Technicalities* 24, no. 4 (2004): 1, 8–10.

Report of a two-week visit to Tbilisi, Georgia, in the former Soviet Union, by a library science professor at Mount Holyoke College in South Hadley, Massachusetts. The tour was sponsored by the Fulbright Senior Specialist Program. Describes the Georgian library environment and the situation at several academic libraries and the National Library of Georgia. Author also gave a seminar at the Georgian Academy of Sciences Central Scientific Library. Notes the benefits achieved in developing relationships and the possibilities for future cooperative activities.

470. Jannetta, Victoria. "Trading places: Library placement and exchange schemes." *The Law Librarian* 28, no. 2 (1997): 70–72.

General discussion of librarian work placements and exchanges. Discusses values of participating, existing schemes in the United Kingdom, other people's experiences, and points to consider when organizing a job exchange. Also provides a contact list for groups organizing exchanges.

471. Jeffries, John. "Exchange program with the American Association of Law Libraries." *Law Librarian* 10, no. 1 (1979): 17.

Brief description of the benefits and problems of exchanges between members of the American Association of Law Libraries (AALL) and the British and Irish Association of Law Librarians (BIALL).

472. Johnson, Eric. "The American Corners program in Russia: Building successful partnerships." *International Leads* 16, no. 4 (2002): 1–2, 8.

Discusses the American Corners and Centers project, which establishes libraries in cities throughout Russia, with English-speaking bilingual librarians and collections focusing on the United States and its way of life. The program is operated by the U.S. Department of State and the U.S. Embassy in Moscow. Article outlines the origin of the program, the locations of libraries, sponsors, and activities. *See also* Grimes, no. 451.

473. Katzenstein, Lisa. "Lessons learned by an exchange librarian in Guadalajara." *Texas Library Journal* 75, no. 2 (1999): 74–76.

Account of a two-week "adventure in Mexican librarianship" in which the author, a librarian at Dallas Public Library, visited a private elementary school library, three public libraries, and nine libraries either run by a university or affiliated with an institution of higher learning in Guadalajara, Mexico. Briefly describes the libraries visited, then discusses issues facing Mexican libraries and librarians and lessons learned.

474. Keane, Nancy J. "Library exchanges in the UK: Considerations when arranging international exchanges." *International Library Review* 21, no. 3 (1989): 441–42.

Briefly describes types of library exchange programs and considers professional and personal issues involved, such as job requirements, salary, living arrangements, and expenses.

475. Keane, Nancy J. "Need a change? Try an exchange." *College and Research Libraries News* 48, no. 10 (1987): 634–37.

Overview of the author's experiences in arranging an exchange between herself, a librarian at the University of Vermont, and a librarian at Trinity College in Dublin, Ireland.

476. Kear, Robin. "International librarianship: Getting there from here." *International Leads* 18, no. 4 (2004): 5, 7.

Discusses working in foreign countries. Includes sections on skills that will help you get a job, types of jobs and job experiences, things to keep in mind when living abroad, and sources of job listings.

477. Kern, Kris. "East meets west in Paris." *OLA Quarterly (Oregon Library Association)* 7, no. 1 (2001): 10–12.

Report of a visit to the library at the Interuniversity Library of Oriental Languages in Paris by an Arabic cataloger at Portland State University in Oregon. Undertaken while the author was visiting Paris on vacation.

478. Kidd, Tony. "International library staff exchanges: How do you organize them and do they do any good?" *Librarian Career Development* 3, no. 1 (1995): 9–13.

Discusses the author's personal experiences and reports on findings from a questionnaire survey of academic library directors and exchange participants from the United Kingdom/Ireland. Discusses such issues as motivation, arranging an exchange, financial aspects, and career development impact. *See also* no. 479.

479. Kidd, Tony, and Karen Roughton. "International staff exchanges for academic libraries." *Journal of Academic Librarianship* 20, no. 6 (1994): 295–99.

Notes that library staff exchanges were becoming more common as a result of internationalization efforts at many universities. Reports on a survey of academic library directors and exchange participants from the United Kingdom/Ireland and the United States/Canada regarding the importance of internationalization. Considers personal characteristics of exchange participants, exchange arrangements, position titles and academic ranks, professional benefits for staff, promotion prospects, motivation, and disadvantages and drawbacks. *See also* no. 478.

480. Kile, Barbara. "The Library/Book Fellow Program—A report." *International Leads* 4, no. 3 (1990): 2–3.

Reflects on the experiences of the author, a librarian at Rice University in Houston, Texas, as an American Library Association Library Fellow at the National Central Library in Taipei, Taiwan. Her job was to assist the staff in developing and organizing their U.S. government publications and to provide staff training in the management and use of government documents.

481. Kipp, Laurence J. "The broadening effect of travelers: A clarion call for action." *Wilson Library Bulletin* 32 (1958): 714.

Early article advocating more support from library organizations for sponsorship of American librarians to go abroad.

482. Knauth, Kristin. "East greets west: 1996 Soros interns arrive at library." *Library of Congress Information Bulletin* 55 (1996): 133.

Describes the three-month visit in the United States of eleven librarians from Eastern Europe and the former Soviet Union as interns in the Soros Foundations–Library of Congress Librarian Intern Program. This program, which superseded the Visiting Fellows Program, was designed to train participants to promote open information access in their home countries.

483. Kniffel, Leonard. "Abandoning overseas fellowships is penny wise, pound foolish." *American Libraries* 28, no. 4 (1997): 30

Editorial expressing concerns over the demise of the American Library Association–administered Library Fellows program, which arranged international exchanges for American librarians.

484. Knobloch, Shirley S. "British–U.S. job exchange." *Bulletin of the Medical Library Association* 73, no. 3 (1985): 285–86.

Describes the experiences of a medical librarian from Washington, D.C., who participated in a two-month job exchange with a medical librarian in Bedfordshire, England. Discusses the settings and operation of the British library. *See also* Hooker, no. 463.

485. Krieger, Michael T. "The context of an American, Catholic, academic library in modern India." *Catholic Library World* 71, no. 3 (2001): 167–75.

An undergraduate academic program in Bangalore, India, was set up in 1997 by the University of Dayton in Ohio. The program was designed to serve a specialized student body of Indian students studying to become religious brothers in the Marianist religious order. In 1998 a librarian was sent to organize a collection and build a library. Article describes the founding of the library and steps involved in building the initial collection. Also discusses the historical context of academic libraries in India and the role of American and Catholic participation in Indian colleges.

486. Laundy, Katherine. "Briefly stepping into another's shoes." *Canadian Library Journal* 43 (1986): 156–60.

Describes a six-month exchange between the author, a librarian at the National Library of Canada in Ottawa, Ontario, and a librarian at the National Library of Wales in Aberystwyth. Discusses how the exchange was arranged and the author's work in the new position and offers tips to consider when planning a job exchange. *See also* Till, no. 552.

487. Lavin, Michael R. "Business libraries in Poland." *Business and Finance Bulletin (Special Libraries Association)* 101 (1996): 15–20.

Report on the state of libraries and library education in Poland. The author, from the State University of New York in Buffalo, traveled to Krakow for two weeks to deliver a series of lectures on American business librarianship at the Jagiellonian University's Department of Library and Information Science. He also had the opportunity to visit the Krakow Academy of Economics Main Library, the Jagiellonian Institute of Economics Library, the Information Department at Jagiellonian University, and the Main Library of the Krakow County Library System.

488. Lees, Ann. "From King's to North Rhine-Westphalia: An exchange through LIBEX." *Focus on International and Comparative Librarianship* 19, no. 1 (1988): 10–11.

Brief account of a six-month exchange between a librarian at King's College, London (England), and a librarian at the university library in Bielefeld, North-rhine-Westphalia, Germany.

489. Little, Sherry K. "Estonia journal: An ALA Fellow in Tallinn." *Texas Library Journal* 74, no. 2 (1998): 90–91.

Report of the author, a doctoral student in library and information studies at Texas Woman's University in Denton, who spent three and a half months as an American Library Association Library Fellow in Estonia. During her time there she presented training workshops, visited academic libraries, lectured on librarianship and library education in the United States and on the role of the public library in a democracy, and worked as a consultant in various library departments on library automation and workflow.

490. Lorkovic, Tanja. "Library consultant in Indonesia." *College and Research Libraries News* 47, no. 10 (1986): 636–40.

The author, then head of cataloging at the University of Iowa in Iowa City, describes her experiences during a year of consulting internationally at the University of North Sumatra in Medan, Indonesia. She served as a library specialist on a development team that was set up to upgrade academic programs, curriculum, teaching management, library service, and physical facilities at the university. Discusses her training for the job and terms of reference for her consultancy, then describes the library facilities and upgrading work undertaken when cataloging and organizing a collection of seven thousand new volumes.

491. Lorkovic, Tanja. "Revolution not over for Eastern European libraries." *American Libraries* 21, no. 8 (1990): 712–13.

Yale University Library's curator of Slavic and East European collections outlines a fact-finding trip to national, university, and academy of sciences libraries and to export/import companies and publishers in Czechoslovakia, Poland, Hungary, Bulgaria, and Yugoslavia.

492. Marra, Toshie. "Internship at Otani University Library and conferences/ meetings related to libraries in Japan." *Journal of East Asian Libraries* 115 (1998): 13–21.

Report of a one-year internship in which the author, a librarian at the University of California, Los Angeles, worked at Otani University Library in Kyoto, Japan. Discusses activities as a library cataloger of old and rare Japanese books, attendance at various conferences and workshops, and participation in study groups and meetings.

493. Max, Patrick. "Just like the movies: University libraries in the Republic of Ireland." *Journal of Academic Librarianship* 24, no. 1 (1998): 69–72.

Describes the experiences of the author, director of the library at Castleton State College in Castleton, Vermont, during a research trip to libraries in Ireland. Considers cultural and professional differences between American and Irish librarians, in particular, the Irish acceptance of state censorship.

494. McBride, Kelly. "A Virginia librarian in Ulster." *Virginia Libraries* 44, no. 2 (1998): 13–15.

Report of a visit by twelve American librarians and one archivist who participated in a ten-day study tour of Northern Ireland sponsored by the British Council. The group visited several public libraries, museum libraries, and the libraries of Queen's University (Belfast and Armagh) and the University of Ulster.

495. McChesney, David L. "Trading places: Planning an international job exchange." *College and Research Libraries News* 50, no. 10 (1989): 919–22.

Discusses a job exchange between the author, a reference librarian at the University of Connecticut in Storrs, and a social sciences librarian at Portsmouth Polytechnic in England. Considers reasons for undertaking an exchange, finding a partner, finances, and communication.

496. McCook, Kathleen de la Peña, Barbara J. Ford, and Kate Lippincott (eds.). *Libraries: Global reach, local touch.* Chicago: American Library Association, 1998. v, 256 p.

Book on international librarianship, with focus on libraries in particular countries or regions around the world. Useful in providing insights into library history and current conditions for librarians preparing to visit or seeking areas in which their skills could be best utilized. Also includes general chapters on issues such as information technology in developing countries, freedom of expression, and women in librarianship. Includes a fourteen-page bibliography.

497. McDermand, Bob, and Jeff Paul. "Job exchange: Two perspectives. A self-interview." *Library Journal* 113, no. 11 (1988): 35–37.

Brief report of a one-year exchange between McDermand, then co-ordinator of public services at Plymouth State College of the University of New Hampshire library system, and Paul, director of media services at San Jose State University library.

498. Miller, Rush G., and Judith Sessions. "A visit to academic libraries in China." *Wilson Library Bulletin* 66, no. 9 (1992): 50–52, 141.

Reports on a 1991 visit by five American librarians to China as part of a program to exchange library administration ideas. Describes experiences at academic libraries in Tianjin, Beijing, and Wuhan. *See also* Rader, no. 522.

499. Mizzy, Danianne. "World Library Partnership." *College & Research Libraries News* 64, no. 11 (2003): 708–9.

Brief report on experiences of three academic librarian volunteers who participated in a four-week World Library Skills Exchange program sponsored by World Library partnership, a nonprofit organization whose mission was to advocate for sustainable, community-based libraries in developing areas of the world. The librarians were paired with local librarians in Central America and South Africa. While placements were not in academic libraries, the participants were able to experience life in another culture while using their skills to further local development projects. The WLP organization suspended operations in 2004 due to lack of funding, but similar kinds of volunteer opportunities are available through a number of church and international aid organizations. *See also* Hytnen, no. 468.

500. Mood, Terry Ann. "An exchange in England." *Reference Services Review* 13 (1985): 9–12.

Describes a three-month exchange between the author, a librarian at the University of Colorado at Denver, and a librarian from the University of Reading in England. Discusses how the exchange was set up, financial considerations, documents required, and experiences while touring various libraries in England.

501. Morton, Marilyn. "Three summers in a row: A work exchange to Australia during the English winter." *Impact: Journal of the Career Development Group* 9, no. 1 (2006): 19–20.

Presents insights of an information assistant at Sheffield Hallam University in Sheffield, England, regarding her participation in a job exchange with a library technician at Southern Cross University in New South Wales, Australia.

502. Myers, Ardie. "LC gets its first exchange librarian: LC and State Library of New South Wales participate." *Library of Congress Information Bulletin* 53, no. 16 (1994): 117.

Brief account of the activities of a librarian from the State Library of New South Wales in Sydney, Australia (Martin Hargous) who participated in a one-year exchange with a librarian from the Library of Congress in Washington, D.C. *See also* no. 503.

503. Myers, Ardie. "Trading places: LC employee returns from Australian exchange." *Library of Congress Information Bulletin* 53, no. 16 (1995): 372–73.

Brief account of the experience of a librarian at the Library of Congress in Washington, D.C. (Art Emerson), who participated in a one-year exchange with a librarian from the State Library of New South Wales in Sydney, Australia. *See also* no. 502.

504. Natsis, James J. "Bridging the technological, language, and cultural gap: Partnering with an academic library in francophone Africa." 157–68 in *The impact of technology on Asian, African, and Middle Eastern library collections,* edited by R. N. Sharma. Lanham, MD: The Scarecrow Press, 2006.

Report of a partnership between the libraries at West Virginia State University in Charleston and the Université Nationale du Bénin in Benin, West Africa. Discusses funding for the three-year project (1999–2002), the universities involved, and activities undertaken, which included exchange visits by librarians (two from WVSU and three from UNB). Project objectives included promoting leadership development and creating a public archive for Benin. Includes an evaluation of the project, which was quite positive. *See also* Sharma and Bess, no. 538.

505. Neff, William B. "La Bibliothéconomie en France: An exchange librarian's report." *College and Research Libraries News* 47, no. 4 (1986): 259–61.

Describes the author's experiences during a one-year exchange at the Conservatoire National des Arts et Métiers in Paris under a program co-sponsored by the Association of College and Research Libraries, the Franco-American Commission for Educational Exchange, and the Direction des Bibliothèques, des Musées et de l'Information Scientifique et Technique, a branch of the French Ministry of Education. *See also* Pailley-Katz, no. 510.

506. Nofsinger, Mary M. "Academic libraries in Sichuan province: An American librarian's perspective." *Journal of Academic Librarianship* 13, no. 6 (1988): 353–56.

Describes an exchange program between academic libraries in Sichuan Province, People's Republic of China, and Washington State University Libraries, then outlines the Chinese approach to academic librarianship in six major areas: management and personnel, staff education and training, access and circulation, automation, reference services, collection development and censorship.

507. North American librarians delegation to the People's Republic of China. *Committee on East Asian Libraries Bulletin* 105 (1995): 16–21.

The delegation, made up of eight American librarians working with Chinese collections from various academic libraries, undertook a ten-day trip to China set up by a representative of the Chinese book trade industry. Report briefly outlines visits made in Beijing (the China National Publishing Industry Trading

Corporation, the China No. 1 Historical Archives, the National Library of China, Peking University Library, the China International Book Trading Corporation) and Shanghai (Shanghai Book Traders, Shanghai Chinese Classics Publishing House).

508. Nystrom, Kathleen A. "What's it like being a librarian in Africa?" *Show-Me Libraries* 45, no. 3/4 (1994): 3–8.

Discusses the experiences of the author, the manager of cataloging at St. Louis Public Library in Missouri, as an American Library Association Library Fellow working at the University of Malawi, where she spent eleven months. Activities included helping initiate the automation of cataloging, training staff in cataloging, and advising on issues of workflow and computer room arrangements. Article describes the country and the project.

509. Oberlander, Mary, and Cyril Oberlander. "Books under glass: The Bibliothèque Nationale de France." *OLA Quarterly (Oregon Library Association)* 7, no. 1 (2001): 4–6, 23.

Report of a tour of the library at the Bibliothèque Nationale de France in Paris by two Portland, Oregon, librarians, one from Linfield College and one from Portland State University. Undertaken while the authors were visiting Paris on vacation.

510. Pailley-Katz, Arlette. "Les relations internationales de la DBMIST: Échanges de personnels." *Bulletin d'Informations de l'association des Bibliothécaires français* 132 (1986): 7–8.

Brief outline of international activities sponsored by the French Ministry of National Education's Direction des Bibliothèques, des Musées et de l'Information Scientifique et Technique (DBMIST), created in 1981 and disbanded in 1988. Among the programs introduced by DBMIST were staff visits to international libraries, promotion of international professional contacts, and exchanges between French and American academic library administrators. *See also* Neff, no. 505.

511. Parker, J. Stephen (ed.). *Information consultants in action.* London: Mansell, 1986. xi, 258 p.

Collection of essays dealing with the development of international consultancy services in the library and information field. Includes sections on cross-cultural work, problems faced by foreign consultants in adapting to conditions in another country, library and information consultancy in general, and more specific examples of information consultancy projects.

512. Parker, J. Stephen (ed.). "The overseas library consultant." *Library Review* 28, no. 4 (1979): 214–25.

Provides an overview of the history of overseas library consultancy, which began on a regular basis in the years between World Wars I and II under the auspices of the Carnegie Corporation of New York. Also considers subsequent developments after World War II, and the work of agencies such as the British

Council, U.S. government aid agencies, and agencies of the United Nations, in particular UNESCO.

513. Pastine, Maureen. "An international library exchange in China." *College and Research Libraries News* 47, no. 6 (1986): 392–99.

Reports on a 1985 visit by a delegation of twenty-four American librarians to the People's Republic of China, arranged through China–U.S. Scientific Exchanges. Participants visited libraries in five major Chinese cities: Beijing, Nanjing, Wuhan, Changsha, and Guangzhou.

514. Patel, Jashu, and Nazar Tiwana. "International cultural exchange of librarians." *Herald of Library Science* 28, no. 4 (1989): 334–37.

Proposal outlining the need for international exchanges, their objectives, and problems. Presents a model for a book development program and a librarian exchange program, designed to be submitted to the Indian Library Association.

515. Peters, Klaus, Hannelore Rader, and Alice Reviere Smith. "The Cologne-Cleveland librarian exchange." *College & Research Libraries* News 6 (1992): 390–91, 393.

Report on the experiences of two librarians, one from the University of Cologne in Cologne, Germany, and the other from Cleveland State University in Cleveland, Ohio, who participated in a one-month job exchange. Describes their activities and compares the two libraries.

516. Picot, Nicole. "Stage dans des bibliothèques." *Art Libraries Journal* 14, no. 1 (1989): 4–8.

Describes the experiences of an art librarian at the Bibliothèque publique d'information in Paris who spent two weeks in London (England), where she visited the National Art Library of the Victoria and Albert Museum and other art libraries in the city. *See also* Varley, no. 557.

517. Popa, Opritsa, and Sandra J. Lamprecht. "Romania and United States library connections." *Advances in Librarianship* 18 (1994): 189–213.

Provides an overview of the state of Romanian libraries following the fall of the Ceausescu regime. Discusses deteriorating collections, antiquated equipment, inadequate buildings, and poor working conditions, then outlines how libraries in the United States and Europe responded. Efforts included setting up programs for study visits and exchanges, Fulbright assignments, technology transfer, preservation, and joint colloquia.

518. Powell, Faye. "A librarian's passage to India." *OLA Quarterly (Oregon Library Association)* 6, no. 4 (2000): 2–4.

The author, social sciences librarian at Portland State University in Portland, Oregon, reports on her experiences in 1989 as an American Library Association Library Fellow at the American Studies Research Centre on the campus of Osmania University in Hyderabad, India. Her library projects included assessing the center's social sciences collection and making recommendations for purchases to bring it up to the graduate level. She also had the opportunity to attend the All-India Library Conference. She returned to India in 1996 and was asked to make presentations to Indian librarians and library science students at three north Indian universities on information technology used in American libraries. At this time she also traveled to Tibet and toured the Tibetan Library. In 1999 she was invited to give a paper at the International Conference on Educational Culture in the 21st Century at Guwahati, Assam, in northeastern India.

519. Powell, Ronald R. "Report on Russia project—Moscow, 1996." *Journal of Education for Library and Information Science* 38, no. 2 (1997): 161–64.

Report of a visit by the author, a professor of library science at Wayne State University in Detroit, Michigan, to the Moscow State University of Culture in Khimki. Describes the university and his activities there, which included giving lectures, meeting with faculty members and university officials, and visiting other libraries.

520. Pupeliene, Janina. "The Klaipeda University Library in Lithuania: An essay by the Washington State University Libraries' Library Fellow." 67–73 in *Coming of age in reference services: A case history of the Washington State University Libraries,* edited by Christy Zlatos. New York: Haworth Press, 1999. Co-published as *The Reference Librarian* 64 (1999): 67–73.

The author, library director at the University of Klaipeda, discusses her library in the context of other Lithuanian academic libraries and emerging consortia in Lithuania and in the European Community. Also offers her impressions of American academic libraries based on her experience as a Washington State University Library Fellow based at Washington State University in Pullman, Washington.

521. Rader, Hannelore. "International personnel exchanges for librarians." *The Bowker Annual of Library & Book Trade Information* 32 (1987): 146–51.

General survey outlining the decline in U.S. organizational support for exchanges and the establishment of the American Library Association Joint Committee on International Exchange of Library and Information Professionals. Also discusses organizations facilitating job exchanges, funding sources, and guidelines for international exchanges. Includes a checklist for preparing for an international exchange.

522. Rader, Hannelore. "The Ohio-China connection." *International Leads* 6, no. 1 (1992): 8–9.

Report of a three-week visit to China by library directors from five Ohio universities as a follow-up to a visit to the United States by six Chinese library directors. Describes their activities in Tianjin, Beijing, Chongqing, and Wuhan and comments on the experience. *See also* Miller and Sessions, no. 498.

523. Rader, Hannelore, and Deborah Greene. "The Heidelberg–Cleveland connection." *College and Research Libraries News* 50, no. 1 (1989): 213–15.

Describes a three-week practicum experience undertaken by a library staff member from the University of Heidelberg in Germany, at Cleveland State University in Ohio, followed by a four-week practicum at Heidelberg Library involving the CSU music librarian (Greene).

524. Riley, Gillian L. "Job exchange in librarianship." *Personnel Training & Education* 8, no. 3 (1991): 49–55.

Provides an overview of overseas exchanges for librarians and what attracts individuals to them. Also considers benefits of overseas job exchanges and other types of exchanges. Produced as part of a project aimed at determining the attitudes and level of interest in job exchange in librarianship in the United Kingdom, with data derived in part from a survey of junior managers at the British Library Document Supply Centre.

525. Roe, John. "The international exchange of library staff." 92–97 in *Developments in international and comparative librarianship, 1976–1985*, edited by Inese A. Smith. Birmingham: International and Comparative Librarianship Group of the Library Association, 1986.

Discusses benefits of temporary job exchanges and organizations set up to facilitate librarian exchanges, then outlines the procedures set up by LIBEX, the British organization that coordinates international job exchanges (see CILIP, no. 575).

526. Rogers, Sharon. "Academics abroad: U.S. librarians visit the People's Republic of China." *College & Research Libraries News* 446, no. 8 (1985): 399–403.

Reports on a 1985 visit by sixty-five American librarians to the People's Republic of China. Tour was sponsored by the China Society of Library Science and arranged by the China Association for Science and Technology. Group included academic, public, special, and school librarians and library educators. Academic librarians traveled to Beijing, Xian, Chengdu, and Shanghai.

527. Sager, Donald J. "An administrator's perspective on foreign exchange." *Law Library Journal* 79 (1987): 722–26.

Discusses international exchange from a library administrator's perspective, including the advantages and benefits to the library and staff members and problems to expect. The author, based in Milwaukee, Wisconsin, has set up a number of exchanges in Western Europe, Great Britain, Scandinavia, Australia, and New Zealand.

528. Salaba, Athena. "A Greek librarian in America: Personal reflections on an eight-month practicum at the Kent State University Libraries." 205–13 in *Academic libraries in Greece: The present situation and future prospects*, edited by Dean H. Keller. New York: Haworth Press, 1993.

Describes the experiences of a librarian from Aristotle University of Thessaloniki while participating in an exchange program at Kent State University in Kent, Ohio. Outlines the exchange program, her technical services training, classes attended, library visits, seminars and meetings in which she participated, and the need for an exchange program for Greek libraries and librarians. *See also* Davis, no. 428; and Tolliver, no. 554.

529. Saule, Mara. "Back to the future." *International Leads* 7, no. 1 (1993): 1–5.

Reports on the experiences of the author, a library associate professor at the University of Vermont in Burlington, while working as an American Library Association Library Fellow at the National Library of Latvia in Riga. Her assignment was to develop a strategic long-range plan for the library's services, collection development, and management. Provides background on the political and economic situation in Latvia and the author's work at the National Library.

530. Sawamoto, Takahisa. "Exchanges of academic librarians between the United States and Japan." 175–87 in *University and research libraries in Japan and the United States*, edited by Thomas R. Buckman, Yukihisa Suzuki, and Warren M. Tsuneishi. Chicago: American Library Association, 1972.

Provides background on the exchange of library personnel between the United States and Japan, noting that it has traditionally been one-sided (i.e., primarily involving Americans going to Japan). Briefly notes some of the individuals who participated in exchanges between the two countries from the early twentieth-century onward and their accomplishments. Also discusses future prospects for exchanges between the two countries.

531. Scott, James Calvert, Warren Eugene Babcock, and Jan Nichols. "Enriching international business faculty exchanges with the library connection." *Journal of Education for Business* 71, no. 2 (1995): 107–9.

Suggests that an innovative way to enrich international business faculty exchanges is by developing a strong library connection. Presents a model in which the exchange of business librarians with their peers abroad complements and facilitates the internationalization of business faculty, instruction, and research. Based on the enriched partnership developed between the College of Business at Utah State University in Logan and the Bristol Business School at the University of the West of England in Bristol. Also discusses the benefits of the relationship for faculty, librarians, their respective institutions, and students.

532. Seeds, Robert. "Academic library service in the Republic of Burundi." *International Information and Library Review* 25, no. 4 (1993): 293–99.

Describes library services and operations at the University of Burundi in Bujumbura, including historical background, branch libraries, collection development, acquisitions, and library organization. Also discusses existing constraints in Burundi, including inadequate facilities, equipment, professional staff, and reference services. Based on the experiences of the author, a librarian at Pennsylvania State University, during a series of five exchange visits between the two university libraries.

533. Segbert, Monika. "A new system for Leninka." *Library Association Record* 101, no. 7 (1999): 414–16.

Report on the experiences of a British librarian sent to Russia by the British Council as team leader on an eighteen-month project to modernize the Russian State Library. Describes the library and its collection, staff, and services and its role as the largest library in Europe and the second largest in the world. Discusses the modernization efforts, stages of development, and special features of the proposed new facility.

534. Seidman, Ruth K. *Building global partnerships for library cooperation.* Washington, DC: Special Libraries Association, 1993. vi, 73 p.

Based on interviews with six North American librarians and information specialists about their international experiences. These included travel overseas to work on a specific project, serving as a short-term adviser on projects in developing countries, taking part in a library staff exchange, and cooperating long-distance with overseas colleagues. Each interview is treated as a case study, with discussion of how to get started, characteristics of successful projects, and benefits. Also discusses factors that support and work against international cooperation.

535. Siegel, Gretta. "Horner Library Staff Exchange still going strong." *International Leads* 21, no. 3 (2007): 5.

Brief outline of the Horner Library Staff Exchange project, which aims to share professional knowledge about library and information science. Partner libraries are the Oregon State Library, the Fujian Provincial Library in China, and the Fujian Library Association. Visiting librarians have the opportunity to tour various libraries. The first staff exchange, involving four delegates from Fujian Province and three Oregon librarians, took place in 2007, though book exchanges have taken place since 1993. *See also* Greey and Wang, no. 449; Shaoning and Zhiminmg, no. 536.

536. Shaoning, Ke and Zheng Zhiminmg. "Libraries in Oregon, USA." *OLA Quarterly (Oregon Library Association)* 7, no. 1 (2001): 16–17.

Report by two librarians from the Fujian Provincial Library in China who took part in a six-week visit to Oregon. During their time in the United States they visited seventeen public, special, and academic libraries in the state. *See also* Greey and Wang, no. 449; Siegel, no. 535.

537. Sharma, R. N. "American librarians visit Gaza Strip." *College and Research Libraries News* 59, no. 1 (1998): 27–28.

Brief report of a fact-finding visit made by a delegation of American librarians to the Gaza Strip in November 1997 aimed at exploring the needs of libraries in the region. Notes that there were twenty-two academic institutions in Palestine, but none had adequate library facilities. *See also* Chepesiuk, no. 419.

538. Sharma, R. N., and Jeannie Bess. "West Virginia to West Africa and back: An international collaboration." *American Libraries* 31, no. 7 (2000): 44–46.

Report of the initial year of a three-year partnership project between the libraries at West Virginia State University in Charleston and the Université Nationale du Bénin in Benin, West Africa. Aims were to share technology, engage in cultural exchanges, and establish a selective depository of Benin government publications in the United States. *See also* Natsis, no. 504.

539. Shearer, James. "Links, exchanges, sharing between U.K. and overseas institutions." *Education for information* 10 (1992): 307–16.

Examines various kinds of links that can be created between British and overseas institutions, using as an example the programs at Thames Valley University (formerly Polytechnic of West London/Ealing College of Higher Education) in London. Links considered include the university's academic partnerships with the Institute of Scientific and Technical Information of China in Beijing and Moi University in Kenya; special short courses offered for library practitioners in Tanzania, India, and South Africa; meetings with educators from Sierra Leone, South Africa, and Turkey; visits by foreign students; staff visits to the West Indies, Kenya, Nigeria, and Mexico; and overseas students. Discusses benefits of these linking efforts for both the UK and international participants involved, funding aspects, and the need to ensure that activities are carefully considered in the context of the ultimate goal of meeting end user needs.

540. Sheridan, John. "A letter from Kiev." *International Leads* 11, no. 2 (1997): 3.

Brief report by a Colorado librarian working for five months at Kiev-Mohyla Academy in Kiev, Russia, as an American Library Association Library Fellow. His primary assignment was to assist with the implementation of an online library system.

541. Shrigley, R. M. "Staff exchange: The UL Libraries experiment." *New Library World* 78 (1977): 148–49.

Discusses the value of job exchanges, especially during periods of low job mobility, and some of the difficulties they present, then comments on an exchange between two librarians at London University, one at Bedford College and one at the School of Oriental and African Studies.

542. Sinitsyna, Olga V., and Thomas E. Hill. "Moscow-Poughkeepsie: Report on a twinning libraries experiment." *IFLA Journal* 23, no. 3 (1997): 192–96.

Reports on the first year of an ongoing relationship between the Vassar College Libraries in Poughkeepsie, New York, and the All Russia State Library for Foreign Literature in Moscow. Activities undertaken included site visits, scrutinizing various areas of practice and service for further collaboration, and developing specific project proposals in the areas of acquisitions, collection development, web projects, library orientation, exhibits, and librarian and faculty visits. Concludes there are many ways libraries can benefit from a twinning arrangement.

543. Smith, George V. "Remembering Angkor . . . meeting the Khmer." *International Leads* 9, no. 4 (1995): 1–4.

The author, deputy director of the Alaska State Library, Archives and Museums, spent eight months in Cambodia as an American Library Association Library Fellow. Describes the impact of civil war in the country and attempts to rebuild, then outlines his activities at the National Library of Cambodia, which included collection-related projects (assessment, weeding, preservation) and administrative duties (reviewing the organizational structure, personnel management, long-range planning, budgeting, political strategizing).

544. Snoeyenbos, Ann, and R. N. Sharma. "American librarians visit Northern Ireland." *College & Research Libraries News* 58, no. 3 (1997): 149.

Brief report of a two-week study tour sponsored by the British Council that was undertaken by fourteen American librarians. The tour was based in Belfast, with day trips to view library and archival collections throughout the country. *See also* Chepesiuk, no. 420.

545. Snyder, Carolyn A., and Larry W. Griffin. "The academic librarian as overseas consultant." 105–15 in *The role of the American academic library in international programs*, edited by Bruce Bonta and James G. Neal. Greenwich CT: JAI Press, 1992.

Discusses questions facing international consultants in developing countries and related issues, including the availability of books in indigenous languages, the importance of fitting in and understanding the culture of libraries in which work is undertaken, and special difficulties of consultants involved in projects where the library aspect has been "tagged on" to larger projects.

546. Snyder, Carolyn A., Larry W. Griffin, Andrea Singer, and Roger Beckman. "The team approach to library consulting in a developing country." *College and Research Libraries News* 46, no. 11 (1985): 629–32.

Summarizes the experiences of four librarians from Indiana University in Bloomington involved in a team consultation for library development at the University of Indonesia in Jakarta. Describes the University of Indonesia and its plans to move to a new campus. The project involved investigating existing conditions, aiding in the design of a library master plan, designing an automated library system, holding regular discussions with relevant parties, and drawing up a final report. Consultations took place over the course of a year.

547. Stanley, Deborah, and Jack Cooper. "Swapping Loughborough for California." *Library Association Record* 99, no. 9 (1997): 488–89.

Report of a nine-month exchange co-written by a librarian at Loughborough University Library in England and a librarian at the University of California, Riverside. Discusses setting up the exchange, aims, the institutions, the jobs, differences observed, and library instruction and orientation.

548. Stine, Diane. *A librarian's directory of exchange programs/study tours/ funding sources and job opportunities outside of the United States.* Chicago: American Library Association, 1982. 15 p.

Brief listing designed for librarians interested in nontraditional employment opportunities such as working in foreign libraries on a permanent basis or participating in a temporary job exchange situation. Also lists opportunities for study tours and information on funding sources. Much material is dated, but background on the history of librarian exchange/study tour programs is of interest, as is the breadth of potential contacts suggested (library schools, government agencies, formal exchange organizations, international school organizations, Christian service agencies, private schools in foreign countries).

549. Tabachnick, B. Robert. "Librarians can play a part in overseas development projects." *College and Research Libraries News* 50, no. 9 (1989): 819–25.

Explores ways in which university librarians can become participants in development projects in developing countries. Provides an overview of changes in developing countries since they achieved independence, in particular the changed view of consultants as colleague-advisors rather than mentor-controllers. Discusses programs that facilitate international work, including the Fulbright program, managed by the Council for the International Exchange of Scholars in Washington, D.C, and university-sponsored projects. Appendices list private development agencies and recruiting companies in the United States and consortia and associations that can provide assistance in tracking down overseas opportunities.

550. Tarr, Hal, and Ivana Kotasek. "Exchange of librarians between the 'City of Brotherly Love' and the 'Land down under.'" *Community & Junior College Libraries* 5, no. 2 (1988): 7–22.

Report of an exchange between librarian Tarr, the technical services librarian at Peirce Junior College in Philadelphia, Pennsylvania, and Kotasek, the head librarian at Port Adelaide College in Australia. Considers such issues as obtaining approval for an exchange project, logistics of the exchange process, the exchange positions, and impressions of a new community and a new country.

551. Thomas, Katherine. *Job swaps and library exchanges.* http://www.llrx .com/node/1448_(November 21, 2008).

Summary of paper presented at the Canadian Association of Law Libraries Annual Conference held in St. John's, Newfoundland, in May 2005. Provides general background on reasons for undertaking a library exchange and lists websites useful in identifying possible exchange partners. Also discusses visiting fellowships and home swaps.

552. Till, Anne. "Muffins, mountains, and multilingual biblioservice." *Canadian Library Journal* 43, no. 3 (1986): 163–66.

Describes a six-month exchange between the author, a librarian at the National Library of Wales, and a librarian at the National Library of Canada. Discusses how the exchange was arranged, the author's work in the new position, and her general impressions of the exchange. *See also* Laundy, no. 486.

553. Tinsley, G. Lynn. "The French connection." *Resources: Carnegie Mellon University Libraries' News* 10, no. 2 (1988): 1–2.

Brief description and comments on exchange visits by computer science librarians at Carnegie Mellon University in Pittsburgh, Pennsylvania, and the University of Grenoble in Grenoble, France.

554. Tolliver, Don L. "International interlibrary cooperation: Exchanging goals, values, and culture." 3–7 in *Academic libraries in Greece: The present situation and future prospects*, edited by Dean H. Keller. New York: Haworth Press, 1993.

Outlines the advantages of cooperation between libraries internationally, pointing out both what American libraries have to offer and what they have to gain. Also describes the staff exchange arrangement set up between Kent State University Libraries in Kent, Ohio, and Aristotle University Library in Thessaloniki, Greece. *See also* Davis, no. 428; and Salaba, no. 528.

555. Tracy, Joan I. "The down under experience: A cataloguer's adventures in Australia." *College & Research Libraries News* 48, no. 7 (1987): 466–67.

Brief report of a six-month exchange between the author, assistant librarian for technical services at Eastern Washington University in Cheney, Washington, and a cataloger at the University of Queensland in Brisbane.

556. Tsuneishi, Warren M. "Exchange of librarians: Past practice and future prospects." 164–74 in *University and research libraries in Japan and the United States*, edited by Thomas R. Buckman, Yukihisa Suzuki, and Warren M. Tsuneishi. Chicago: American Library Association, 1972.

Provides general background on the exchange of librarians between the United States and Japan, then outlines accomplishments of Americans in Japan and the Japanese in the United States. Also discusses mechanisms for making international contacts and arranging exchanges between the two countries.

557. Varley, Gillian. "An English art librarian in Paris: A report and diary." *Art Libraries Journal* 14, no. 1 (1989): 9–15.

Describes the experiences of an art librarian from the Victoria and Albert Museum in London during two weeks spent at the Bibliothèque publique d'information in Paris. During this time she also visited eight other art libraries in Paris. Notes differences between the Parisian libraries and her home institution in the areas of automated cataloging, online union cataloging of serials, and reader services. *See also* Picot, no. 516.

558. Warth, Terry. "You're the librarians—you know the rules! A tour of British libraries." *Kentucky Libraries* 44, no. 4 (1980): 4–9.

Report of a three-week study tour of British libraries undertaken by three librarians from the University of Kentucky in Lexington and one from St. Mary and Elizabeth Hospital Library in Louisville, Kentucky. Discusses visits to Durham University Library, York University Library, Warwickshire County Library,

Coventry Public Library, Westminster Abbey Library, and Brasenose College library and the Bodleian Library in Oxford. *See also* Foster, no. 441.

559. Weeks, Gerald M. "Time for a change—Try a job exchange." *Canadian Library Journal* 40, no. 3 (1983): 165–67.

Outlines the experiences of a British Columbia Institute of Technology librarian on a six-month job exchange with a New South Wales Institute of Technology (Australia) counterpart. Offers planning hints for librarians interested in preparing for a mid-career move.

560. Weeraperuma, Susunaga. *Staff exchanges in librarianship*. London: Poets and Painters Press, 1970. 71 p.

Guidebook for librarians interested in exchange. Discusses such issues as feasibility of arranging exchanges, specific exchange schemes, timing of exchanges, preparation, language difficulties, organization of work, and financial aspects. Written from the perspective of a British librarian. Provides interesting comments on early experiences with job exchanges (1940s–1960s).

561. Welch, Theodore, and Eizaburo Okuizumi. "Form and substance: How Japanese and American academic librarians have shaped a relationship." 227–60 in *The role of the American academic library in international programs*, edited by Bruce Bonta and James G. Neal. Greenwich, CT: JAI Press, 1992.

Examines the development of a binational library relationship between the United States and Japan. Discusses Japan–U.S. staff exchanges and internship programs, international meetings and conferences, and the development of Japanese studies collections in U.S. academic libraries and vice versa. Also considers the role of government agencies and funding agencies.

562. Westerman, Mel. "The librarian as Fulbright Scholar." *Special Libraries Association Business and Finance Division Bulletin* 86 (1991): 10–11.

The Pennsylvania State University business librarian describes his experiences during a four-month visit to the Management Library at Cranfield Institute of Technology in Cranfield, England, where he carried out a research project on academic library services to small businesses.

563. Will, Grinton I. "When assistants exchange positions." *American Library Association Bulletin* 34 (1940): 11–16, 50.

Early discussion of librarian exchanges, including purposes and practical points to consider. Exchanges under consideration are between two libraries in the United States. Includes commentary by two library administrators and two staff members who participated in a six-month staff exchange.

564. Williamson, Linda E. *Going international: Librarians' preparation guide for a work experience/job exchange abroad*. Chicago: American Library Association, 1988. vi, 74 p.

Guidebook compiled under the auspices of the American Library Association's International Relations Committee/ International Relations Round Table Committee on International Exchange of Librarians and Information Professionals. Discusses general preparations for going abroad; passport and other official documentation; financial considerations; host programming; maintenance of insurance, health, and other plans; living arrangements; arrangements for pets; transportation concerns; medical considerations; communications; concerns with respect to accompanying family members (e.g., schooling); tax considerations; and miscellaneous tips. Appendices list groups that arrange international exchange of librarians and possible funding sources. *See also* no. 565.

565. Williamson, Linda. "Guidelines for planning an exchange." *Law Library Journal* 79, no. 4 (1987): 727–31.

The author, a member of the Joint Committee on International Exchange of Librarians and Information Professionals of the International Relations Committee/International Relations Round Table of the American Library Association, discusses preparations for those planning a foreign exchange and presents scenarios involving issues that may arise, such as visa problems, tax planning, medical coverage, and insurance for personal property. *See also* no. 564.

566. Worley, Loyita. "Hastings exchange." *Law Librarian* 18, no. 3 (1987): 91–92.

Brief account of the experiences of the author, the assistant librarian for the Law Society in London, England, on an eleven-week exchange with a reference librarian from Hastings College of the Law at the University of California, San Francisco.

567. Wright, Patrick. "A library job exchange." *Manitoba Library Association Bulletin* 14, no. 2 (1984): 12–13.

Discusses the experience of the author, the head of St. John's College Library, University of Manitoba (Winnipeg), in setting up a seven-month job exchange with the assistant librarian at Luton Central Library in Bedfordshire, England. Written prior to the exchange. *See also* Wright, no. 568.

568. Wright, Patrick. "A library job exchange (part 2)." *Manitoba Library Association Bulletin* 15, no. 3 (1985): 11–12.

Follow-up article to no. 567 discussing the author's exchange experience.

569. Xu, Ye. "Bailin Temple Library: Rare glimpses of a unique institution." *OLA Quarterly (Oregon Library Association)* 7, no. 1 (2001): 13–15.

Report of a study term spent at one of China's national treasures, the Bailin Temple Library in northeastern Beijing. The author, a librarian at Portland State University Library in Oregon, was engaged in a research project to produce a textbook.

570. Yackle, Jeanette. "Living and working in Germany." *Law Library Journal* 79, no. 4 (1987): 740–47.

Discusses the experiences of the author, a reference librarian at Harvard Law School in Cambridge, Massachusetts, who participated in a one-month exchange with the assistant director of the library at the Max Planck Institute for Comparative Public Law and International Law in Heidelberg, West Germany. This was a rotational exchange, in which the partners visited each other's libraries at different times. Describes the institute and its work and practical considerations involved, including spending a year studying German prior to the exchange.

571. Yealy, Gretchen. "Springtime in Germany." *College and Research Libraries News* 48, no. 6 (1987): 341–43.

Describes a three-month exchange between the author, a librarian at Brown University in Providence, Rhode Island, and a librarian at the Universität Bamberg in Germany. *See also* Doksansky, no. 429.

572. Zainuddin, H. R. Lenggang, Chan Sirdi, and Antoinette Paris Powell. "Management techniques for developing libraries: Teaching library management techniques to Indonesian librarians." *IAALD (International Association of Agricultural Information Specialists) Quarterly Bulletin* 34 (1989): 167–70.

Describes a short course team taught by a library consultant from the University of Kentucky in Lexington and two Indonesian librarians. Undertaken as part of a University of Kentucky project to improve agricultural education in the western islands of Indonesia. *See also* nos. 216, 217, 323, 330, 332, 574, 575, 576, 577, 581, 584.

WEB RESOURCES

573. American Library Association. *Multilingual glossary.* http://www.ala.org/ala/acrlbucket/is/publicationsacrl/multilingualglossarydefinitions.cfm.

Glossary of eighty-five terms commonly used in libraries, with definitions in six languages: English, Chinese, Korean, Japanese, French, and Spanish.

574. American Library Association. International Relations Round Table International Exchanges Committee. http://www.ala.org/ala/mgrps/rts/irrt/index.cfm.

Mission of the committee is to promote interest in library issues and librarianship worldwide. The committee website provides links to sources of library employment worldwide, including exchange opportunities and funding sources. This information can also be found on the ALA website on the International Relations Office web page under the Awards, Grants and Exchanges link: http://www.ala.org/ala/aboutala/offices/iro/awardsactivities/awardsgrants.cfm.

575. Chartered Institute of Library and Information Professionals (CILIP). *LIBEX international library and information job exchange.* http://www.cilip.org.uk/jobscareers/libex.

LIBEX acts as a clearinghouse for CILIP members and library and information staff in other countries who are interested in arranging a job exchange between a UK-based post and a non-UK-based post.

576. Deutscher Akademischer Austausch Dients/German Academic Exchange Service (DAAD). http://www.daad.org/.

DAAD is the German national agency for the support of international academic cooperation. Offers programs and funding for students, faculty, researchers, and others in higher education.

577. Fulbright Specialists Program. http://www.cies.org/specialists/

The Fulbright programs, administered by the Council for the International Exchange of Scholars based in Washington, D.C., provide opportunities for international educational exchanges. The Specialists Program is designed to provide funding for short-term postings (two to six weeks) for U.S. faculty and professionals, including librarians. Website provides links to program information and applications. In addition, the Canada–U.S Fulbright Program (http://www.fulbright.ca), which aims to enhance understanding between Canada and the United States, provides support to faculty and professionals who wish to conduct research, lecture, or enroll in academic programs in the other country.

578. Hickok, John. "ESL (English as a second language) web sites, resources for library administrators, librarians, and ESL users." *Journal of Library Administration* 43, no. 3–4 (2005): 247–62.

Annotated listing of web resources for English-as-a-second-language (ESL) students and those who teach them. Discusses the sites in the context of how they may be of help to libraries. Includes professional and organizations' ESL sites, ESL webographies, ESL publisher sites, and resource sites for ESL educators and ESL students/learners.

579. iliinternational. http://ilinternational.pbwiki.com/.

Wiki focusing on teaching information literacy to non-native English speakers.

580. Institute of International Education (IIE). http://www.iie.org/.

IIE is an independent nonprofit organization focusing on international education and training organizations. Website provides links to various programs and resources, including study abroad options, funding sources (mainly for U.S. students), and opportunities for international professional exchange.

581. International Federation of Library Associations and Institutions (IFLA). http://www.ifla.org/.

IFLA has been involved in various projects to facilitate the exchange of resources and personnel between member countries, including the IFLA Twinning Database (closed down in 2000 due to lack of funding). The IFLA strategic plan 2006–2009 lists the revitalization of its website for professional development and exchange as one of its strategic actions.

582. International Federation of Library Associations and Institutions (IFLA). Library Services to Multicultural Populations Section. http://www.ifla.org/VII/s32/index.htm.

Provides information for libraries and institutions interested in the development and availability of library services designed to meet the needs of cultural and linguistic minorities. Links include the section's strategic plans, work schedule, the IFLA Multicultural Library Manifesto, and guidelines for library services to multicultural communities.

583. International Graduate Insight Group (IGI). http://www.i-graduate.org/.

I-graduate is an independent benchmarking and research service focusing on the education sector worldwide. Established in 2005, it aims to assess trends in demand from international markets, monitor expectations and experiences of students, and assist international educators with the planning process.

584. International Research and Exchanges Board (IREX). http://www.irex .org/.

IREX is "an international non-profit organization providing leadership and innovative programs to improve the quality of education, strengthen independent media, and foster pluralistic civil society development." IREX and its partner IREX Europe provide programs and consulting expertise in more than fifty countries. Website includes information for those interested in working abroad or in participating in projects to assist libraries in developing countries.

585. Open Doors Online: Report on International Educational Exchange. http://opendoors.iienetwork.org/.

Website provides various statistical reports with respect to international students in the United States and U.S. students abroad.

586. Shastri Indo-Canadian Institute. www.sici.org.

This binational organization aims to promote understanding between India and Canada through academic activities and exchanges. The Librarian Fellowship is awarded to Canadian university librarians to undertake intensive programs of study at an Indian institution, to enhance knowledge of an Indian language, or to enhance research support for South Asian studies.

587. Vega García, Susan A. "Latino resources on the web." 207–27 in *Library services to Latinos: An anthology*, edited by Salvador Guereña. Jefferson, NC: MacFarland, 2000.

Report of research project designed to identify and evaluate the most useful Latino web resources and to analyze which Latino groups were making use of the web and for what reason. Discusses types of Latino web resources and Latino web resources as reference and research tools, then provides an annotated listing of recommended U.S. Latino websites. *See also* nos. 10, 35, 322, 366, 370, 551.

WORK WITH INTERNATIONAL FACULTY

588. Osborne, Nancy Seale, and Maria Helena Maier. "Service to international users: The case of a Brazilian biologist." *Research Strategies* 10 (1992): 84–87.

Describes the author's personal relationship with an international researcher and its impact on improving the researcher's library skills. Includes discussion on training the researcher in the use of the library and in communication differences.

589. Pal, Gabriel, Jim Brett, Tom Flemming, and Michael Ridley. "Providing electronic library reference service: Experiences from the Indonesia-Canada Tele-Education Project." *Journal of Academic Librarianship* 15, no. 5 (1989): 274–78.

Describes and evaluates a project in which librarians from McMaster University in Hamilton, Ontario, and the University of Guelph, Ontario, offered reference service to scientists at academic institutions in Indonesia. Discusses implications of electronic reference service between developed and developing countries.

590. Roberts, Anne. "Indonesians in the library: Unity in diversity, or, One library's experience." *The Bookmark* 46 (1987): 42–46.

Describes a semester-long program for twenty-six faculty members from Indonesia who came to the University of Albany, New York, to study, make contacts, and write textbooks in their fields. Participants had faculty mentors and a librarian was assigned to assist with library instruction and textbook writing and editing. Language barriers and common library problems are outlined.

591. Roberts, Anne. "Indonesians in the library: Unity and diversity: Diversity in unity." 96 in *Reaching and teaching diverse library user groups: Papers presented at the Sixteenth National LOEX Library Instruction Conference held at Bowling Green State University, 5 & 6 May 1988*, edited by Teresa B. Mensching. Ann Arbor, MI: Pierian Press, 1989.

Brief summary of program outlined in no. 590. See also no. 218.

Author Index

Subject Index

About the Author

Diane E. Peters is a librarian at Wilfrid Laurier University in Waterloo, Ontario, Canada. She is a member of the library reference department and has collection responsibilities for medieval studies, music, and religion/theology. She holds degrees in music, literature, and religion from Wilfrid Laurier University and in library science from the University of Western Ontario (London) and has an associate diploma in piano from the Royal Conservatory of Music, Toronto, Ontario. She also did graduate work in musicology at Oxford University. She is involved with various committees at Wilfrid Laurier University and is a past chair of both the Canadian Association of Music Libraries, Archives and Documentation Centres and the Librarians' Committee of the Canadian Association of University Teachers. Ms. Peters's current research focuses on the biblical figure Lazarus of Bethany and his impact on literature and popular culture.

Breinigsville, PA USA
01 April 2010
235337BV00001B/4/P

9 780810 874299